An Introduction to Discourse Analysis

"If you only read one book on discourse analysis, this is the one to read. If you're a specialist, you'll find much to enjoy here as well. Gee's book shows us that discourse analysis is about a lot more than linguistic study; it will help us all to see how to keep from, as he says, 'getting physically, socially, culturally, or morally "bitten" by the world'."

Ron Scollon, *Georgetown University, USA*

James Paul Gee presents here his unique, integrated approach to discourse analysis: the analysis of spoken and written language as it is used to enact social and cultural perspectives and identities.

Assuming no prior knowledge of linguistics, James Paul Gee presents both a theory of language-in-use, as well as a method of research. This method is made up of a set of "tools of inquiry" and strategies for using them.

Clearly structured and written in a highly accessible style, the book presents these tools of inquiry alongside the theory of language-in-use. They are then placed in the framework of an overall approach to discourse analysis. Finally, an extended example of discourse analysis is presented using some of the tools and strategies developed earlier in the book.

Perspectives from a variety of approaches and disciplines – including applied linguistics, education, psychology, anthropology, and communication – are incorporated to help students and scholars from a range of backgrounds formulate their own views on discourse and engage in their own discourse analyses.

James Paul Gee is the Tashia Morgridge Professor of Reading at the University of Wisconsin at Madison. His previous publications include *Social Linguistics and Literacies*, *The Social Mind* and *The New Work Order* (with Glynda Hull and Colin Lankshear).

An Introduction to Discourse Analysis

Theory and Method

James Paul Gee

London and New York

First published 1999
by Routledge
11 New Fetter Lane, London EC4P 4EE

Simultaneously published in the USA and Canada
by Routledge
29 West 35th Street, New York, NY 10001

Reprinted 2000 (twice), 2001, 2002

Routledge is an imprint of the Taylor & Francis Group

Typeset in Palatino by
BC Typesetting, Bristol
Printed and bound in Great Britain by
St Edmundsbury Press Ltd, Bury St Edmunds Suffolk

British Library Cataloguing in Publication Data
A catalogue record for this book is available from the British Library

Library of Congress Cataloguing in Publication Data
Gee, James Paul.
    An introduction to discourse analysis: theory and method/James
Paul Gee.
        p.   cm.
    Includes bibliographical references.
    ISBN 0–415–21186–7. – ISBN 0–415–21185–9 (hbk.)
    1. Discourse analysis.   I. Title.
P302.G4   1999
401'.41–dc21   98-54719
                                                         CIP

ISBN 0–415–21186–7 (pbk)
ISBN 0–415–21185–9 (hbk)

Contents

Acknowledgments

The viewpoint on language in this book has evolved over a good many years. It arose, initially, not out of any desire to contribute to discourse analysis as a method of inquiry, but rather, out of my own attempts to understand how language works in a fully integrated way as simultaneously a mental, social, cultural, institutional, and political phenomenon. I first became interested in these matters when I was teaching linguistics in the School of Language and Communication at Hampshire College in Amherst, Massachusetts. When I moved to the Applied Psycholinguistics Program at Boston University, I became interested in how such an integrated understanding of language could be applied to problems in society, especially to problems in education. It was while I was in Boston that I first met Courtney Cazden, Sarah Michaels, Eliot Mishler, Cathy O'Connor, and Dennis Wolf, colleagues who worked at other institutions, but whose work and viewpoints have deeply influenced my own ever since. When I joined the linguistics department at the University of Southern California, I had the great good fortune to work with a set of colleagues in the department who profoundly advanced my education. I am grateful, too, to Elaine Andersen and Ed Finegan for advice and encouragement in my years at USC and thereafter. Moving from USC to the Hiatt Center for Urban Education at Clark University in Worcester, Massachusetts allowed me to rejoin Sarah Michaels, founder of the Hiatt Center, both as a colleague and co-researcher, and to have the privilege of working with Jim Wertsch before he departed to head the Education Department at Washington University in St. Louis. Coming to the University of Wisconsin at Madison has continued my great good fortune of inheriting wonderful colleagues. Michael Apple, Deborah Brandt, Ann DeVaney, Ceci Ford, Mary-Louise Gomez, Gloria Ladson-Billings, Rich Lehrer, Marty Nystrand, Leona Schauble, and Tom Popkewitz, in particular, have made me feel welcome and have influenced my work on this book here in Madison.

I have been blessed over the years with being able to work with a number of inspiring friends and colleagues in Australia, Canada, England, New Zealand, and the United States. I will not name names for fear I might inadvertently leave someone out. But, perhaps ironically, as an "isolate" in academics, I all the more treasure the friendship and support my colleagues, at a variety of institutions, have shown me.

I must thank David Bloome, for a very insightful and helpful review of an earlier draft of this manuscript, as well as one of his graduate students, Sheila Otto, who helpfully reviewed the original manuscript from the point of view of a student. Another, but anonymous, reviewer from Routledge, also offered quite helpful suggestions for revision. I have to thank David Barton for helping me to "place" this book in the first place, as well as for very useful feedback. Judith Green collaborated with me on a project at a time and in a way that helped me to clarify my views on a variety of issues.

Of my friends and colleagues, Norman Fairclough, Gunther Kress, Jay Lemke, Allen Luke, Brian Street, and Jim Wertsch have been the major influences on the theoretical and linguistic aspects of this book, though they probably won't fully recognize (and maybe won't even like) what I have "done" with their influence. Much of my work, too, has been formed by trying to understand for myself and to relate together the seminal work of people like Bernstein, Bourdieu, Foucault, Gumperz, Halliday, and Hymes.

My graduate student "project assistants" here at the University of Wisconsin, Anna-Ruth Allen and Katherine Clinton, students whom I brought with me from Clark University, have been an immense help throughout the production of this book. Furthermore, they were co-researchers with me on the data dealt with in Chapter 7. My newest "project assistants," Kerrie Kephart and Cathleen Schultz, have offered me important insights that helped me in finishing this book.

Colin Lankshear has been more than a colleague; his support, often over e-mail, has helped me stay in academia, though he has bravely left his university home for new horizons. Donaldo Macedo has done more than his share, too, to keep me in the "game."

I owe a deep debt to Maggie Hawkins for reading an earlier version of this book and for much helpful discussion as the book was being written. I owe my "baby" Sam, who turned three as I was working on this book, an immense debt for dramatically reintroducing me, first hand, to the miracle of children learning language and building worlds with it.

1 Introduction

1.1 Language as action and affiliation

In a moment, I will issue a "truth in lending" statement about what this book is and is not meant to do. But first, let me say something about the viewpoint on language that I will take in this book. Many people, including many linguists, think that the primary purpose of human language is to "communicate information." In fact, I believe this is simply a prejudice on the part of academics who believe, often falsely, that what they themselves primarily do to and with each other is "exchange information." Language, in fact, serves a great many functions and "giving and getting information," yes, even in our new "Information Age," is but one, and, by no means, the only one.

If I had to single out a primary function of human language, it would be not one, but the following two: to scaffold the performance of social activities (whether play or work or both) and to scaffold human affiliation within cultures and social groups and institutions.

These two functions are connected. Cultures, social groups, and institutions shape social activities: there are no activities like "water-cooler gossip sessions" or "corridor politics" without an institution whose water cooler, social relations, corridors, and politics are the sites of and rationale for these activities. At the same time though, cultures, social groups, and institutions get produced, reproduced, and transformed through human activities. There is no institution unless it is enacted and reenacted moment-by-moment in activities like water-cooler gossip sessions, corridor politics, meetings, and numerous other sorts of social interactions, all of which partly (but only partly) have a life all of their own apart from larger cultural and institutional forces.

This book is concerned with a theory and a method for studying how the details of language get recruited, "on site," to "pull off" specific social activities and social identities ("memberships" in various social groups, cultures, and institutions). In the process, we will see that language-in-use is everywhere and always "political."

By "politics" I mean something that Aristotle would have recognized, though not, perhaps, today's "Democrats" and "Republicans." By "politics" I mean anything and anyplace where human social interactions and relationships have implications for how "social goods" are or ought to be distributed. By "social goods" I mean anything that a group of people believes to be a source of power, status, or worth (whether this be "street smarts," academic intelligence, money, control, possessions, verbal abilities, "looks," age, wisdom, knowledge, technology, literacy, morality, "common sense," and so on and so forth through a very long list indeed).

When we speak or write we always take a particular *perspective* on what the "world" is like. This involves us in taking perspectives on what is "normal" and not; what is "acceptable" and not; what is "right" and not; what is "real" and not; what is the "way things are" and not; what is the "ways things ought to be" and not; what is "possible" and not; what "people like us" or "people like them" do and don't do; and so on and so forth, again through a nearly endless list. But these are all, too, perspectives on how we believe, wish, or act as if potential "social goods" are, or ought to be, distributed.

There is nothing special, then, about politics. Politics is part and parcel of using language. Furthermore, far from exonerating us from looking at the empirical details of language and social action and allowing us simply to pontificate, an interest in politics demands that we engage in the empirical details of language and interaction. Politics has its lifeblood in such details. It is there that social goods are created, sustained, distributed and redistributed. It is there that people are harmed and helped.

Let me give a brief example of how language details lead to social activities, identities, and politics, far beyond "giving and getting information." My example here will involve a written text, though most of the examples later in this book will come from speech. Consider the following sentences chosen at random from Paul Gagnon's book *Democracy's Untold Story: What World History Textbooks Neglect* (1987: 65–71). I have highlighted in bold some aspects of the text that I will discuss below:

> **Also secure, by 1689**, was the principle of representative government, as tested against the two criteria for valid constitutions proposed in the previous chapter. **As to the first criterion**, there was a genuine balance of power in English society, expressing itself in the Whig and Tory parties. **As narrowly confined to the privileged classes as these were**, they none the less represented different factions and tendencies. Elections meant real choice among separate, contending parties and personalities.

In his book, sponsored by the American Federation of Teachers, the Education Excellence Network, and Freedom House, Gagnon speaks of what he thinks ought to be the "essential plot" of Western history as taught in schools. In the sentences quoted above, and in the passage as a whole from which they are taken, Gagnon uses certain aspects of English grammar as a resource with which to "design" his sentences in a certain way. He uses English grammar to see to it that the *subject* of his sentences is not in its "normal" place at the beginning of the sentence, except for his last sentence, whose subject is "elections" and at the beginning. I have highlighted in bold the beginnings of the other sentences, none of which are the subjects of those sentences.

It is clear that Gagnon's use of English grammar to design his text this way creates connections in his text, allowing it to flow from sentence to sentence in a certain, rather artful, way. However, Gagnon's use of English grammar does much more than this. The sorts of features of English grammar that Gagnon is using often function to create a *background context* against which other information is *foregrounded* as the main or focal point. Thus, material like "Also secure, by 1689" and "As to the first criterion" is background material. Placed where they are, these phrases allow Gagnon to "flow" to his main foregrounded information in each sentence (i.e. to representative government as he has defined it earlier and the balance of power represented by the Tories and Whigs), while providing the contextual scaffolding needed to frame (or, as we will see below, "cushion") his main points.

Having used such "backgrounding–foregrounding" features twice (and several times earlier), Gagnon does it again in the sentence "**As narrowly confined to the privileged classes as these were**, they [the Whig and Tory parties] none the less represented different factions and tendencies." This allows him to treat the fact that the Whig and Tory parties were confined "to the privileged classes" as connecting tissue and background information, a mere concession, despite the fact that some other historians might see this as a focal piece of information. His final sentence about elections can now be issued with no "background." The major reason to contest that these were meaningful elections has already been relegated to the background.

In other words, Gagnon has relegated to a "background consideration" what some other historians would have placed in the foreground of their arguments [and, I admit, it is somewhat devious that I have highlighted in bold what his grammar has tried to background!]. And indeed, we can really only understand him "deeply" and "critically" if we understand his "ways with words" in relationship to the different "ways with words" of other historians, historians who might claim, for instance, that elections are not meaningful or democratic if confined to elites.

Am I accusing Gagnon of using English grammar for "political purposes?" If by this we mean that I am saying that Gagnon is using the resources of English grammar to create a *perspective* with implications, the answer is most certainly "yes." But it could not be otherwise. The whole point of grammar, in speech or writing, is, in fact, to allow us to create just such "political" perspectives. Grammar simply does not allow us to speak or write from no perspective.

Is Gagnon "just" communicating information? Hardly – he is engaging in a very real "project," a social activity, an attempt to create new affiliations and transform old ones over who will teach and what will be taught in the schools, and over what is and what is not "real history." This, too, could not be otherwise. To read Gagnon without regard for the way he recruits design features for his social and, yes, political "purposes" is, for better and worse, to have missed most of the action. In fact, we can hardly have a "discussion" with Gagnon, engage with his views, if we have missed this action.

Gagnon is, in and through language, enacting a particular activity. He is also enacting a specific social identity as a particular type of historian (against other types of historians), an historian who connects history, citizenship, patriotism, and schools together in a certain way. Furthermore, his text is only a part of a larger project in which he is engaged, a project in setting "standards" for school history and fighting the "history wars" against those who hold radically different perspectives on the nature, purposes, and goals of history, schooling, and society than he does.

Note too, by the way, that an historian who wants to "rise above" debates about standards in public schools and "history wars" and write as an "objective" and "dispassionate" scholar simply retailing the "facts" will only have designed a text whose language enacts a different set of perspectives and a different politics. That text will be designed to render texts like Gagnon's "unprofessional," "mere politics," "just about schools," not "real history." Writing as if all you have to offer are "the facts" or "the truth" is also *a way of writing*, a way of using language to enact an activity and an identity, too.

This does not mean that "nothing is true" or that "everything is equally good." No, for better or worse, physicists' bombs do go off and astrologists' don't. Rather, it means that "truth" (really, "doing better, rather than worse, in not getting physically, socially, culturally, or morally 'bitten' by the world") is a matter of taking, negotiating, and contesting perspectives created in and through language within social activities.

1.2 About this book: theory and method

Now it is time to turn to our "truth in lending" disclaimers. These are all the more appropriate here, as this book is meant to "lend" readers certain tools of inquiry, fully anticipating that these tools will be transformed, or even abandoned, as readers invent their own versions of them or meld them with other tools embedded in somewhat different perspectives.

This book is an introduction to *one* approach to discourse analysis, that is, to the analysis of language as it is used to enact activities, perspectives, and identities. There are many different approaches to discourse, none of them, including this one, uniquely "right." Different approaches often fit different issues and questions better or worse than others. And, too, different approaches sometimes reach similar conclusions though using somewhat different tools and terminologies connected to different "micro-communities" of researchers.

Furthermore, the approach to discourse analysis in this book is not "mine." No set of research tools and no theory belongs to a single person, no matter how much academic style and our own egos sometimes force (or tempt) us to write that way. I have freely begged, borrowed, and patched together. If there is any quality in my work, it is primarily in the "taste" with which I have raided others' stores and in the way I have adapted and mixed together the ingredients and, thereby, made the soup. Some will, of course, not recognize the ingredient they have contributed, or, at least, not want to admit they do after they taste my soup. If there are occasional "inventions," their only chance for a "full life" is that someone else will borrow them and mix them into new soup.

A note on the soup: the approach to discourse analysis in this book seeks to balance talk about the mind, talk about interaction and activities, and talk about society and institutions more than is the case in some other approaches. So, some may think my approach too "cognitive," others may think it too "social."

However, I believe we have to get minds, bodies, interactions, social groups, and institutions all in the soup together. Of course, there are other ways than mine to do this, and, in fact, this is currently a "cutting-edge" topic and an important one for the future. Whatever approach we take, it holds out the hope that various micro-communities of researchers working in diverse fields can begin to come together, seeing that, using somewhat different, but related, tools, terminologies, and theories, we are all contributing to a "big picture."

This book is partly about a "method" of research. However, I hasten to point out that the whole issue of research methods is, as far as I am concerned, badly confused. First of all, any method always goes with a *theory*. Method and theory cannot be separated, despite the fact that methods are often taught as if they could stand alone. Any method of research is a way to investigate some particular domain. In this case, the domain is language-in-use. There can be no sensible method to study a domain, unless one also has a theory of what the domain is. Thus, this book offers, as it must, a theory about the nature of language-in-use.

People with different theories about a domain will use different methods for their research. The reason this is so is because a research method is made up essentially of various "tools of inquiry" and strategies for applying them. Tools of inquiry are designed to describe and explain what the researcher takes to exist and to be important in a domain. Thus, when theories about a domain differ – for instance, a theory about what language-in-use is, or about what evolution is – tools of inquiry will differ, as well. For example, if your theory is that evolution works at the level of cells, you will use different methods of research in biology than if you believe it works at the level of genes. You will have different methods again if you believe it operates at the level of species.

Since methods go with theories, there really are no grand categories of research like "quantitative research" and "qualitative research." On the one hand, some physicists use different research methods than do chemists and biologists (and then, there are "biophysicists" and "biochemists" – hybrids). On the other hand, biologists with different theories about organisms, cells, species, or evolution use different methods. By the same token, people engaged in forms of research that involve interpreting language, as any version of discourse analysis does, use different methods if and when they have different theories about what language and interpretation are, or what the important questions to pursue in regard to them are.

Besides seeing that methods change with theories, it is also important to see that research, whether in physics, literary criticism, or in discourse analysis, is *not* an algorithmic procedure, a set of "rules" that can be followed step-by-linear-step to get guaranteed "results." There is no "scientific method," even in the "hard" sciences, if by this we mean such a set of rules to follow. Rather, research adopts and adapts specific tools of inquiry and strategies for implementing them. These tools and strategies ultimately reside in a "community of practice" formed by those engaged in such research.

Such tools and strategies are continually and flexibly adapted to specific issues, problems, and contexts of study. They are continually transformed as they are applied in practice. At the same time, new researchers in an area are normed by examples of research that more advanced others in the area take (for the time) to be "prototypical" examples of that area's tools and strategies in operation. Methods are social and communal through and through.

This book will introduce various tools of inquiry for what I will (for the moment) call "D/discourse analysis" and strategies for using them (and in a moment I will say why the odd "D/d"). It will give a number of examples of the tools in action, as well. But the reader should keep in mind that these tools of inquiry are not meant to be rigid definitions. Rather, they are meant to be "thinking devices" that guide inquiry in regard to specific sorts of data and specific sorts of issues and questions. They are meant to be adapted for the reader's own purposes. They are meant, as well, to be transformed as the reader adapts them to his or her own theory of the domain (of course, if the reader's theory gets too far away from mine, the tools will be less and less easily or sensibly adaptable and useful).

The distinction between "Discourse" with a "big D" and "discourse" with a "little d" plays a role throughout this book. This distinction is meant to do this: we, as "applied linguists" or "sociolinguists," are interested in how language is used "on site" to enact activities and identities. Such language-in-use, I will call "discourse" with a "little d." *But* activities and identities are rarely ever enacted through language alone.

To "pull off" being an "X" doing "Y" (e.g. a Los Angeles Latino street-gang member warning another gang member off his territory, or a laboratory physicist convincing colleagues that a particular graph supports her ideas, or, for that matter, a laboratory physicist warning another laboratory physicist off her research territory) it is not enough to get just the words "right," though that is crucial. It is necessary, as well, to get one's body, clothes, gestures, actions, interactions, ways with things, symbols, tools, technologies (be they guns or graphs), and values, attitudes, beliefs, and emotions "right," as well, and all at the "right" places and times.

When "little d" discourse (language-in-use) is melded integrally with non-language "stuff" to enact specific identities and activities, then, I say that "big D" Discourses are involved. We are all members of many, a great many, different Discourses, Discourses which often influence each other in positive and negative ways, and which sometimes breed with each other to create new hybrids.

When you "pull off" being a culturally-specific sort of "everyday" person, a "regular" at the local bar, a certain type of African-American or Greek-Australian, a certain type of cutting-edge particle physicist or teen-age heavy-metal enthusiast, a teacher or a student of a certain sort, or any of a great many other "ways of being in the world," you use language and "other stuff" – ways of acting, interacting, feeling, believing, valuing, together with other people and with various sorts of characteristic objects, symbols, tools, and technologies – to recognize yourself and others as meaning and meaningful in certain ways. In turn, you produce, reproduce, sustain, and transform a given "form of life" or Discourse. All life for all of us is just a patchwork of thoughts, words, objects, events, actions, and interactions in Discourses.

So, this book will introduce tools of inquiry with which to study discourse in Discourses. Let me close this section with a note on "validity" and then, on "having a point." While we will discuss the contentious question of validity for D/discourse analysis and related interpretive enterprises in Chapter 5, I want to point out here that validity does not consist in how any one tool of inquiry works on its own. Rather, validity primarily consists in how our various tools of inquiry work together. What we test when we worry about why we should trust an analysis of some data is not each claim or the result of each tool separately. We test the whole analysis in terms of how much data it covers, how well it works on new sources of data, how much agreement we can gather from others, how well tied the analysis is to a wide variety of linguistic details, and whether or not there are competing analyses that work better in any or all these respects than ours.

Finally, let me say that in D/discourse analysis we are not interested in specific analyses of data just in and for themselves. A D/discourse analysis must have a point. We are not interested in simply describing data so that we can admire the intricacy of language, though this is, indeed, admirable. Rather, we are interested, beyond description, in two things: illuminating and gaining evidence for our theory of the domain, a theory that helps to explain how and why language works the way it does when it is put into action; and contributing, in terms of understanding and intervention, to important issues and problems in some "applied" area (e.g. education) that interests and motivates the researcher.

Thanks to the fact that D/discourse analyses must have a "point," this book will have relevance to "applied" issues throughout, many of which are germane to education, though these issues are not always in the foreground of attention. In D/discourse analysis, at least, any notion that applications and practice are less "prestigious" or less "important" or less "pure" than theory has no place. Such a notion has no place, because, as the reader will see, the theory of language in this book is *that language has meaning only in and through practices*, practices which often leave us morally complicit with harm and injustice unless we attempt to transform them. It is a tenet of this book that any proper theory of language is a theory of practice.

1.3 About this book: readers and reading

This book is directed at three audiences. It is meant to introduce students and researchers in other areas to one form of discourse analysis that I hope they can use and experiment with as they learn other forms of discourse analysis and come up with their own ideas. It is meant, as well, for people interested in language, culture, and institutions, but who have not focused their own work on discourse analysis. Finally, it is meant for my colleagues in discourse studies, so that they can compare and contrast their own views to those developed here, and so that, together, we can advance our common enterprise of understanding how language works in society to create better and worse worlds, institutions, and human relationships.

The book is structured in, perhaps, a somewhat odd way. The "method" is fully sketched out in Chapter 5, the heart of the book. Chapters 2–4 discuss, with many examples, specific tools of inquiry that are part of the overall method and strategies for using them. These tools and strategies are fully embedded in a theory of language-in-use in culture and society. Thus, that theory is also laid out in Chapters 2–4. Chapter 5 briefly recapitulates our tools of inquiry and places them in the framework of an overall approach to D/discourse analysis. I also discuss the issue of validity for D/discourse analysis in this chapter.

Chapter 6 deals with some linguistic details (various aspects of grammar and discourse) that play an important role in D/discourse analysis. Here, issues about how speech is planned and produced, intonation, lines and stanzas, and narrative structure are taken up. These linguistic details will, hopefully, make more sense once the "big picture" is made clear in Chapters 2–5, and will give readers some additional tools with which to deal with the empirical details of discourse analysis. Chapter 7 is an extended example of D/discourse analysis using some of the tools and strategies developed earlier in the book. This chapter is by no means meant to be a step-by-step "how to" manual; it is simply meant to exemplify in practice a few of the tools discussed in this book.

My analyses throughout this book do not assume any specific theory of grammar or, for that matter, any great depth of knowledge about grammar. However, readers may want to supplement their reading of this book with some additional reading about grammar, preferably grammar as it functions in communication and social interaction. The best known such "functional" approach to grammar is that developed by M. A. K. Halliday (1994). Good introductory secondary sources exist on Halliday's approach to grammar (e.g. see Thompson 1996). For readers who want a quick overview of how grammar works in communication, I have given a brief introduction to this topic as an appendix to this book. Different readers may want to read this appendix (if at all) at different points in the reading of the main material in the book.

Since this book is meant to be an "introduction," I have tried not to clutter up the chapters with long lists of interpolated references. The downside of this policy is that I will have to leave out references to the more specialized work of many colleagues whose work I value greatly. The upside is that people new to discourse analysis may actually read some of the material I cite and will have good places to start their further investigations. The material I do cite is, in most cases, replete with further references to the literature. Some chapters end with a note containing further references to the literature. Otherwise, I have eschewed footnotes.

Since the word "method" so triggers in our minds ideas of a "step-by-step" set of "rules" to follow, I want to stress, once again, in closing, that that is not what "method" means here. Rather, it means sets of "thinking devices" with which one can investigate certain sorts of questions, with due regard for how others have investigated such questions, but with adaptation, innovation, and creativity, as well. "Validity" is communal: if you take risks and make mistakes, your colleagues will help you clean up the mess – that's what they're for. The quality of research often resides in how fruitful our mistakes are, that is, in whether they open up paths that others can then make more progress on than we have.

Finally, having repeatedly used the term "D/discourse analysis" to make the point that we are interested in analyzing language as it is fully integrated with all the other elements that go into social practices (e.g.

ways of thinking or feeling, ways of manipulating objects or tools, ways of using non-linguistic symbol systems, etc.), we can dispense with this device. It will just clutter up the text and the point is now made. Throughout this book I will simply use the phrase "discourse analysis," but will mean by this phrase analyses that deal with both "little d" discourse and "big D" Discourse.

2 Discourses and social languages

2.1 Building things through language

Language has a magical property: when we speak or write we craft what we have to say to *fit* the situation or context in which we are communicating. But, at the same time, how we speak or write *creates* that very situation or context. It seems, then, that we fit our language to a situation or context that our language, in turn, helped to create in the first place.

This is rather like the "chicken and egg" question: Which comes first? The situation we're in (e.g. a committee meeting)? Or the language we use (our committee ways of talking and interacting)? Is this a "committee meeting" *because* we are speaking and acting this way, or are we speaking and acting this way *because* this is a committee meeting? After all, if we did not speak and act in certain ways, committees could not exist; but then, if institutions, committees, and committee meetings didn't already exist, speaking and acting this way would be nonsense. The answer here is that this magical property is real and language and institutions "boot strap" each other into existence in a reciprocal process through time.

Another way to look at the matter is this: we always actively use spoken and written language to create or build the world of activities (e.g. committee meetings) and institutions (committees) around us. However, thanks to the workings of history and culture, we often do this in more or less routine ways. These routines make activities and institutions, like committees and committee meetings, seem to (and, in that sense, actually) exist apart from language and action in the here and now. None the less, these activities and institutions have to be continuously and actively rebuilt in the here and now. This is what accounts for change, transformation, and the power of language-in-action in the world.

We continually and actively build and rebuild our worlds not just through language, but through language used in tandem with actions, interactions, non-linguistic symbol systems, objects, tools, technologies, and distinctive ways of thinking, valuing, feeling, and believing. Sometimes what we build is quite similar to what we have built before; sometimes it is not. But language-in-action is always and everywhere an active building process.

Whenever we speak or write, we always and simultaneously construct or build six things or six areas of "reality":

1   *The meaning and value of aspects of the material world:* I enter a plain, square room, and speak and act in a certain way (e.g. like someone about to run a meeting), and, low and behold, where I sit becomes the "front" of the room.
2   *Activities*: We talk and act in one way and we are engaged in formally opening a committee meeting; we talk and act in another way and we are engaged in "chit-chat" before the official start of the meeting.
3   *Identities and relationships:* I talk and act in one way one moment and I am speaking and acting as "chair" of the committee; the next moment I speak and talk in a different way and I am speaking and acting as one peer/colleague speaking to another.
4   *Politics (the distribution of social goods):* I talk and act in such a way that a visibly angry male in a committee meeting (perhaps it's me!) is "standing his ground on principle," but a visibly angry female is "hysterical."
5   *Connections:* I talk and act so as to make what I am saying here and now in this committee meeting about whether we should admit more minority students connected to or relevant to (or, on the other hand, not connected to or relevant to) what I said last week about my fears of losing my job given the new government's turn to the right.
6   *Semiotics (what and how different symbol systems and different forms of knowledge "count"):* I talk and act so as to make the knowledge and language of lawyers relevant (privileged), or not, over "everyday language" or over "non-lawyerly academic language" in our committee discussion of facilitating the admission of more minority students.

In Chapter 5 I will elaborate these "building tasks" and their relevance for discourse analysis. But in the next three chapters, I want to develop several "tools of inquiry" (ways of looking at the world of talk and interaction) that will help us study how these building tasks are carried out and with what social and political consequences. The tools of inquiry I will introduce in this chapter are primarily relevant to how we (together with others) build identities and activities and recognize the identities and activities that are being built around us. However, the tools of inquiry introduced here are most certainly caught up with all the other building tasks above, as well, as we will see progressively in this book. The tools to be discussed in this chapter are:

(a)   *"Situated identities,"* that is, different identities or social positions we enact and recognize in different settings.
(b)   *"Social languages,"* that is, different styles of language that we use to enact and recognize different identities in different settings; different

social languages also allow us to engage in all the other building tasks above (in different ways, building different sorts of things).

(c) *"Discourses"* with a capital *"D,"* that is, different ways in which we humans integrate language with non-language "stuff," such as different ways of thinking, acting, interacting, valuing, feeling, believing, and using symbols, tools, and objects in the right places and at the right times so as to enact and recognize different identities and activities, give the material world certain meanings, distribute social goods in a certain way, make certain sorts of meaningful connections in our experience, and privilege certain symbol systems and ways of knowing over others (i.e. carry out all the building tasks above).

(d) *"Conversations"* with a capital *"C,"* that is, long-running and important themes or motifs that have been the focus of a variety of different texts and interactions (in different social languages and Discourses) through a significant stretch of time and across an array of institutions.

2.2 *Whos* and *whats*

When you speak or write anything, you use the resources of English to project yourself as a certain kind of person, a different kind in different circumstances. You also project yourself as engaged in a certain kind of activity, a different kind in different circumstances. If I have no idea who you are and what you are doing, then I cannot make sense of what you have said, written, or done.

You project a different identity at a formal dinner party than you do at the family dinner table. And, though these are both dinner, they are none the less different activities. The fact that people have differential access to different identities and activities, connected to different sorts of status and social goods, is a root source of inequality in society. Intervening in such matters can be a contribution to social justice. Since different identities and activities are enacted in and through language, the study of language is integrally connected to matters of equity and justice.

An oral or written "utterance" has meaning, then, only if and when it communicates a *who* and a *what* (Wieder and Pratt 1990a). What I mean by a "who" is a *socially-situated identity*, the "kind of person" one is seeking to be and enact here and now. What I mean by a "what" is a socially-situated *activity* that the utterance helps to constitute.

Lots of interesting complications can set in when we think about identity enacted in and through language. *Whos* can be multiple and they need not always be people. The President's Press Secretary can issue an utterance that is, in fact, authored by a speech writer and authorized (and even claimed) by the President. In this case, the utterance communicates a sort of overlapping and compound *who*. The Press Secretary, even if she is directly quoting the speech writer, must inflect the remark with her own voice. In turn, the speech writer is both "mimicking" the President's "voice" and creating an identity for him.

Not just individuals, but also institutions, through the "anonymous" texts and products they circulate, can author or issue "utterances." For example, we will see below that the warning on an aspirin bottle actually communicates multiple *whos*. An utterance can be authored, authorized by, or issued by a group or a single individual.

Finally, we can point out that *whos* and *whats* are not really discrete and separable. You are *who* you are partly through *what* you are doing and *what* you are doing is partly recognized for what it is by *who* is doing it. So it is better, in fact, to say that utterances communicate an integrated, though often multiple or "heteroglossic," *who-doing-what*.

2.3 "Real Indians"

Though I have focused on language, it is important to see that making visible and recognizable *who* we are and *what* we are doing always requires more than language. It requires, as well, that we act, think, value, and inter-act in ways that together with language render *who* we are and *what* we are doing recognizable to others (and ourselves). In fact, to be a particular *who* and to pull off a particular *what* requires that we act, value, interact, and use language *in sync with* or *in coordination with* other people and with various objects ("props") in appropriate locations and at appropriate times.

To see this wider notion of language as integrated with "other stuff" (other people, objects, values, times and places), we will briefly consider Wieder and Pratt's (1990a, b) fascinating work on how Native Americans (from a variety of different groups, though no claim is made that the follow-ing is true of all Native American groups) recognize each other as "really Indian." Wieder and Pratt point out that real Indians "refer to persons who are 'really Indian' in just those words with regularity and standardiza-tion" (1990a: 48). Wieder and Pratt's work will also make clear how the identities (the *whos*) we take on are flexibly negotiated in actual contexts of practice.

The term "real Indian" is, of course, an "insiders' term." The fact that it is used by some Native Americans in enacting their own identity work does not license non-Native Americans to use the term. Thus, though it may clutter the text, I will below always place the term "real Indian" in scare quotes to make clear that I am talking about the term and not claiming that I have the "right" to actually use it of anyone. In any case, however I might use it, it certainly would do different work than it does for the Native Americans we will discuss below. Finally, let me say that I am not discussing Native Americans here because I think they are "esoteric." In fact, I am using this example, because I think it is a clear and dramatic example of what we *all* do all the time, though in different ways.

The problem of "recognition and being recognized" is very consequential and problematic for Native Americans. While in order to be considered a "real Indian," one must be able to make some claims to kinship with others who are recognized as "real Indians," this by no means settles the matter. People with such (biological) ties can fail to get recognized as a "real Indian," and people of mixed kinship can be so recognized.

Being a "real Indian" is not something one can simply be. Rather, it is something that one becomes in and through the doing of it, that is, in carrying out the actual performance itself. Though one must have certain kinship ties to get in the "game," beyond this entry criterion, there is no *being* (once and for all) a "real Indian," rather there is only doing *being-or-becoming-a-"real-Indian."* If one does not continue to "practice" being a "real Indian," one ceases to be one.

Finally, doing being-and-becoming-a-"real-Indian" is not something that one can do all by oneself. It requires the participation of others. One cannot be a "real Indian" unless one appropriately recognizes "real Indians" and gets recognized by others as a "real Indian" in the practices of doing being-and-becoming-a-"real-Indian." Being a "real Indian" also requires appropriate accompanying objects (props), times, and places.

There are a multitude of ways one can do being-and-becoming-a-"real-Indian." Some of these are (following Wieder and Pratt 1990a): "Real Indians" prefer to avoid conversation with strangers, Native American or otherwise. They cannot be related to one another as "mere acquaintances," as some "non-Indians" might put it. So, for "real Indians," any conversation they do have with a stranger who may turn out to be a "real Indian" will, in the discovery of the other's "Indianness," establish substantial obligations between the conversational partners just through the mutual acknowledgment that they are "Indians" and that they are now no longer strangers to one another.

In their search for the other's "real Indianness" and in their display of their own "Indianness," "real Indians" frequently engage in a distinctive form of verbal sparring. By correctly responding to and correctly engaging in this sparring, which "Indians" call "razzing," each participant further establishes cultural competency in the eyes of the other.

"Real Indians" manage face-to-face relations with others in such a way that they appear to be in agreement with them (or, at least, they do not overtly disagree); they are modest and "fit in." They show accord and harmony and are reserved about their own interests, skills, attainments, and positions. "Real Indians" understand that they should not elevate themselves over other "real Indians." And they understand that the complex system of obligations they have to kin and other "real Indians" takes priority over those contractual obligations and pursuit of self-interest that some "non-Indians" prize so highly.

"Real Indians" must be competent in "doing their part" in participating in conversations that begin with the participants exchanging greetings and other amenities and then lapsing into extended periods of silence. They must know that neither they nor the others have an obligation to speak – that silence on the part of all conversants is permissible.

When they are among "Indians," "real Indians" must also be able to perform in the roles of "student" and "teacher" and be able to recognize the behaviors appropriate to these roles. These roles are brought into play exclusively when the appropriate occasion arises for transmitting cultural knowledge (i.e. things pertinent to being a "real Indian"). Although many "non-Indians" find it proper to ask questions of someone who is instructing them, "Indians" regard questions in such a situation as being inattentive, rude, insolent, and so forth. The person who has taken the role of "student" shows attentiveness by avoiding eye contact and by being silent. The teaching situation, then, as a witnessed monologue, lacks the dialogical features that characterize some Western instruction.

While the above sort of information gives us something of the flavor of what sorts of things one must do and say to get recognized as a "real Indian," such information can lead to a bad mistake. It can sound as if the above features are necessary and sufficient criteria for doing being-and-becoming-a-"real-Indian." But this is not true.

These features are not a test that can be or ever is administered all at once, and once and for all, to determine who is or is not a "real Indian." Rather, the circumstances under which these features are employed by "Indians" emerge over the course of a developing history among groups of people. They are employed always in the context of actual situations, and at different times in the life history of groups of people. The ways in which the judgment, "He (or she) is (or is not) a 'real Indian'," is embedded within situations that motivate it make such judgments intrinsically provisional. Those now recognized can spoil their acceptance or have it spoiled and those not now accepted can have another chance, even when others are reluctant to extend it.

The same thing applies, in fact, in regard to many other social identities, not just being "a real Indian." There are no once and for all tests for who is a "real" feminist, gang member, patriot, humanist, cutting-edge scientist, "yuppie," or "regular" at the local bar. These matters are settled provisionally and continuously, in practice, as part and parcel of shared histories and on-going activities. When I was young, my community certainly had (very rigid) tests through which we continually, always provisionally, and sometimes contentiously, displayed and recognized who was and was not a "real Catholic" (versus being a "Catholic in name only" or being a non-Catholic). That community, and those tests, have, over the least several decades, changed radically, however much we then viewed them as static and eternal.

Different social identities (different *whos*) may seriously conflict with one another. For instance, Scollon and Scollon (1981) point out that for the Native Americans they studied (Athabaskans in Canada and the U.S.), writing essays, a practice common in school, can constitute a crisis in identity. To produce an essay requires the Athabaskan to produce a major self-display, which is appropriate to Athabaskans only when a person is in a position of dominance in relation to the audience (in the case of school, the teacher, not the student).

Furthermore, in essayist prose, the audience and the author are "fictionalized" (not really me and you, but decontextualized and rather generic readers and writers) and the text is decontextualized from specific social networks and relationships. Where the relationship of the communicants is decontextualized and unknown, Athabaskans prefer silence.

The paradox of prose for Athabaskans, the Scollons point out, is that if it is communication between known author and audience it is contextualized and compatible with Athabaskan values, but not good essayist prose. To the extent that it becomes decontextualized and thus good essayist prose, it becomes uncharacteristic of Athabaskans to seek to communicate. What is required to do and be an Athabaskan is in large part mutually exclusive with what it is required to do and be a writer of school-based essayist prose. This doesn't mean Athabaskans cannot do both (remember, we are all multiple), it simply means that they may face very real conflicts in terms of values and identity. And, as the Scollons point out, many other groups of people have similar or related "identity issues" with essayist literacy.

2.4 Discourses (with a big "D")

I want to argue that the problem of "recognition and being recognized" is very consequential, not only for Native Americans, but for all of us all the time. And, as we saw above, making visible and recognizable *who* we are and *what* we are doing always involves a great deal more than "just language." It involves acting-interacting-thinking-valuing-talking-(sometimes writing-reading) in the "appropriate way" with the "appropriate" props at the "appropriate" times in the "appropriate" places.

Such socially accepted associations among ways of using language, of thinking, valuing, acting, and interacting, in the "right" places and at the "right" times with the "right" objects (associations that can be used to identify oneself as a member of a socially meaningful group or "social network"), I will refer to as "Discourses," with a capital "D" (Gee 1990b, 1992, 1996; see also Bourdieu 1990b; Foucault 1985). I will reserve the word "discourse," with a little "d," to mean language-in-use or stretches of language (like conversations or stories). "Big D" Discourses are always language *plus* "other stuff." There are innumerable Discourses in any modern, technological, urban-based society: for example, (enacting) being something as general as a type of African-American or Anglo-Australian or something as specific as being a type of modern British young second-generation affluent Sikh woman. Being a type of middle-class American, factory worker, or executive, doctor or hospital patient, teacher, administrator, or student, student of physics or of literature, member of a club or street gang, regular at the local bar, or, as we saw earlier, "real Indian" are all Discourses.

The key to Discourses is "recognition." If you put language, action, inter-action, values, beliefs, symbols, objects, tools, and places together in such a way that others *recognize* you as a particular type of who (identity) engaged in a particular type of what (activity) here and now, then you have pulled off a Discourse (and thereby continued it through history, if only for a while longer). Whatever you have done must be similar enough to other per-formances to be recognizable. However, if it is different enough from what has gone before, but still recognizable, it can simultaneously change and transform Discourses. If it is not recognizable, then you're not "in" the Discourse.

Discourses are always embedded in a medley of social institutions, and often involve various "props" like books and magazines of various sorts, laboratories, classrooms, buildings of various sorts, various technologies, and a myriad of other objects from sewing needles (for sewing circles) through birds (for bird watchers) to basketball courts and basketballs (for basketball players). Think of all the words, symbols, deeds, objects, clothes, and tools you need to coordinate in the right way at the right time and place to "pull off" (or recognize someone as) being a cutting-edge particle physicist or a Los Angeles Latino street gang member or a sensitive high-culture humanist (of old).

It is sometimes helpful to think about social and political issues as if it is not just us humans who are talking and interacting with each other, but rather, the Discourses we represent and enact, and for which we are "carriers." The Discourses we enact existed before each of us came on the scene and most of them will exist long after we have left the scene. Discourses, through our words and deeds, carry on conversations with each other through history, and, in doing so, form human history.

Think, for instance, of the long-running and ever-changing "conversa-tion" in the U.S. and Canada between the Discourses of "being an Indian" and "being an Anglo" or of the different, but equally long-running "conversation" in New Zealand between "being a Maori" and "being an Anglo" (or, for that matter, think of the long-running conversation between "being a British Anglo" and "being an American Anglo"). Think of the long-running and ever-changing "conversation" between creationists and biologists. Think of the long-running and ever-changing "conversa-tion" in Los Angeles between African-American teenage gang members and the L.A. police (some of whom, for instance, are leading experts, even academically speaking, on the "grammar" of gang graffiti, which varies significantly, by the way, between African-American gangs and Latino gangs). Intriguingly, we humans are very often unaware of the his-tory of these conversations, and thus, in a deep sense, not fully aware of what we mean when we act and talk.

When we discussed being a "real Indian," we argued that "knowing how" to be a "real Indian" rests on one's being able to "be in sync with other 'real Indians'" and with objects (e.g. the material items of the culture) in the appropriate times and places. Recent studies of science suggest much the same thing is true for scientists.

For example, these studies argue the physics experimental physicists "know" is, in large part, *not* in their heads. Rather, it is spread out (distributed), inscribed in (and often trapped in) apparatus, symbolic systems, books, papers, and journals, institutions, habits of bodies, routines of practice, and other people (Latour 1987; Traweek 1988). Each domain of practice, each scientific Discourse – for example, a specific area within physics or biology – *attunes* actions, expressions, objects, and people (the scientists themselves) so that they become "workable" *in relation* to each other (Knorr Cetina 1992). They are "in sync."

Just as there were verbal and non-verbal ways to be a "real Indian," there are ways to be a "real experimental physicist." They are both (being an experimental physicist or being a "real Indian") ways with words, feelings, values, beliefs, emotions, people, actions, things, tools, and places that allow us to display and recognize characteristic *whos* doing characteristic *whats*. They are both, then, Discourses.

The scientist's "know how" is the ability to *coordinate and be coordinated by* constellations of expressions, actions, objects, and people. In a sense, the scientist is *both* an actor (coordinating other people and various things, tools, technologies, and symbol systems) and a *patient* (being coordinated by other people and various things, tools, technologies, and symbol systems). Scientists become *agent-patients* "in sync with," "linked with," "in association with," "in coordination with," however we want to put it, other "actants" (adapting a term from Callon and Latour 1992), such as particular forms of language, other people, objects (e.g. scientific equipment, atoms, molecules, or birds), places (e.g. labs or fields), and non-verbal practices.

In the end a Discourse is a "dance" that exists in the abstract as a co-ordinated pattern of words, deeds, values, beliefs, symbols, tools, objects, times, and places and in the here and now as a performance that is recognizable as just such a coordination. Like a dance, the performance here and now is never exactly the same. It all comes down, often, to what the "masters of the dance" will allow to be recognized or will be forced to recognize as a possible instantiation of the dance.

2.5 Discourses are not "units" with clear boundaries

The notion of Discourses will be important throughout this book. It is important, therefore, to make some points clear to avoid some common misunderstandings. Imagine I freeze a moment of thought, talk, action, or interaction for you, in the way in which a projector can freeze a piece of film. To make sense of that moment, you have to recognize the identities and activities involved in it. Perhaps, for this frozen moment you can't do so, so you move the film back and forward enough until you can make such a recognition judgment.

"Oh, now I see," you say, "it's a 'real Indian' razzing another 'real Indian'," or "it's a radical feminist berating a male for a crass male remark" or "it's a laboratory physicist orienting colleagues to a graph" or "it's a first-grader in Ms. X's class starting a sharing time story." Perhaps, if you now move the film backwards and forwards a bit more, you will change your judgments a little, a lot, or not at all.

Perhaps, you aren't sure. You and I even argue about the matter. You say that "It's a skinhead sending intimidating glances to a passing adult on the street" and I say, "No, it's just a wanna-be trying to act tough." You say, "It's a modern classroom teacher leading a discussion" and I say, "No, it's a traditional teacher giving a lecture in the guise of a series of known-answer questions."

This is what I call "recognition work." People engage in such work when they try to make visible to others (and to themselves, as well) who they are and what they are doing. People engage in such work when they try to recognize others for who they are and what they are doing. People engage in such work within interactions, moment by moment. They engage in such work when they reflect on their interactions later. They engage in such work, as well, when they try to understand human interaction as researchers, practitioners, theoreticians, or interventionists.

Sometimes such recognition work is conscious, sometimes it is not. Sometimes people have labels they can articulate for the *whos* and *whats* they recognize, sometimes they don't. Sometimes they fight over the labels, sometimes they don't. And the labels change over time.

Thanks to the fact that we humans engage, inside and outside interactions, in recognition work, Discourses exist in the world. For example, there is a way of being a kindergarten student in Ms. X's class with its associated activities and ways with words, deeds, and things. Ms. X, her students, her classroom, with its objects and artifacts, and characteristic activities, are all *in* the Discourse she and her students create. These same people and things, of course, can be in other Discourses as well.

Recognition work and Discourses out in the world go hand-in-hand. Ms. X and her students engage in recognition work, for example, a certain sort of sharing time story isn't recognized as "acceptable" in this class, another type is. That recognition work creates a Discourse, that is, ways with words, actions, beliefs, emotions, values, interactions, people, objects, tools, and technologies that come to constitute "being and doing a student in Ms. X's class." In turn, this Discourse renders recognition work possible and meaningful. It's another "chicken and egg" question, then: Which comes first, recognition work or Discourses? Neither. They are reflexively related, such that each creates the other.

Discourses have no discrete boundaries because people are always, in history, creating new Discourses, changing old ones, and contesting and pushing the boundaries of Discourses. You, an African-American male, speak and act here and now in an attempt to get recognized as a "new capitalist manager coaching a project team." If you get recognized as such, then your performance is *in the Discourse* of new capitalist management. If you don't, it isn't.

If your performance has been influenced, intentionally or not, by another one of your Discourses (say, your membership in the Discourse of doing and being a jazz fan or your membership in a certain version of African-American culture as a Discourse), and it gets recognized in the new capitalist management Discourse, then you have just, at least for here and now, "infected" one Discourse with another and widened what "counts" in the new capitalist management Discourse. You pushed the boundaries. In another time and place they may get narrowed.

You can get several of your Discourses recognized all at once. You (thinking of one of my esteemed colleagues at a university where I previously worked) "pull off" being here and now, in a class or meeting, for example, "a British, twice-migrant, globally oriented, traditional and modern, fashionable, female, Sikh, American Professor of cultural studies and feminist postmodern anthropology" by weaving strands of your multiple Discourses together. If this sort of thing gets enacted and recognized enough, by enough people, then it will become not multiple strands of multiple Discourses interleaved, but a single Discourse whose hybridity may ultimately be forgotten. The point is not how we "count" Discourses; the point is the performance, negotiation, and recognition work that goes into creating, sustaining, and transforming them, and the role of language (always with other things) in this process.

Let me make several other brief, but important points about Discourses:

1   Discourses can split into two or more Discourses. For example, medieval "natural philosophy" eventually split into philosophy, physics and other sciences.
2   Two or more Discourses can meld together. For example, after the movie *Colors* came out some years ago, mixed Latino, African-American, and white gangs emerged. Prior to that, Latinos, African-Americans, and whites had quite separate ways of being and doing gangs, as they still do in the case of segregated gangs.
3   It can be problematic whether a Discourse today is or is not the same as one in the past. For example, modern medicine bears little resemblance to medicine before the nineteenth century, but perhaps enough to draw some important parallels for some purposes, though not for others.
4   New Discourses emerge and old ones die all the time. For example, in Palmdale, California (a desert community outside Los Angeles), and I assume other places as well, an anti-racist skinhead Discourse is

dying because people, including the police, tend to confuse its members with a quite separate, but similar looking, racist Neo-Nazi skinhead Discourse.

5   Discourses are always defined in relationships of complicity and contestation with other Discourses, and so they change when other Discourses in a society emerge or die. For example, the emergence of a "new male" Discourse in the 1970s (ways of doing and being a "new male") happened in response to various gender-based Discourses (e.g. various sorts of feminism) and class-based Discourses (the baby-boom middle class was too big for all young males to stay in it, so those who "made it" needed to mark their difference from those who did not), and, in turn, changed the meanings and actions of these other Discourses.

6   Discourses need, by no means, be "grand" or large scale. I used to eat regularly at a restaurant with a long bar. Among the regulars, there were two different Discourses at opposite ends of the bar, that is, ways of being and doing that end of the bar. One involved young men and women and a lot of male-dominated sexual bantering; the other involved older people and lots of hard luck stories. The restaurant assigned different bartenders to each end (always a young female at the young end) and many of the bartenders could fully articulate the Discourse at their end of the bar and their role in it.

7   Discourses can be hybrids of other Discourses. For example, the school yards of many urban middle and high schools are places where teenagers of different ethnic groups come together and engage in what I have elsewhere called a "borderland Discourse" of doing and being urban teenager peers (Gee 1996), when they cannot safely go into each other's neighborhoods and when they each have their own neighborhood peer-based Discourses. The borderland Discourse is quite manifestly a mixture of the various neighborhood peer Discourses, with some emergent properties of its own.

8   There are limitless Discourses and no way to count them, both because new ones, even quite non-grand ones, can always emerge and because boundaries are always contestable.

One way to think about the role of Discourses is this: Imagine you have a giant map. Each Discourse is represented on the map like a country, but with movable boundaries that you can slide around a bit. You place the map on top of any language, action, or interaction you participate in or want to think about. You move the boundaries of the Discourse areas on the map around in negotiation with others or as your reflections change.

The map gives you a way to understand what you are seeing in relationship to the full set of Discourses in an institution (maybe it is just a map of all the Discourses in a given community, business, school, or university) or the society as a whole (if it's a map of the whole society), at least as far as you know it. Wherever on the map you line up the current thought, action, interaction, or language, it is immediately placed in relation to all the other countries (Discourses) on the map (though "fuzzily," since you can move the boundaries around or others can try to make you do so).

Such a map is a Discourse grid against which you understand your own and others' thought, language, action, and interaction. It is an ever changing map with which you can engage in recognition work. It is, as it exists across people and social groups, both the origin and the product of the reality of actual Discourses in the world, aligning and disaligning themselves with each other through history.

Understanding is always relative to the whole grid or map. The complex relationships among Discourses, which we can imagine as intricate criss-crossing lines connecting the various Discourse-areas on the map in complex positive and negative ways, define and demarcate individual Discourses. Your own Discourse grid is the limit of your understanding, and it is the fundamental job of education to give people bigger and better Discourse maps, ones that reflect the working of Discourses through-out society, the world, and history in relationship to each other and to the learner.

So Discourses are out in the world and in history as coordinations ("a dance") of people, places, times, actions, interactions, verbal and non-verbal expression, symbols, things, tools, and technologies that betoken certain identities and associated activities. Thus, they are material realities. But Discourses also exist as the work we do to get people and things recognized in certain ways and not others, and they exist as maps that constitute our understandings. They are, then, social practices and mental entities, as well as material realities.

2.6 A heteroglossic aspirin bottle

I want now to return to how *whos* and *whats* are communicated in *language* (keeping in mind that language alone is rarely enough and is always put together with "other stuff" to pull off a Discourse). It is time, then, to turn to examples in order to make my points about *whos-doing-whats* more concrete. Consider, then, the warning on my aspirin bottle (Gee 1996), reprinted below (italics and capitals are on the warning):

> Warnings: *Children and teenagers should not use this medication for chicken pox or flu symptoms before a doctor is consulted about Reye Syndrome, a rare but serious illness reported to be associated with aspirin.* Keep this and all drugs out of the reach of children. In case of accidental overdose, seek professional assistance or contact a poison control center immediately. As with any drug, if you are pregnant or nursing a baby, seek the advice of a health professional before using this product. IT IS ESPECIALLY IMPORTANT NOT TO USE ASPIRIN DURING THE LAST 3 MONTHS OF PREGNANCY

UNLESS SPECIFICALLY DIRECTED TO DO SO BY A DOCTOR BECAUSE IT MAY CAUSE PROBLEMS IN THE UNBORN CHILD OR COMPLICATIONS DURING DELIVERY. See carton for arthritis use[+] and Important Notice.

My interpretation of this text is that there are two *who-doing-whats* in this warning, and they are interleaved. The first is made up of the following sentences:

Children and teenagers should not use this medication for chicken pox or flu symptoms before a doctor is consulted about Reye Syndrome, a rare but serious illness reported to be associated with aspirin. It is especially important not to use aspirin during the last 3 months of pregnancy unless specifically directed to do so by a doctor because it may cause problems in the unborn child or complications during delivery.

Here things are referred to quite specifically ("children or teenagers," "this medication," "chicken pox," "flu," "Reye Syndrome," "aspirin," "last 3 months," "unborn child," "delivery"), doctors are called "doctor," and matters are treated emphatically (italics, capitals, "should not," "rare but serious," "especially important," "specifically directed").

The second *who-doing-what* is made up of the following sentences, placed in the middle of the other two:

Keep this and all drugs out of the reach of children. In case of accidental overdose, seek professional assistance or contact a poison control center immediately. As with any drug, if you are pregnant or nursing a baby, seek the advice of a health professional before using this product.

Here things are referred to more generally and generically ("this and all drugs," "any drug," and "this product," rather than "this medication" and "aspirin"; "children" rather than "children and teenagers," "pregnant" rather than "last 3 months of pregnancy"), doctors are not mentioned, rather the health profession is referred to more generally ("professional assistance," "poison control center," "health professional"), and matters are treated less stridently with the exception of that "immediately" (small print, "keep out of reach," "accidental overdose," "seek . . . assistance," "seek advice," rather than "should not" and "important not to use").

These two *who-doing-whats* "feel" different. The are authorized and issued by different "voices" to different purposes and effects. The first speaks with a lawyerly voice responding to specific court cases; the second speaks with the official voice of a caring, but authoritatively knowledgeable company trying to avoid anyone thinking that aspirin in particular is a potentially harmful drug. Of course, this second *who-doing-what* partly contradicts the first. By the way, the second *who-doing-what* on the aspirin bottle used to be the only warning on the bottle (with the order of the sentences a bit different).

This warning, like all utterances, reflects the company it has kept, or, to put the matter another way, it reflects a history that has given rise to it. In this case, presumably, the new sterner, more direct *who-doing-what* was added to the more general and avuncular one because the company got sued over things like Reye Syndrome.

The warning on the aspirin bottle is heteroglossic. That is, it is "double-voiced," since it interleaves two different *whos-doing-whats* together. Of course, in different cases, this sort of interleaving could be much more intricate, with the two (or more) *whos-doing-whats* more fully integrated, and harder to tease apart.

2.7 Social languages

There is another term that it is useful in place of the cumbersome phrase "who-doing-what," at least as far as the *language* aspects of "who-doing-whats" are concerned (remembering that language is caught up with "other stuff" in Discourses). This term is "social language" (Gee 1996: ch. 4; Bakhtin 1986). Each of the *who-doing-whats* we saw on the aspirin bottle is linguistically expressed in different "social languages." All languages, like English or French, are composed of many (a great many) different social languages. Social languages are what we learn and what we speak.

Keep in mind that "social languages" and "Discourses" are terms for different things. I will use the term "social languages" to talk about the role of language in Discourses. But as I said above, Discourses always involve more than language. They always involve coordinating language with ways of acting, interacting, valuing, believing, feeling, and with bodies, clothes, non-linguistic symbols, objects, tools, technologies, times, and places.

Let me give a couple of examples of social languages at work, beyond the example of the two different social languages in the warning on the aspirin bottle, examples I have used over the years as particularly clear instances of different social languages (e.g. Gee 1996). Consider, for instance, the following case of an upper-middle-class, Anglo-American young woman named "Jane," in her twenties, who was attending one of my courses on language and communication. The course was discussing different social languages and, during the discussion, Jane claimed that she herself did not use different social languages in different contexts, but rather, was consistent from context to context. In fact, to do otherwise, she said, would be "hypocritical," a failure to "be oneself."

In order to support her claim that she did not switch her style of speaking in different contexts and for different conversational partners, Jane decided to record herself talking to her parents and to her boyfriend. In both cases, she decided to discuss a story the class had discussed earlier, so as to be sure that, in both contexts, she was talking about the same thing.

In the story, a character named Abigail wants to get across a river to see her true love, Gregory. A river boat captain (Roger) says he will take her only if she consents to sleep with him. In desperation to see Gregory, Abigail agrees to do so. But when she arrives and tells Gregory what she has done, he disowns her and sends her away. There is more to the story, but this is enough for our purposes here. Students in my class had been asked to rank order the characters in the story from the most offensive to the least.

In explaining to her parents why she thought Gregory was the worst (least moral) character in the story, the young woman said the following:

> Well, when I thought about it, I don't know, it seemed to me that Gregory should be the most offensive. He showed no understanding for Abigail, when she told him what she was forced to do. He was callous. He was hypocritical, in the sense that he professed to love her, then acted like that.

Earlier, in her discussion with her boyfriend, in an informal setting, she had also explained why she thought Gregory was the worst character. In this context she said:

> What an ass that guy was, you know, her boyfriend. I should hope, if I ever did that to see you, you would shoot the guy. He uses her and he says he loves her. Roger never lies, you know what I mean?

It was clear – even to Jane – that she had used two very different forms of language. The differences between Jane's two social languages are everywhere apparent in the two texts.

To her parents, she carefully hedges her claims ("I don't know," "it seemed to me"); to her boyfriend, she makes her claims straight out. To her boyfriend, she uses terms like "ass" and "guy," while to her parents she uses more formal terms like "offensive," "understanding," "callous," "hypocritical" and "professed." She also uses more formal sentence structure to her parents ("it seemed to me that . . . ," "He showed no understanding for Abigail, when . . . ," "He was hypocritical in the sense that . . .") than she does to her boyfriend (". . . that guy, you know, her boyfriend," "Roger never lies, you know what I mean?").

Jane repeatedly addresses her boyfriend as "you," thereby noting his social involvement as a listener, but does not directly address her parents in this way. In talking to her boyfriend, she leaves several points to be inferred, points that she spells out more explicitly to her parents (e.g. her boyfriend must infer that Gregory is being accused of being a hypocrite from the information that though Roger is bad, at least he does not lie, which Gregory did in claiming to love Abigail).

All in all, Jane appears to use more "school-like" language to her parents. Her language to them requires less inferencing on their part and distances them as listeners from social and emotional involvement with what she is saying, while stressing, perhaps, their cognitive involvement and their judgment of her and her "intelligence." Her language to her boyfriend, on the other hand, stresses social and affective involvement, solidarity, and co-participation in meaning making.

This young woman is making visible and recognizable two different versions of *who* she is and *what* she is doing. In one case she is "a dutiful and intelligent daughter having dinner with her proud parents" and in the other case she is "a girlfriend being intimate with her boyfriend." Of course, I should add, that while people like Jane may talk at dinner this way to their parents, not all people do; there are other identities one can take on for one's parents, other social languages one can speak to them. And, indeed, there may well be others that Jane would use with her parents in different settings.

Let me give one more example of social languages at work, an example taken from Greg Myers' work (1990). Biologists, and other scientists, write differently in professional journals than they do in popular science magazines. These two different ways of writing do different things and display different identities. The popular science article is *not* merely a "translation" or "simplification" of the professional article.

To see this, consider the two extracts below, the first from a professional journal, the second from a popular science magazine, both written by the same biologist on the same topic (Myers 1990: 150):

> Experiments show that *Heliconius* butterflies are less likely to ovipost on host plants that possess eggs or egg-like structures. These egg-mimics are an unambiguous example of a plant trait evolved in response to a host-restricted group of insect herbivores.
>
> (Professional journal)

> *Heliconius* butterflies lay their eggs on *Passiflora* vines. In defense the vines seem to have evolved fake eggs that make it look to the butterflies as if eggs have already been laid on them.
>
> (Popular science)

The first extract, from a professional scientific journal, is about the *conceptual structure* of a specific *theory* within the scientific *discipline* of biology. The subject of the initial sentence is "experiments," a *methodological* tool in natural science. The subject of the next sentence is "these egg-mimics": note how plant-parts are named, not in terms of the plant itself, but in terms of the role they play in a particular *theory* of natural selection and evolution, namely "coevolution" of predator and prey (that is, the theory that predator and prey evolve together by shaping each other). Note also, in this regard, the earlier "host plants" in the preceding sentence, rather than the "vines" of the popular passage.

In the second sentence, the butterflies are referred to as "a host-restricted group of insect herbivores," which points simultaneously to an aspect of scientific methodology (like "experiments" did) and to the logic of a theory (like "egg-mimics" did). Any scientist arguing for the theory of co-evolution faces the difficulty of demonstrating a causal connection between a particular plant characteristic and a particular predator when most plants have so many different sorts of animals attacking them. A central methodo-logical technique to overcome this problem is to study plant groups (like *Passiflora* vines) that are preyed on by only one or a few predators (in this case, *Heliconius* butterflies). "Host-restricted group of insect herbi-vores," then, refers to both the relationship between plant and insect that is at the heart of the theory of coevolution and to the methodological technique of picking plants and insects that are *restricted* to each other so as to "control" for other sorts of interactions.

The first passage, then, is concerned with scientific methodology and a particular theoretical perspective on evolution. On the other hand, the second extract, from a popular science magazine, is not about methodology and theory, but about *animals* in *nature*. The butterflies are the subject of the first sentence and the vine is the subject of the second. Further, the butter-flies and the vine are labeled as such, not in terms of their role in a particular theory.

The second passage is a story about the struggles of insects and plants that are transparently open to the trained gaze of the scientist. Further-more, the plant and insect become "intentional" actors in the drama: the plants act in their own "defense" and things "look" a certain way to the insects, they are "deceived" by appearances as humans sometimes are.

These two examples replicate in the present what, in fact, is an historical difference. In the history of biology, the scientist's relationship with nature gradually changed from telling stories about direct observations of nature to carrying out complex experiments to test complex theories (Bazerman 1989). Myers (1990) argues that professional science is now concerned with the expert "management of uncertainty and complexity" and popular science with the general assurance that the world is knowable by and directly accessible to experts.

The need to "manage uncertainty" was created, in part, by the fact that mounting "observations" of nature led scientists not to consensus, but to growing disagreement as to how to describe and explain such observations (Shapin and Schaffer 1985). This problem led, in turn, to the need to con-vince the public that such uncertainty did not damage the scientist's claim to professional expertise or the ultimate "knowability" of the world.

This example lets us see, then, not just that ways with words are connected to different *whos* (here the experimenter/theoretician versus the careful observer of nature) and *whats* (the professional contribution to science and the popularization of it), but that they are always acquired within and licensed by specific social and historically shaped practices representing the *values* and *interests* of distinctive groups of people.

So, it is clear now, I hope, that in using language what is at stake are *whos-doing-whats*. But, you cannot be any old *who* you want to. You cannot engage in any old *what* you want to. That is to say that *whos* and *whats* are creations in history and change in history, as we have just seen in the examples from biology.

2.8 Two grammars

Each social language has its own distinctive grammar. However, two different sorts of grammars are important to social languages, only one of which we ever think to study formally in school. One grammar is the traditional set of units like nouns, verbs, inflections, phrases and clauses. These are real enough, though quite inadequately described in traditional school grammars. Let's call this "grammar one."

The other – less studied, but more important – grammar is the "rules" by which grammatical units like nouns and verbs, phrases and clauses, are used to create *patterns* which signal or "index" characteristic *whos-doing-whats-within-Discourses*. That is, we speakers and writers design our oral or written utterances to have patterns in them in virtue of which interpreters can attribute situated identities and specific activities to us and our utterances. We will call this "grammar two."

These patterns, I hasten to add, are not fancy devices of postmodern social science. They have been named in linguistics for a long time. Linguists call them "collocational patterns." This means that various sorts of grammatical devices "co-locate" with each other. The patterns I am trying to name here are "co-relations" (correlations) among many grammatical devices, from different "levels" of grammar one. These correlations, in turn, also co-relate to (coordinate with) other non-language "stuff" to constitute (for historical, i.e. *conventional* reasons) *whos-doing-whats-within-Discourses*.

For example, in Jane's utterance to her boyfriend, "What an ass that guy was, you know, her boyfriend," note how informal terms like "ass" and "guy," the vague reference "that guy," the informal parenthetical device "you know," and the informal syntactic device of "right dislocation" (i.e. letting the phrase "her boyfriend" hang out at the end of the sentence) all pattern together to signal that this utterance is in an informal social language used to achieve solidarity.

The situation here is much like choosing clothes that go together in such a way that they communicate that we are engaged in a certain activity or are taking up a certain style connected to such activities. For example, consider how thongs, bathing suit, tank top, shades, and sun hat "co-locate" together to "signal" to us things like outdoor and water activities and the situated identities we take up in such situations.

2.9 Grammar and conversations

Let me give you another example of grammar one being used to create grammar two, that is, to create co-locational patterns in virtue of which we recognize a specific social language and its concomitant social identities and activities. Consider the sentence below (adapted from Halliday and Martin 1993: 77):

> 1   Lung cancer death rates are clearly associated with an increase in smoking.

A whole bevy of linguistic features mark this sentence as part of a distinctive academic social language (though without more connected text we can't actually tell exactly which one). Some of these are: a heavy subject ("lung cancer death rates"), deverbal nouns ("increase," "smoking"), a complex compound noun ("lung cancer death rates"), a "low transitive" relational predicate ("are associated with"), passive or passive-like voice ("are associated"), the absence of agency (no mention of who does the associating), an abstract noun ("rates"), and an assertive modifier to the verb ("clearly").

No single grammatical feature marks the social language of this sentence. Rather, all these features (and a great many more if we took a larger stretch of text, including many discourse-level features) form a distinctive *configuration* (a correlation or, better, co-relation) that marks the social language. This co-relational (co-locational) *pattern* is part of the *grammar* of this social language (in the sense of "grammar two").

I hasten to point out that the configuration of features that mark a social language are too complex and *too situated in the specific context they are helping to create* (after all, there is no such thing as a "general social science context") to be open to much generalized and rote learning. Linguistic relationships like these do not exist, and are not learned, outside the distinctive social practices (whats) of which they are an integral part. They are part and parcel of the very "voice" or "identity" (*whos*) of people who speak and write and think and act and value and live *that* way (e.g. as a social scientist) for a given time and place. To learn such relationships is part of what it means to learn to recognize the very social context one is in (and helping to create). This is not to say there is no role here for overt instruction (there is). It is only to say that there is no way we can leave out immersion in situated practices if we want to teach people new social languages.

It is sometimes said that what distinguishes "informal" social languages like the one Jane used to her boyfriend from more "formal" ones character- istic of literacy and "literate talk," like the social language Jane used to her parents, or the smoking example on p. 30, is that, in the "informal" case, "context" determines meaning and you just have to have been there to understand what was being said. In the more "formal" cases, it is held that the words and sentences mean in a more explicit, less contextual way. In fact, it is sometimes said that such language is "decontextualized." Some people in education claim that what many minority and lower socio- economic children who do not succeed in school fail to know is how to use such "decontextualized language."

All this is seriously in error, and in ways that not only mislead us, but actually damage some people (e.g. the children just referred to). Consider sentence 1 again. This sentence is no more explicit than informal language. It is no less contextualized. It is simply inexplicit and contextualized in a different way.

Though we tend to think of writing, at least academic writing, as clear, unambiguous, and explicit in comparison to speech, sentence 1, in fact, has at least 112 different meanings! What is odder still is that anyone read- ing sentence 1 (at least anyone reading this book) hits on only *one* of these meanings (or but one of a select few) without any overt awareness that the other 111 meanings are perfectly possible.

There are theories in psycholinguistics that claim that what happens in a case like sentence 1 is that we unconsciously consider all 112 possible meanings and rule out all but one, but we do this so fast and so below the level of consciousness that we are completely unaware of it. Be that as it may, how can sentence 1 have so many meanings and why do we all, none the less, hit on one and, in fact, exactly the same one?

This fact is due to the grammar (in the grammar one sense) of the sentence. The subject of sentence 1 ("Lung cancer death rates") is a "nom- inalization" made up of a compound noun. Nominalizations are like trash compactors: they allow one to take a lot of information – indeed, a whole sentence's worth of information – and compact it into a compound word or a phrase. One can then insert this compacted information into another sentence (thereby making bigger and bigger sentences). The trouble is this: once one has made the compacted item (the nominalization), it is hard to tell what information exactly went into it. Just like the compacted trash in the trash compactor, you can't always tell exactly what's in it.

"Lung cancer death rates" could be a compaction of any of the following more expanded pieces of information:

2a [lung cancer] [death rates] = rates (number) of people dying from lung cancer = how many people die from lung cancer

2b [lung cancer] [death rates] = rates (speed) of people dying from lung
    cancer = how quickly people die from lung cancer
2c [lung] [cancer death] [rates] = rates (number) of lungs dying from
    cancer = how many lungs die from cancer
2d [lung] [cancer death] [rates] = rates (speed) of lungs dying from cancer
    = how quickly lungs die from cancer

The first two meanings (2a/b) parse the phrase "lung cancer death rates"
as "lung-cancer (a disease) death-rates," that is "death-rates from lung-
cancer," where "rates" can mean number of people dying or the speed of
their death from the disease. The second two meanings (2c/d) parse the
phrase "lung cancer death rates" as "lung cancer-death-rates," that is
"cancer-death-rates for lungs," where, once again, "rates" can mean
number of (this time) lungs dying from cancer or the speed with which
they are dying from cancer. This way of parsing the phrase is analogous
to the most obvious reading of "pet cancer death rates" (i.e. "cancer-
death-rates for pets," that is, how many/how fast pets are dying from
cancer). Of course, everyone reading this paper interpreted "lung cancer
death rates" to be a compaction of 2a. Our question is, why?

Consider now the verbal phrase "are clearly associated with" in sentence
1. Such rather "colorless" relational predicates are typical of certain social
languages. Such verbal expressions are ambiguous in two respects. First,
we cannot tell whether "associated with" indicates a relationship of *causa-
tion* or just *correlation*. Thus, does sentence 1 say that one thing causes
another (e.g. smoking causes cancer) or just that one thing is correlated
with another (smoking and cancer are found together, but, perhaps, something else causes both of them)? Second, even if we take "associated with"
to mean *cause*, we still cannot tell what causes what. You and I may know,
in fact, that smoking causes cancer, but sentence 1 can perfectly mean that
lung cancer death rates *lead to* increased smoking. "Perhaps," as Halliday
remarks, "people are so upset by fear of lung cancer that they need to
smoke more in order to calm their nerves" (Halliday and Martin 1993:
77–8). It is even possible that the writer did not want to commit to a
choice between *cause* and *correlate*, or to a choice between smoking causing
cancer or fear of cancer causing smoking. This gives us at least the following
meaning possibilities for the verbal phrase "are clearly associated with":

3a cause
3b caused by
3c correlated with
3d writer does not want to commit herself

Now, let's finish with the phrase "increased smoking." This is another
nominalization, compacting information. Does it mean "people smoke
more" (smokers are increasing the amount they smoke), or "more people

smoke" (new smokers are being added to the list of smokers), or is it a combination of the two, meaning "more people smoke more"?

We can also ask, in regard to the death rates and the increased smoking
taken together, if the people who are increasing their smoking (whether old
smokers or new ones) are the people who are dying from lung cancer, or
whether other people dying as well (e.g. people who don't smoke, but, perhaps, are "associated with" smokers). Finally, we can ask of the sentence as
a whole, whether it is representing a "real" situation (*"because* more people
are smoking more people are dying") or just a hypothetical one (*"if* more
people were to smoke we know more people would die")? This gives us
at least seven more meaning possibilities:

4a increased smoking = people smoke more
4b increased smoking = more people smoke
4c increased smoking = more people smoke more
4d the same people are smoking and dying
4e the people smoking and dying are not all the same
4f the situation being talked about is real (*because*)
4g the situation being talked about is hypothetical (*if*)

We now have considered four possible meanings for the subject ("lung
cancer death rates"), four possible meanings for the verbal phrase ("are
clearly associated with") and seven possibilities for the complement
("increased smoking"). Like an old-fashioned Chinese menu, you can
take one from list A and another from list B and yet another from list C
and get a specific combination of meanings. This gives us four times four
times seven possibilities, that is, 112 different possible meanings.

All of these meanings are perfectly allowed by the grammar of sentence 1
in the "grammar one" sense of grammar. And, in fact, there are other
possibilities I have not discussed, e.g. taking "rates" to mean "monetary
costs" or "lung cancer death rates" to be the rates at which lung cancer
is dying. And yet – here's our mystery again – everyone reading this
paper in a micro second hit on just one of these many meanings and the
same one (or, at worst, considered a very few of the possibilities). Why?

The answer to the mystery I am discussing here may be perfectly obvious
to you, but I want to suggest that, none the less, it is important for how we
view language and language learning. We all hit on only one (and the same
one) of the 112 meanings because we have all been part of – we have all
been privy to – the ongoing discussion or *conversation* in our society
about smoking, disease, tobacco companies, contested research findings,
warnings on cartons, ads that entice teens to smoke, and so on and so forth.

Given this conversation as background, sentence 1 has one meaning.
Without that conversation – with only the grammar of English in one's
head – the sentence has more than 112 meanings. Obviously, however important grammar is, the conversation is more important. It leaves

open one meaning (or a small number of possibilities, like allowing that sentence 1 also covers people getting lung cancer from secondary smoke).

A more technical way to put this point is this: Meaning is not merely a matter of decoding grammar, it is also, and more importantly, a matter of knowing which of the many inferences that one can draw from an utterance are *relevant* (Sperber and Wilson 1986). And relevance is a matter deeply tied to context, point of view, and culture. One knows what counts for a given group of people at a given time and place as "relevant" by having been privy to certain "conversations" those people have heretofore had. If there had been a major conversation about environmentally induced lung cancer in a nervous society, then sentence 1 could perfectly well have been taken to mean that the prevalence of lung cancer is causing many more people to turn to smoking to calm their nerves (2a + 3a + 4b).

So, we have concluded, we speak and write not in English alone, but in specific *social languages*. The utterances of these social languages have meaning – or, at least, the meanings they are taken to have – thanks to being embedded in specific *social conversations*. Though I have established these points in regard to a single sentence (sentence 1), I take them to be generally true.

To teach someone the meaning of sentence 1 – or any sentence for that matter – is to embed them in the conversational sea in which sentence 1 swims. To teach someone the sort of social language in which sentences like sentence 1 occur is to embed them in the conversations that have recruited (and which, in turn, continually reproduce) that social language.

2.10 Big "C" Conversations: Conversation among Discourses

Now it is time to become clearer about what I mean by "conversation." The word "conversation," as I am using it here, can be misleading. We tend to think of conversations as "just words." But the sorts of conversations I am talking about involve a lot more than words; they involve, in fact, Discourses. It is better, perhaps, to call them "Conversations" with a "big C," since they are better viewed as (historic) conversations between and among Discourses, not just among individual people. Think, for instance, as we mentioned above, of the long-running, historic Conversation between biology and creationism, or between the Los Angeles police department and Latino street gangs.

More than people, and more than language, are involved in Conversations. They involve, as well, at least the following three non-verbal things:

1   controversy, that is, "sides" we can identify as constituting a debate (Billig 1987);
2   values and ways of thinking connected to the debate; and

3   the "symbolic" value of objects and institutions that are what we might call non-verbal participants in the Conversation (Latour 1987).

Let me give you an example of what I am trying to get at here. It is fashionable today for businesses to announce (in "mission statements") their "core values" in an attempt to create a particular company "culture" (Collins and Porras 1994, examples below are from pp. 68–9). For instance, the announced core values of Johnson & Johnson, a large pharmaceutical company, include "The company exists to alleviate pain and disease" and "Individual opportunity and reward based on merit," as well as several others.

One might wonder, then, what the core values of a cigarette company might be. Given the Conversations that most of us are familiar with – about the U.S. and its history in this case, as well as about smoking – we can almost predict what they will be. For example, the espoused core values of Philip Morris, a large company which sells cigarettes among a great many other products, include "The right to personal freedom of choice (to smoke, to buy whatever one wants) is worth defending," "Winning – being the best and beating others," and "Encouraging individual initiative," as well as (in a statement similar to one of Johnson & Johnson's statements) "Opportunity to achieve based on merit, not gender, race, or class."

We all readily connect Philip Morris's core value statements to themes of American individualism and freedom. Note how the values of "individual initiative" and "reward for merit," which are part of the core values of both Johnson & Johnson and Philip Morris, take on a different coloring in the two cases. In the first case, they take on a humanistic coloring and in the other the coloring of "every man for himself." This coloring is the effect of our knowledge of the two sides to the "smoking Conversation" in which, we all know, individual freedom is pitted against social responsibility.

Note, then, here how values, beliefs, and objects play a role in the sorts of Conversations I am talking about. We know that in this Conversation some people will hold values and beliefs consistent with expressions about individualism, freedom, the "American way," and so forth, while others will express values and beliefs consistent with the rights of others, social responsibility, and protecting people from harm, even harm caused by their own desires. In turn, these two value and belief orientations can be historically tied to much wider dichotomies centering around beliefs about the responsibilities and the role of governments.

Furthermore, within this Conversation, an object like a cigarette or an institution like a tobacco company, or the act of smoking itself, takes on meanings – symbolic values – within the Conversation, but dichotomous meanings. Smoking can be seen as an addiction, an expression of freedom, or a lack of caring about others. The point is that those familiar with the Conversation know, just as they can select the meaning of sentence 1 out of 112 possibilities, the possible meanings of cigarettes, tobacco companies, and smoking.

When we teach literature or physics, or anything else, for that matter, we index a multiple, but specific world of Conversations, though it is no easy matter in classrooms to get most of these Conversations going "for real." When we teach language – whether this be French, English as Second Language, composition, basic skills, literacy, or what have you – we face in the purest and hardest form the question of what Conversation or Conversations make words and phrases meaningful and relevant here and now.

The themes and values that enter into Conversations circulate in a multitude of texts and media and have done so in the past. They are the products of historic meaning making within Discourses. Of course, people today often know these themes and values without knowing the historical events that helped create or sustain them in the past and pass them down to us today.

For example, throughout the latter half of the nineteenth century in Massachusetts, courts were asked to return escaped slaves to their Southern "owners" (von Frank 1998). These court battles, and the accompanying controversies in newspapers and public meetings, engaged two distinctive Discourses among several others (for example, several Discourses connected to Black churches and to Massachusetts' significant nineteenth-century population of free Black people, some of them professionals, such as ministers, doctors, and lawyers – note that it is hard to know what to call these people, they were of African descent, born in the U.S., of all different colors, but were not full citizens).

One Discourse, connected to people like Emerson and Thoreau, championed freedom, personal responsibility, and morality as constituting a "higher law" than the law of states, the federal government, or the courts. They argued and fought, not only to not return the slaves, but to disobey the court and the federal officials seeking to enforce its mandate. The other Discourse, heavily associated with nationally-oriented political and business elites, championed the rule of law at the expense of either the slave's freedom or one's own personal conscience.

These two Discourses were, by no means, just "statements" and "beliefs." There were, for example, distinctive ways, in mind, body, and social practice, to mark oneself in nineteenth-century Massachusetts as a "Transcendentalist" (i.e. a follower of Emerson and his colleagues) and to engage in social activities seen as part and parcel of this identity.

Many people today have no knowledge of the debates over escaped slaves in Massachusetts and nationally in the nineteenth century (though these debates, of course, helped lead to the Civil War). However, these debates sustained, transformed, and handed down themes and values that are quite recognizable as parts of ongoing Conversations in the mid-twentieth century (e.g. in the Civil Rights Movement) and today.

Of course, I must hasten to add, again, that a number of other important Discourses played a significant role in the escaped slave cases in Massachusetts. Blacks were part of some integrated Discourses, as well as their own distinctive Discourses. Furthermore, all these Discourses interacted with each other, in complex relations of alliance and contestation, with some important overlaps between Discourses (e.g. between the Transcendentalists and John Brown's distinctive and violent Discourse in regard to slavery and abolition).

Because people are often unaware of historical clashes among Discourses, it is often easier to study Conversations, rather than Discourses directly, though it is always important and interesting to uncover the historical antecedents of today's Conversations. Conversations are the precipitates of what we will call, in subsequent chapters, "situated meanings" and "cultural models" as these have circulated with and across Discourses in history.

The way in which I have used the term "Conversation" here is a use that is sometimes covered in other work by the term "discourse." People who use the term "discourse" this way mean something like this: the range of things that count as "appropriately" "sayable" and "meaning-able," in terms of (oral or written) words, symbols, images, and things, at a given time and place, or within a given institution, set of institutions, or society, in regard to a given topic or theme (e.g. schools, women's health, smoking, children, prisons, etc.). Such a use of the term "discourse" or "Conversation" (the term I will use) concentrates on themes and topics as they are "appropriately" "discussible" within and across Discourses at a particular time in history, across a particular historical period, within a given institution or set of them, or within a particular society or across several of them (Foucault 1985).

2.11 Social languages and Discourses as tools of inquiry

In this chapter, I have treated the terms "social languages," "Discourses," and "Conversations" realistically. That is, I have spoken about them as things that exist in the mind and in the world. And indeed, this is, I believe, both true and the easiest way to grasp what they mean and how and why they are significant for discourse analysis.

But it is important to realize that, in the end, these terms are ultimately our ways as theoreticians and analysts of talking about, and, thus, constructing and construing the world. And it is in this guise that I am primarily interested in them. They are "tools of inquiry." "Social languages," "Discourses," and "Conversations" are "thinking devices" that guide us to ask certain sorts of questions. Faced with a piece of oral or written language, we ask the following sorts of questions:

- What social languages are involved? What sorts of "grammar two" patterns indicate this? Are different social languages mixed? How so?
- What socially situated identities and activities do these social languages enact?
- What Discourse or Discourses are involved? How is "stuff" other than language ("mind stuff" and "emotional stuff" and "world stuff" and "interactional stuff" and non-language symbol systems, etc.) relevant in indicating socially situated identities and activities?
- What sort of performance and recognition work (negotiations and struggles) has gone on in interactions over this language? What are the actual or possible social, institutional, and political consequences of this work?
- In considering this language, what sorts of relationships among different Discourses are involved (institutionally, in society, or historically)? How are different Discourses aligned or in contention here?
- What Conversations are relevant to understanding this language and to what Conversations does it contribute (institutionally, in society, or historically)?

Note: The term "Discourse" (with a big "D") is meant to cover important aspects of what others have called: discourses (Foucault 1966, 1969, 1973, 1977, 1978, 1980, 1984, 1985); communities of practice (Lave and Wenger 1991); cultural communities (Clark 1996); discourse communities (Berkenkotter and Huckin 1995; Miller 1984); distributed knowledge or distributed systems (Hutchins 1995; Lave 1988); thought collectives (Fleck 1979); practices (Barton and Hamilton 1998; Bourdieu 1977, 1985, 1990a, b; Heidegger 1962); cultures (Geertz 1973, 1983); activity systems (Engestrom 1987, 1990; Leont'ev 1981; Wertsch 1998); actor-actant networks (Callon and Latour 1992; Latour 1987); and (one interpretation of) "forms of life" (Wittgenstein 1958). Discourses, for me, crucially involve:

- situated identities;
- ways of performing and recognizing characteristic identities and activities;
- ways of coordinating and getting coordinated by other people, things, tools, technologies, symbol systems, places, and times;
- characteristic ways of acting-interacting-feeling-emoting-valuing-gesturing-posturing-dressing-thinking-believing-knowing-speaking-listening (and, in some Discourses, reading-and-writing, as well).

A given Discourse can involve multiple identities (e.g. a teacher, Ms. X , and her kindergarten students take on different situated identities, and different, but related, ones in diverse activities within the "Ms. X-and-her-students classroom Discourse," provided that Ms. X has, in fact, created a coherent Discourse in and around her classroom). Some people dislike the term "situated identity" and prefer, instead, something like "(social) position" or "subjectivity" (they tend to reserve the term "identity" for a sense of self that is relatively continuous and "fixed" over time). I use the term "identity" (or, to be specific, "socially-situated identity") for the multiple identities we take on in different practices and contexts and would use the term "core identity" for whatever continuous and relatively "fixed" sense of self underlies our contextually shifting multiple identities.

3 Situated meanings and cultural models

3.1 Meaning

The primary tools of inquiry we will discuss in this chapter are "situated meanings" and "cultural models." Both of these involve ways of looking at how speakers and writers give language specific meanings within specific situations. I will argue in this chapter that the meanings of words are not stable and general. Rather, words have multiple and ever changing meanings created for and adapted to specific contexts of use. At the same time, the meanings of words are integrally linked to social and cultural groups in ways that transcend individual minds.

This chapter will also discuss a perspective on the human mind at work in the social world. Traditional views of the mind in cognitive science have tended to view the human mind as a "rule following" device that very often works in quite abstract and general ways. The perspective taken here views the human mind as a "pattern recognizing" device that works primarily by storing experiences and finding patterns in those experiences, patterns that often stay fairly close to the experiences from which they were extracted (i.e. they are not always all that abstract or general) and that shape how we engage with (and store in our minds) our subsequent experiences.

To begin to develop a "situated" viewpoint on meaning ("situated" means "local, grounded in actual practices and experiences"), I will consider two areas where it is clear that meaning is multiple, flexible, and tied to culture. In the first case, dealt with in section 3.2, we look at how children acquire the meanings of words. In the second case, which we turn to in section 3.5, we look at how scientists and "everyday" people use the "same" words to mean different things.

In sections 3.3 and 3.4, I introduce the two tools of inquiry (ways of looking at language-in-action in the world) focused on in this chapter. These two tools will play a major role throughout the rest of this book: "situated meanings" and "cultural models." In subsequent sections, I extend the discussion of situated meanings in several directions. I first develop the particular perspective on the human mind that underlies the approach to meaning taken in this book and discuss some of the implications it holds. Then, after a brief discussion of the role of "situated meaning" in discourse analysis, I close this chapter with a discussion of how meanings are situated in relationship to history and in relationship to other texts and voices. This latter discussion will introduce a third tool of inquiry, namely "intertextuality," that is, the ways in which different sorts of texts and styles of language intermingle to create and transform meaning.

To make matters clearer here, I will often write stressing the ways in which language-in-use is fitted or adapted to the contexts or situations in which it is used. However, as we saw at the outset of Chapter 2, when we use language we both create contexts or situations (make things meaningful in certain ways and not others) and fit or adapt our language to these ongoing contexts or situations (which, after all, often get created in relatively similar ways from time to time and usually stay in existence, thanks to people's interactional work, for a shorter or longer period of time). In fact, it is because children learn how to fit their language to the contexts primarily created by others in their social and cultural groups that they learn that certain forms of language can create and transform such contexts in quite active ways.

3.2 A child acquiring the meaning of a word

Consider the case of a little girl learning the word "shoe." At first, she uses the word only for the shoes in her mother's closet. Eventually, however, she "overextends" the meaning of the word (beyond what adults would use it for). Now she uses it, not only in situations where shoes are involved, but also while handling her teddy bear's shoeless feet, passing a doll's arm to an adult to be refitted on the doll, putting a sock on a doll, and when looking at a picture of a brown beetle (Griffiths 1986: 296–7).

At this point, the little girl associates the word "shoe" with a variety of different contexts, each of which contains one or more salient "features" that could trigger the use of the word. The picture of the beetle is associated with the word "shoe" presumably in virtue of features like "shiny" and "hard" and "oval shaped"; the doll's arm merits the word "shoe" in virtue of features like "fittable to the body" and "associated with a limb of the body," and so forth.

What the little girl is doing here is typical even of how adults deal with meaning. Of course, she still must learn the full range of features she ought to consult in a context in order to call something a "shoe," but more importantly, she must also come to realize that the features associated with different contexts which trigger the application of a word are not just a random list. Rather, they "hang together" to form a *pattern* that specific sociocultural groups of people find significant.

For example, in the case of shoes, features like "hard," "shiny," "formal," "rigid soles," "solid color," "with thin laces" tend to "hang together." They form a pattern, picking out a certain set of shoes, i.e. formal shoes. On the other hand, features like "soft," "thick laces," "perhaps with colored trim," "flexible soles," "made of certain sorts of characteristic materials," "having certain sorts of characteristic looks/designs," tend to "hang together" to form another sort of pattern. This pattern picks a different set of shoes, i.e. athletic shoes. There are other patterns that pick out other sorts of shoes.

I should point out, as is clear already in any case, that it is no easy matter to put these patterns into words. As we will see below, such patterns are really a matter, in many cases, of *unconscious recognition*, rather than conscious thought. Furthermore, some features in a pattern are always present, while some are present in some cases and not in others (e.g. note our "perhaps with colored trim" above).

There are patterns of features like "having a shape contoured to a human foot," "covering a significant amount of the foot," "flexible enough to fit on foot," but "relatively rigid" that "hang together" in such a way that they pick out a very large class of the whole set of shoes. However, even these are not a necessary and sufficient set of conditions for shoes in general. There are still borderline cases, like moccasins (not really hard enough) and sandals (don't really cover enough). When the child reaches this point, she is finding patterns and sub-patterns in the contexts in which the word "shoe" is used.

3.3 Situated meanings

So one important aspect of word meaning is this: we humans *recognize* certain patterns in our experience of the world. These patterns (such as "soft," "thick laces," "perhaps with colored trim," "flexible soles," "made of certain sorts of characteristic materials," "having certain sorts of characteristic looks/designs", etc. = athletic shoes) constitute one of the many *situated meanings* of a word like "shoe." In the context of a teenager saying something like "I can't play basketball today, I haven't got any shoes," the situated meaning of "shoes" is something like the pattern above for athletic shoes (actually, a much more customized pattern for acceptable teenage basketball shoes). The sentence certainly does not mean that the teenager has no shoes whatsoever in the closet.

3.4 Cultural models

There is more to meaning than patterns, children learning the meanings of words cannot stop there. For adults, words involve, in addition to patterns, a sometimes rather "rough and ready" *explanation* of these patterns (Anglin 1977; Keil 1979, 1989): Why do these things hang together this way (at least, for people in our social group)?

That is, the patterns are required to make sense within some kind of cause–effect model or "theory" of the domain – in the case of shoes, the domain is feet and footwear. That is, "everyday" people form, transform, and deal with "theories" just as much as scientists do. However, everyday people's "explanations," "models," or "theories" are very often largely unconscious, or, at least, not easily articulated in any very full fashion, and often incomplete in some ways. This does not mean that they are not also often deep and rich in their own way.

For example, why does the word "shoe" have the different situated meanings it has and on what basis can we change them and add new ones? The "explanatory theory" that goes with "shoe" has to do with things like the fact that humans wear clothes (and shoes, in particular) for protection, but that they are also items of fashion (style) and that different sorts of clothes are better or worse suited for different tasks and activities. Different social and cultural groups, as well as different age groups and genders, have different "explanatory theories" about shoes. Furthermore, all these theories themselves encapsulate viewpoints on who wears what sorts of shoes to what purposes and with what "status."

The child eventually comes to form a "theory" (really, we should say comes to share with her community a more or less tacit "theory") of the shoe domain. In this theory "higher-order" concepts like "protection," "style," and "activities" play a role. This theory makes sense of the patterns the child has found, and, in turn, may well lead the child to discern yet deeper or more complicated patterns.

Such theories are rooted in the practices of the sociocultural groups to which the learner belongs. For example, some African-American teenagers have a different theory of shoes in general, and athletic shoes, in particular, than do some groups of white teenagers (though both groups influence each other over time).

Because these theories are rooted in the practices of socioculturally defined groups of people, I will refer to them as *cultural models* (D'Andrade 1995; D'Andrade and Strauss 1992; Holland and Quinn 1987; Shore 1996; Strauss and Quinn 1997). It is important to see, as well, that bits and pieces of cultural models are in people's heads (different bits and pieces for different people), while other bits and pieces reside in the practices and settings of cultural groups and, thus, need not take up residence inside heads at all. We will return to this issue below. [For reasons that will become clear as we go on, I would prefer to replace the term "cultural model" with something like the term "Discourse model," since the word "culture" is connected to too many diffuse and controversial meanings and because these cultural theories/models are often connected to groups not so grand or fixed as "cultures." However, since the term "cultural model" – or "cultural schema" – is used in the relevant literature, I will retain it.]

So, in addition to situated meanings, each word is also associated with a cultural model. A cultural model is usually a totally or partially unconscious explanatory theory or "storyline" connected to a word – bits and pieces of which are distributed across different people in a social group – that helps to explain why the word has the different situated meanings and possibilities for the specific social and cultural groups of people that it does.

3.5 Meanings in and out of science

If we turn now to another area – how scientists and "everyday" people understand the "same" words differently – we will see again how the meaning of a word varies across different contexts, both within a given Discourse (e.g. that of physicists) and across different Discourses (e.g. between physicists and "everyday" people). We will see, how the situated meanings of words are connected to different cultural models linked to specific social groups and their characteristic Discourses. We will also see that these different social groups are often in competition with each other over things like power, status, and the "right" to claim to know.

The topic of "everyday" people's understanding of science is currently a "hot topic" in education (e.g. Bruer 1993; Gardner 1991). Let us consider briefly a specific study bemoaning how poorly we "everyday" "lay" people think about "scientific concepts," namely Osborne and Freyberg's discussion of children's understandings of light in their (now classic) *Learning in Science* (1985: 8–11).

Children's views about light were investigated by showing them a set of pictures, one of which showed a person (actually a "stick figure") facing a candle on a table. The children were asked questions like "Does the candle make light?," "What happens to the light?," and "How far does the light from the candle go?" Some children gave answers "acceptable to the scientific community" (ibid.: 9), while others did not. Furthermore, this did not correlate with age. Some nine- and ten-year-olds gave "acceptable" answers, while some fifteen-year-olds gave "unacceptable" answers, though many of them could successfully define such terms as "reflection" and "refraction." This is not actually surprising since on these sorts of tasks many adults give "immature" answers.

Many children claimed that the light from the candle travels only a short distance ("One metre at the most," "About one foot") or stays where it is at the candle ("Just stays there and lights up," "Stays there," ibid.: 9). Some children suggested that the distance the light travels from the candle depends on whether or not it is daytime or night-time, claiming that the light travels further at night. Views like these are held even by many students who have studied the topic of light in school: "While teaching may have had some influence on pupils' views about this phenomenon it can be seen that the effect is not great" (ibid.: 9):

How are we to explain the rather 'strange' ideas that some children have about light? From our study it became clear that children's ideas are strongly influenced by their egocentric or human-centred view of the world. Light from a candle, for example, is deemed to travel as far as any object which is obviously illuminated by it. If *they* (the children) can't see the illumination, then the light hasn't got as far as that. In the daytime, objects more than about 0.5 metres from a candle do not appear illuminated by it, but the situation is different at night.

(ibid.: 11)

How, you might ask, can people (namely, in respect to many of these sorts of tasks, us) be so stupid? I would argue that people are not, in fact, so stupid. We can see this if we note that, in one perfectly good sense, the *correct* answer to the question "How far does the light from the candle go?" *is* the one our science educators count as "incorrect," namely, "not very far" (though the "correct" scientific answer is that a ray of light travels indefinitely far unless and until it strikes an object). This is so because in many "everyday" contexts "light" *means* (or is "confounded with" or, to use a less invidious term, "compounded with") *illumination*, and illumination is the range through which an observer can see visible effects of the light. Further, this range is, indeed, greater at night than in the daytime.

Let me give another example to make my point clear. Here is another remark from Osborne and Freyberg: ". . . some children consider that, when sugar is dissolved in hot water, there is 'nothing left but the taste' (ibid.: 58)." But, when a solid is put into a liquid and dissolves so that no parts of it are visible, the correct *everyday* way to describe this *is* to say that the solid has "disappeared." In everyday, non-scientific practice, "disappeared" does not mean "all material, including any esoteric material discoverable by scientists (such as molecules or atoms), has gone out of existence." Rather, it means that some object I formerly saw is now no longer visible. The everyday word "disappear" does not refer to science or scientists at all. Descriptions like "there is nothing left but the taste" are perfectly correct in our everyday contexts of communication.

There is another way to look at what is happening here. Let us call "the lifeworld" all those contexts in which we humans think, act, and communicate as "everyday" people and not as "specialists" (e.g. physicists, doctors or lawyers, etc.). Of course, even specialists spend lots of their time in their lifeworld, outside their professional, specialist worlds (e.g. the world of physics). In actuality, there are many different socioculturally-specific lifeworlds, different lifeworld Discourses, because people from different social and cultural groups have different ways of thinking, acting, and talking as "everyday," non-specialist people.

What's happening in the sort of cognitive science research we are considering here is that one form of language, practice, and thinking, namely, that of "professional physicists," is being substituted for another form, namely that of the "lifeworld." The lifeworld form is claimed to be a mistaken version of the scientific form, when, in fact, the lifeworld form is not actually trying to be "correct" in the same way in which the scientific form is.

This move is most certainly an attempt on the part of science to "colonize" the lifeworld and denigrate everyday ways of knowing. This is, indeed, one reason so many children do so poorly in science in school. It also suggests, I believe, an incorrect view of how thinking works. Both this example, and our earlier discussion of children acquiring the meanings of words, suggest that words are not associated with general concepts that accompany them wherever they go.

Earlier in this chapter we argued that the meanings with which words are associated are situated meanings. In the context of the lifeworld and questions like "How far does the light go?," asked while staring at a lamp or a picture of a candle, the situated meaning associated with "light" has to do with "illumination" and spaces "bathed" in illumination. In the context of physical science, there are a number of different situated meanings that could be associated with "light," one of which (but only one of which) is "waves" that travel indefinitely far and which can reflect off surfaces. In the context of theater, "light" is associated with yet different situated meanings, e.g. with various lighting effects.

Furthermore, the multiple situated meanings for "light" in our "lifeworld" are connected to a "cultural model" (theory) of light (e.g. light "fills" spaces that are otherwise "filled" with darkness; light is healthy and good; light sources produce light, and much more). The multiple situated meanings for "light" in the physicist's world (e.g. waves versus particles) are also connected to a theory. In this case it is a "formal theory" which we might say is physicists' "cultural model" of light when they are being physicists and not "everyday" people.

What this discussion should make clear is that the situated meanings a word has are relative to a specific Discourse. The Discourse of physics has a different set of situated meanings for the word "light" than do lifeworld Discourses.

3.6 Situated meanings as "assemblies"

Thus far, I have talked about humans recognizing various patterns in their experience in virtue of which a word has specific situated meanings. But this way of talking can, in fact, become too static. Another way to talk about situated meanings is to say that they are *assembled* out of diverse features, "on the spot," as we speak, listen, and act (Barsalou 1987; 1991, 1992; Clark

1993). Instantly, in context, we assemble the features that will constitute the pattern or situated meanings that a word will have in that context.

Different contexts invite different assemblies. A formal wedding invites one to assemble one sort of situated meaning for "shoe" and a pick-up game of basketball at the park invites one to assemble a different sort of situated meaning. If one were unfortunate enough to become poor and homeless, one might soon learn to assemble a new and quite different situated meaning for "shoe."

"Concepts" or "meanings" are "jerry-rigged" on the spot in integral interaction with context. Sometimes these assemblies are fairly routine and automatic thanks to having been done more or less in the same way on many past occasions; other times they require new work to come up with novel assemblies for new contexts. Novel assemblies are always a possibility as features of the context or the world in which we live change or as one faces relatively novel contexts. The assembly process is guided by, and, in turn, helps to transform and change, a cultural model that explains (often partially and sometimes inconsistently) why and how certain assemblies are linked to certain sorts of contexts.

So we can either talk about people recognizing patterns of features or assembling patterns of features. These are two ways of talking about the same thing. However, the latter way has the advantage of stressing meaning as an active process. Even if the assembly is, in many cases, rather routine and conventional, there is always the potential for less routine assemblies.

The "assembly" way of talking has a further advantage. So far, we have treated the relationship between language and context itself in too static and unidimensional a way. We have talked as if the "context" is just "out there" and language is adapted to it. But the relationship between language and context is, as said in Chapter 2, much more two-way and dynamic than this. We do recognize or assemble situated meanings based on context, but we also construe the context to be a certain way and not another based on the situated meanings we assemble.

If I utter "sweet nothings," assembling the situated meanings they imply, in a certain situation, I am both taking and making the context as a romantic one. We see here, too, that situated meanings are not just in our heads. They are negotiated by people in interaction. My "sweet nothings" can be seen as a "bid" to *create a certain context* (and to get the other person to attribute certain sorts of situated meanings to my words and deeds) that is accepted, rejected, or countered in certain ways by the person with whom I am interacting.

A situated meaning is an image or pattern that we assemble "on the spot" as we communicate in a given context, based on our construal of that context and on our past experiences (Agar 1994; Barsalou 1991, 1992; Clark 1993; Clark 1996; Hofstadter 1997; Kress 1985; Levinson 1983). One can even "feel" one's mind assemble different situated meanings.

For example, consider these two utterances about "coffee": "The coffee spilled, get a mop"; "The coffee spilled, get a broom."

In the first case, triggered by the word "mop" and your experience of such matters, you assemble a situated meaning something like "dark liquid, perhaps quite hot" for "coffee." In the second case, triggered by the word "broom" and your experience of such matters, you assemble either a situated meaning something like "dark dry grains" or something like "dark reddish beans." Of course, in a real context, there are many more signals as to how to go about assembling situated meanings for words and phrases.

3.7 A pattern-recognition view of the mind

Our discussion of situated meanings is based on a particular perspective on the nature of the human mind. This perspective takes the mind to be basically an adept *pattern recognizer and builder*. That is to say, first and foremost, that the mind operates primarily with (flexibly transformable) *patterns* extracted from experience, not with highly general or decontextualized *rules* (for a variety of perspectives, see: Bechtel and Abrahamsen 1990; P. M. Churchland 1995; P. S. Churchland and Sejnowski 1992; Clark 1993, 1997; Elman, Bates, Johnson, Karmiloff-Smith, Parisi, and Plunkett 1996; Gee 1992; Hofstadter and the Fluid Analogies Research Group 1995; Margolis 1987, 1993; Minksy 1985; Nolan 1994; Rumelhart, McClelland, and the PDP Group 1986). It recognizes (or assembles) in context patterns like "hard – shiny – formal – solid color – with thin laces" as the situated meaning of "shoe," though ever ready to adapt and transform such patterns as contexts, times, and worlds change.

This view of the mind has important consequences for areas like education, consequences which we cannot fully pursue here. The mind is no longer viewed as a rule-following logic-like calculator. In fact, the human mind does not deal well with general rules and principles that do not come out of and tie back to real contexts, situations, practices, and experiences. It is crucial, however, to realize that the patterns most important to human thinking and action follow a sort of "Goldilocks Principle": they are not too general and they are not too specific. Situated meanings are *mid-level patterns or generalizations* between these two extremes (Barsalou 1992).

Think about recognizing faces. If you see your friend when she is sick as a different person than when she is well, your knowledge is too specific. If, on the other hand, you see all your female friends as the same, your knowledge is too general. The level at which knowledge is most useful for practice is the level at which you see your friend's many appearances as one person, though different from other people like her. So, too, there is little you can do in physics, if all you can do is recognize specific refraction patterns: your knowledge is too specific. There is, also, little you can effectively do, beyond passing school tests, if all you can do is recite the general theory of electromagnetism: your knowledge is too general.

Really effective knowledge, then, is being able to recognize, work on, transform, and talk about mid-level generalizations such as, to take physics as an example once again: "light as a bundle of light waves of different wave lengths combinable in certain specific ways" or "light as particles (photons) with various special properties in specific circumstances" or "light as a beam that can be directed in specific ways for various specific purposes (e.g. lasers)" or "light as colors that mix in certain specific ways with certain specific results." Note the mix of the general and the specific in these patterns.

And it is not just in technical areas, like physics, that mid-level generalizations are crucial. In everyday life as well, they are the basis of thinking for practice. For example, the word (concept) "coffee" is primarily meaningful as a set of mid-level generalizations that simultaneously define and are triggered by experience: dark-liquid-in-a-certain-type-of-cup; beans-in-a-certain-type-of-bag; grains-in-a-certain-sort-of-tin; berries-on-a-certain-type-of-tree; flavoring-in-certain-type-of-food (Clark 1989).

As I have said, situated meanings are not static and they are not definitions. Rather, they are flexibly transformable patterns that come out of experience and, in turn, construct experience as meaningful in certain ways and not others.

To see the dynamic nature of situated meanings, imagine a situated meaning (mid-level generalization) that comes to mind when you think of a *bedroom* (Clark 1989; Rumelhart, McClelland, and the PDP Research Group 1986). You conjure up an image that connects various objects and features in a typical bedroom, relative, of course, to your sociocultural experience of bedrooms and homes. Now I tell you to imagine that the bedroom has a refrigerator in it. At once you transform your situated meaning for a bedroom, keeping parts of it, deleting parts of it, and adding, perhaps, things like a desk and a college student. Your original situated meaning is quickly replaced by another one.

You can even make up (assemble) situated meanings *de novo*: e.g. say that I tell you to form a meaning for the phrase (concept) "things you would save first in a fire" (Barsalou 1991). You have no trouble putting together a pattern – again based on your sociocultural experiences – of things like children, pets, important documents, expensive or irreplaceable items, and so forth. You have just invented a mid-level generalization (situated meaning) suitable for action, a new "concept," one to which we could even assign a new word, but a "concept" tied intimately to your sociocultural experiences in the world.

The moral is this: thinking and using language is an *active* matter of *assembling* the situated meanings that you need for action in the world. This assembly is always relative to your socioculturally-defined experiences in the world and, *more or less,* routinized ("normed") through cultural models and various social practices of the sociocultural groups to which you belong (Gee 1992). The assembly processes for "coffee" (in "everyday life") and "light" (in physics) are fairly routinized, but even here the situated meanings are adapted each time to the specific contexts they are used in and are open to transformations from new experiences. The situated meanings behind words (concepts) like "democracy," "honesty," "literacy," or "masculine" are, of course, less routinized.

Having argued that the meanings of words are not general concepts, we might very well ask now why, if situated meanings drive learning and practicing on the world, do we have the feeling that the word "coffee" is associated with something more general, something that unites and rises above these mid-level patterns? Part of the answer is simply the fact that the single word exists, and we are misled by this fact to think that a single, general meaning exists. But, another part of the answer lies in "cultural models." The cultural model associated with "coffee" gives us this feeling of generality.

This cultural model associated with "coffee" tells us that coffee grows, is picked, and is then prepared as beans or grain to be made into a drink, as well as into flavorings for other foods. It tells us, as well, the when, where, who, and how about coffee from the perspective of our sociocultural groups (and their view of other groups).

Of course, none of us need know the cultural models associated with words fully. I, for one, have no idea what sort of tree (or is it another sort of plant?) coffee grows on, nor could I recognize a "coffee berry" if I saw one (Aren't there berries on those trees? Are they berries in the way in which strawberries and blueberries are berries? I don't know.) I really have no idea how "coffee flavoring" gets made, nor even what the limits are of what counts as "coffee" (this is something that really confuses me in the case of "tea").

But it is no matter. Other people know the bits I don't or these bits could be looked up in books or other media. The "storyline" (cultural model) that makes sense of all the different situated meanings for "coffee" (and new ones that may arise) is "out there" in social space, somewhat different for different groups (think of "coffee bars" and yuppies), and itself ever changing.

It is crucial to realize that to "know" a situated meaning is not merely to be able to "say certain words," e.g. "a cup of coffee," but to be able to *recognize a pattern* (e.g. a cup of coffee) in a variety of settings and variations. This is what makes situated meanings both contextualized and somewhat general.

To see this point in another domain, one more important for education, consider again the notion of "light" in physics. First of all, our everyday cultural model for "light" is not, as we have seen, the same as the model (theory) of "light" in physics. That model is the specialized theory of electromagnetic radiation. It is more overt and articulated than most cultural models.

In physics, "light" is associated with a variety of situated meanings – e.g. as a bundle of waves of different wave lengths; as particles (photons) with various special (quantum-like) properties; as a beam that can be directed in various ways and for various purposes (e.g. lasers); as colors that can mix in various fashions, and more. If one wants to start "practicing" with light so as to learn physics, then one has to get *experiences* that lead to the acquisition of a few situated meanings (mid-level, contextualized patterns in one's pattern recognizer that can guide action). Otherwise, one really cannot understand what the theory of light has to explain, at least not in any way that could efficaciously guide pattern recognition and action and reflection.

But I must admit now that I myself do not understand (in any embodied way) these various physically-situated meanings well enough to really have a deep understanding, despite the fact that I have read and can recite lots of the scientific theory behind light in physics. To really teach me, you would have to insure that I got experiences that allowed my mind/brain to really recognize patterns at the level of situated meanings.

And what does it mean to "recognize" these? Situated meanings are correlations of various features, they are patterns that associate various features with each other, e.g. light-as-a-particle-that-behaves-in-terms-of-various-sorts-of-contrived-(experimental)-observations-in-certain-characteristic-quantum-like-ways. To recognize such things is to be able to re-cognize (reconstruct in terms of one's pattern-recognizing capabilities) and to be able to act-on-and-with these various features and their associations in a range of contexts. One's body and mind have to be able to be situated with (coordinated by and with) these correlated features in the world. Otherwise you have my sort of understanding.

As it is, I cannot really understand what it means to say that light is a wave, even less that it is composed of various waves of different wave lengths, though I can say it. I just have not had the action-and-reflection experiences that would have made this pattern, this correlation of features, meaningful and recognizable in a way useful for practice, and thus, useful for building on in the further development of patterns and theories. Therefore, I cannot, in any deep way, be said to understand the theory of light in physics (though I could pass some tests on it, perhaps), since that theory is what makes (partial) sense of the various patterns connected to the word "light."

Situated meanings are, then, a product of the bottom-up action and reflection with which the learner engages the world and the top-town guidance of the cultural models or theories the learner is developing. Without both these levels, the learner either ends up with something too general (a cultural model or theory poorly connected to contextualized, mid-level patterns) or with something too specific and contextualized, something that functions too much like a proper name (the word applies just here, I don't really know why).

We argued above that cultural models don't just exist in people's heads, but are often shared across people, books, other media, and various social practices (more on this later). So, too, situated meanings don't just reside in individual minds; very often they are *negotiated* between people in and through communicative social interaction, as our example about uttering "sweet nothings" was meant to suggest. To take another example, consider that if a partner in a relationship says something like "I think good relationships shouldn't take work," a good part of the ensuing conversation might very well involve mutually negotiating (directly or indirectly through inferencing) what "work" is going to mean for the people concerned, in this specific context, as well as in the larger context of their ongoing relationship. Furthermore, as conversations, and, indeed, relationships, develop, participants often continually revise their situated meanings.

3.8 The social mind

As we have just discussed above, I have taken the view, which is becoming progressively more common in work in cognitive science and the philosophy of mind, that the human mind is, at root, a pattern recognizer and builder (see references at opening of Section 3.6, p. 46). However, since the world is infinitely full of potentially meaningful patterns and sub-patterns in any domain, something must *guide* the learner in selecting which patterns and sub-patterns to focus on. And this something resides in the cultural models of the learner's sociocultural groups and the social practices and settings in which they are rooted.

Because the mind is a pattern recognizer, and there are infinite ways to pattern features of the world, of necessity, though perhaps ironically, the mind is social (really cultural). It is social (cultural) in the sense that sociocultural practices and settings guide and norm the patterns in terms of which the learner thinks, acts, talks, values, and interacts (Gee 1992).

This need not, however, mitigate each learner's own agency. Since each individual belongs to multiple sociocultural groups, the cultural models and patterns associated with each group can influence the others in unique ways, depending on the different "mix" for different individuals (Kress 1985). And, of course, each individual is biologically and, in particular, neurally quite different from every other (Crick 1994).

Thus, we see that, from this perspective, talk about the mind does not lock us into a "private" world, but rather, returns us to the social and cultural world. If the patterns a mind recognizes or assembles stray too far from those used by others in a given Discourse (whether this be the Discourse of physics, bird watching, or a lifeworld Discourse), the social practices of the Discourse will seek to "discipline" and "renorm" that mind. Thus, in reality, situated meanings and cultural models exist out in the social practices of Discourses as much as, or more than they do inside heads.

3.9 "Situated meanings" as a tool of inquiry

In this chapter, I have treated the terms "situated meaning" and "cultural model" realistically. That is, I have spoken about them as things that exist in the mind and in the world. Indeed, this is, I believe, both true and the easiest way to grasp what they mean and how and why they are significant for discourse analysis.

But it is important to realize that, in the end, these terms are ultimately our ways as theoreticians and analysts of talking about, and, thus, constructing and construing the world. And it is in this guise that I am primarily interested in them. They are "tools of inquiry." I will discuss cultural models as tools of inquiry more thoroughly in the next chapter. Here I want to sketch out what I mean by "situated meaning" as a tool of inquiry.

"Situated meaning" is a "thinking device" that guides us to ask certain sorts of questions. Faced with a piece of oral or written language, we consider a certain key word or a family of key words, that is, words we hypothesize are important to understanding the language we wish to analyze. We consider, as well, all that we can learn about the context that this language is both used in and helps to create or construe in a certain way. We then ask the following sorts of questions:

- What specific, situated meanings is it reasonable, from the point of view of the Discourse in which these words are used, to attribute to their "author"?
- What specific, situated meanings is it reasonable, from the point of view of the Discourse in which these words are used, to attribute to their "receiver(s)" (interpreter(s))?
- What specific, situated meanings is it reasonable, from the point of view of *other* Discourses than the one in which the words were uttered or written (Discourses which would or do bring different values, norms, perspectives, and assumptions to the situation) to attribute to actual or possible interpreters from these other Discourses? (e.g. what sorts of situated meanings might a creationist give to a text in biology or a Native American to an American history text if they chose to interpret the text from the point of view of their Discourse and not the one from which the text had originally been produced?)
- What specific, situated meanings is it reasonable, from the point of view of the Discourse in which these words were used or of other Discourses, to assume are *potentially* attributable to these words by interpreters, whether or not we have evidence that anyone actually activated that potential in the current case?

Our answers to these questions are always tentative. They are always open to revision as we learn more about the context, and we can nearly always learn more about the material, social, cultural, and historical contexts in which the words were uttered or written. However, at some point, what we learn may well cease to change our answers to these sorts of questions in a very substantive way.

Our tentative answers are testable in a variety of different ways, including (but not exhausted by) asking actual and possible producers and receivers what they think (remembering that many, but not all, aspects of situated meanings and cultural models are unconscious); looking at the verbal and non-verbal effects of the language in the present and future; looking at how the past led up to these words and deeds; looking at similar and contrasting uses of language; and appealing to a wide and diverse array of linguistic and contextual factors, as well as different tools of inquiry, at different levels, that we hope converge on the same answer. These sorts of concerns lead us to issues about validity, issues which I will take up in Chapter 5, after I have introduced a variety of other tools of inquiry.

3.10 Context: intertextual and historical

The context of an utterance (oral or written) is everything in the material, mental, personal, interactional, social, institutional, cultural, and historical situation in which the utterance was made that could conceivably influence the answer to any of the questions in section 3.9. Thus, context is nearly limitless. However, as I pointed out, learning more about what producers and interpreters think, believe, value, and share, and how they are situated materially, interactionally, socially, institutionally, culturally, and historically will eventually cease to change the sorts of answers to these questions all that much. The answers cease to change because we have reached the limits of what contextual information was relevant to the producers and interpreters of the utterance or to our research interests.

However, the final question in section 3.9 raises an important issue. Words have *histories*. They have been in other people's mouths and on other people's pens. They have circulated through other Discourses and within other institutions. They have been part of specific historical events and episodes. Words bring with them as *potential situated meanings* all the situated meanings they have picked up in history and in other settings and Discourses.

Producers and receivers may know and use only some of these potential situated meanings. They may not activate them or only partially activate them. But such meanings are always potentially open to being activated or more fully activated. They are like a virus that may remain inactive for a long while, but that is always there and potentially able to infect people, situations, social practices, and Discourses with new situated meanings (ironically, the meanings are actually old, but previously un-activated or only partially activated in the Discourse under consideration).

This is the "bite" of theories of "intertextuality." Any text (oral or written) is infected with the meanings (at least, as potential) of all the other texts in which its words have comported. Studying the meaning potential of texts, in this sense, is an important part of discourse analysis. Such potential situated meanings can have effects even when they are not fully activated by producers and interpreters.

In previous work I have used as an example of such intertextuality a sentence uttered by a scientist during an undergraduate classroom presentation on the neuroanatomy of finches. Let me briefly recap this example here.

In finches, only males sing, not females. The scientist was interested in the way in which the development of the male's song relates to the structure of its brain. In the course of her presentation, she drew a diagram of the male finch's brain on the board. The diagram was a large circle, representing the bird's brain, with three smaller circles inside it, marked "A," "B," and "C," representing discrete localized regions of neurons that function as units in the learning and production of the male's song.

When the young bird hears its song (in the wild or on tape), it tries to produce the various parts of the song (engages in something like "babbling"). As the young bird's own productions get better and better, the neurons in region A are "tuned" and eventually respond selectively to aspects of the song the young bird was exposed to and not other songs. The regions marked "B" and "C" also play a role in the development of the song and in its production.

The scientist went on to discuss the relationship between the male's brain and the hormones produced in the bird's gonads. The A, B, and C regions each have many cells in them that respond to testosterone, a hormone plentifully produced by the testes of the male bird.

In this context, the scientist uttered the following sentence: "If you look in the brain [of the finch] you see high sexual dimorphism – A/B/C regions are robust in males and atrophied or non-existent in females." The word "atrophied" in this sentence is a technical term, the correct term required by the current Discourse of biology. Note that one *could* have viewed the male brain as containing "monstrous growths" and thus as having deviated from the "normal" female brain. Instead, however, the terminology requires us to see the male brain as having developed fully ("robust") and the female brain as having either "atrophied" or failed to develop ("non-existent").

The words "robust" and "atrophied" carry potential situated meanings with them from history. It is not an historical accident that "atrophied" has ended up a technical term for the female finch brain (and other similar cases), though this brain is simply less "localized" in terms of discrete regions like A, B, and C.

Females, in medical and biological Discourses in the West from the time of Galen to the present, have been seen as either inferior to males or, at the least, deviant from the male as the "norm" or "fully developed" exemplar of the species (Fausto-Sterling 1985; Laqueur 1990). Rather than retrace this immense history, let me simply point to one very salient moment of it. Consider the following quote from Darwin:

> It is generally admitted that with woman the powers of intuition, of rapid perception, and perhaps of imitation, are more strongly marked than in man; but some, at least, of these faculties are characteristic of the lower races, and therefore of a past and lower state of civilization. The chief distinction in the intellectual powers of the two sexes is shewn by man's attaining to a higher eminence, in whatever he takes up, than can woman – whether requiring deep thought, reason, or imagination, or merely the use of senses and hands.
>
> (1859: 873; see also Gould 1993: 297–368)

Though Darwin usually did not himself interpret "evolution" as a linear development upward to "better things," many of his followers did (Bowler 1990). The competition men have faced in their environments has caused their bodies and brains to "develop" further than those of women, so that it was a commonplace by the nineteenth century and in the early decades of the twentieth that "anthropologists regard[ed] women intermediate in development between the child and the man" (Thomas 1897, cited in Degler 1991: 29). This logic, of course, leads us to see the whole woman, in body and brain, as an "atrophied" man (exactly as Aristotle and Galen did), less developed because less challenged by her environment.

The technical term "atrophied" has its own specific situated meanings in the Discourse of biology. But, thanks to its history, it carries, like a virus, a bevy of additional potential situated meanings and associated cultural models. While the scientist may be unaware or only partially aware of these meanings and models, they have effects none the less.

For example, there are a nearly limitless number of things worth studying at one time in any science. What gets time, money, and attention – what is seen as normal, natural, and important to study – is, in part, an artifact of the long histories of words, situated meanings, cultural models, and theories.

The history of females and development could have been different. So too, could the history of brains. This is a part of the story I have left out here, but see Gee (1996). The history of the development of clinical medicine, surgery, and brain research (Star 1989) led to the localized aspects of brains being considered more important for study than the holistic aspects (and this, as it happens, is changing a bit in current neuroscience). For one thing, tools existed for studying isolated neurons, but not for studying large parts of the brain acting in concert (tools which now do exist). For another, the emergence of modern medical schools and standardized training give rise to a pedagogical system intolerant of complex pictures of the brain and happy with localized diagrams that associate each part of the brain with a clear and discrete function (however inaccurate many of these diagrams are).

If the history of females, development, and brains had been different, perhaps we would be studying female finches as important sites of holistic brains that represent a form of development, unlike the male's, that is not overly specialized and special-purpose. Here, too, important things would have been discovered, just as they have been in the current science of birds and brains. I am not claiming that today's science is "wrong" and the alternative we could come up with by imagining a different history is "right." There are an endless number of facts to be discovered and different routes to the same or similar theories.

Our alternative imaginings simply show us that situated meanings, meaning potential, cultural models, and theories could have been different. Thus, the present is, indeed, partly an artifact of a very specific past. The present is an outcome of previous situated meanings and cultural models, meanings and models which continue to inhabit the present in more or less overt ways. They always have the potential for further effects in a given Discourse (e.g. someone refers to studies of bird brains and hormones to reinstantiate the "old" story about women as less developed than men).

4   Cultural models

4.1 Bachelors

This chapter will focus exclusively on cultural models and their social and political implications. Cultural models are an important tool of inquiry because they mediate between the "micro" (small) level of interaction and the "macro" (large) level of institutions. They mediate between the local interactional work we do in carrying out the six building tasks discussed in Chapter 2 (p. 12) and Discourses as they operate to create the complex patterns of institutions and cultures across societies and history.

For example, when I was growing up, the Discourse of heterosexual romance (i.e. enacting and being recognized as an acceptable "date" and potential partner) and actual dating practices were mediated by a bevy of cultural models, one of which held that women brought "beauty" as their prime asset to a relationship and men brought "intelligence" and potential career success as their prime asset. This model has changed a good bit, and so too have both actual practices and various (culturally specific and class-based) Discourses of romance.

The role of cultural models was first made clear in a classic paper by the linguist Charles Fillmore (1975). Fillmore used a deceptively simple example: the word "bachelor." All of us think we know what the word "bachelor" means: like dictionaries (e.g. Webster Handy College Dictionary 1972), we all think it means "an unmarried man."

Fillmore, however, asks questions like: Is the Pope a bachelor? Is a thrice-divorced man a bachelor? Is a young man who has been in an irreversible coma since childhood a bachelor? What about a eunuch? A committed gay man? An elderly senile gentleman who has never been married? The answer to all these questions is either "no" or "I'm not sure" (as I have discovered by asking a variety of people). Why? After all, all these people are unmarried men.

The reason why the answer to these questions is "no," despite the fact that they all involve cases of clearly unmarried males, is that we actually use the word "bachelor" (and any other word) in relation to a largely taken-for-granted "theory," which in the last chapter, I called a "cultural model." One way to look at cultural models is as images or storylines or descriptions of simplified worlds in which prototypical events unfold. They are our "first thoughts" or taken-for-granted assumptions about what is "typical" or "normal."

We will see below that when cultural models are brought to our attention, we can often acknowledge that they are really simplifications about the world, simplifications which leave out many complexities. But then, all theories, even theories in science, are simplifications useful for some purposes and not others. Unfortunately, the simplifications in cultural models can do harm by implanting in thought and action unfair, dismissive, or derogatory assumptions about other people.

The most commonly used cultural model for the word "bachelor" is (or used to be) something like the following (Fillmore 1975):

> Men marry women at a certain age; marriages last for life; and in such a world, a bachelor is a man who stays unmarried beyond the usual age, thereby becoming eminently marriageable. We know that this simplified world is not always true, but it is the one against which we use the word 'bachelor', that is, make choices about what other words are excluded as applicable or not, and make assumptions about what the relevant context is in a given case of using the word. Thus, the Pope is not a bachelor because he just isn't in this simplified world, being someone who has vowed not to marry at any age. Nor are gay men, since they have chosen not to marry women.

Cultural models often involve us in exclusions that are not at first obvious and which we are often unaware of making. In the case of "bachelor" we are actually excluding people like gay individuals and priests as "normal" men, and assuming that men come in two "normal" types: those who get married early and those who get married late. This assumption, of course, marginalizes people who do not want to get married or do not want to marry members of the opposite sex. It is part of the function of cultural models to set up what count as central, typical cases, and what count as marginal, non-typical cases.

There is, of course, another exclusion that is made via the cultural model for "bachelor." If men become "eminently marriageable" when they stay unmarried beyond the usual age, then this can only be because we have assumed that after that age there is a shortage of "desirable" men and a surplus of women who want them, women who aren't "eminently marriageable," or, at least, not as "eminently marriageable" as the men. Hence, we get the most common cultural model associated with "spinster."

Fillmore's example raises another important point that further illustrates the connection between cultural models and "politics." Thanks to feminism, lots of people have become consciously aware of the cultural model behind the word "bachelor." Many have come to reject it, thereby either dropping the word or changing its meaning. For example, many people now use the word "bachelor" for unmarried women, thus, giving the word new situated meanings and applying it against a new cultural model. Other people use a word like "spinster" as a badge of honor and respect, once again creating new situated meanings and cultural models.

The "bite" of Fillmore's example is this: if any word in English seems to have a clear "definition," it is a word like "bachelor." But this word is not used in terms of a definition, but rather against a set of social and cultural assumptions that constitute a cultural model. If this is true of a word like "bachelor," how much more likely is it to be true of words like "democracy," "justice," "intelligent," or "literate," for instance?

4.2 Videotapes in the mind

The "bachelor" example is, of course, too simple. There are lots of different sorts of cultural models and lots of different ways to think and talk about them. Another way to think about cultural models is this: Cultural models are rather like "movies" or "videotapes" in the mind, tapes of experiences we have had, seen, read about, or imagined. We all have a vast store of these tapes, the edited (and, thus, transformed) records of our experiences in the world or with texts and media. We treat some of these tapes as if they depict prototypical (what we take to be "normal") people, objects, and events. We conventionally take these "prototypical" tapes to be the "real" world, or act as if they were, overlooking many of the complexities in the world in order to get on with the business of social action and interaction.

Cultural models can become emblematic visions of an idealized, "normal," "typical" reality, in much the way that, say, a Bogart movie is emblematic of the world of the "tough guy" or an early Woody Allen movie of the "sensitive, but klutzy male." Cultural models are also variable, differing across different cultural groups, including different cultural groups in a society speaking the same language. They change with time and other changes in the society, as well as with new experience. But we are usually quite unaware we are using them and of their full implications, unless challenged by someone or by a new experience where our cultural models clearly don't "fit."

The "videotapes in the mind" metaphor should not be taken too rigidly. We have cultural models within cultural models, like Chinese boxes, and can switch among them quite rapidly. In the last chapter we took a "pattern-recognition" view of the mind. Such a perspective argues that thinking is not a matter of following general rules and engaging in logic-like computations on abstract representations (the viewpoint of traditional cognitivist perspectives). Rather, pattern-recognition perspectives argue that the mind stores connected "images" of actual experiences, problem-solves through finding patterns in that experience, applies these patterns in a "customized" (adapted) way to understand new experiences, and dynamically changes these patterns in the face of those new experiences.

Recall, for instance, our example in the last chapter of how you think about bedrooms (p. 49). Your "image" of a prototypical bedroom is a compendium (something rather like an edited collection of what you take to be your most typical bedroom videotapes) of your many experiences of bedrooms, linking, at a lower level, many smaller images, such as types of beds and carpets, and linking, at a larger level, to other sorts of images, such as types of adjoining bathrooms and closets.

When I tell you the bedroom has a small sink and refrigerator in it, you immediately transform your image and "customize" it for this new setting, forming an image, perhaps, of something like a college dorm room. The two different images you have formed are what I called, in the last chapter, "situated meanings" (for "bedroom"). But each one is used against or in relation to different cultural models. In one case, your cultural model of what you take to be typical adults and their bedrooms and houses, in the other case your cultural model of what you take to be typical college students, and their living quarters.

Both of these cultural models will vary significantly based on your social class and other sociocultural memberships. In fact, you may very well have not formed a situated meaning involving college students at all in the second case. And, indeed, your situated meaning of bedrooms with and without refrigerators in them will vary a good bit based on your class-based and other sociocultural experiences and the cultural models about people, bedrooms, and houses to which they have given rise.

Any situated meanings and cultural models active in a given context bring with them (are linked to) a good many other related situated meanings and cultural models. When you think about bedrooms, you activate (more or less strongly) related situated meanings and cultural models having to do with houses, homes, relationships, and a good deal more. Any situated meaning or any cultural model is like a ball attached to a great many other balls on a string. When you pick up the ball (situated meaning or cultural model) you drag along all the other balls (some more closely attached to the original ball than others).

In the rest of this chapter we will see other sorts of cultural models and other ways to think about cultural models. We will also see an array of psychological, social, and political issues that arise, in different cases, when we study cultural models and the situated meanings they help to organize, and lead us to form and transform.

4.3 All meaning is local

It is difficult to appreciate the importance and pervasiveness of cultural models, or to understand how they work, if we stick only to examples from cultures close to our own. So let me give an example of cultural models at work adapted from William Hanks' excellent book, *Language and Communicative Practices* (1996). This example will also let us see that cultural models are at work in even the "simplest" cases of communication and in regard to even the simplest words.

When we watch language-in-action in a culture quite different from our own, even simple interactions can be inexplicable, thanks to the fact that we do not know many of the cultural models at play. This means that even if we can figure out the situated meanings of some words, we cannot see any sense to why these situated meanings have arisen (why they were assembled here and how). So let's move, with Hanks, to Yucatan, Mexico.

In a small town in Yucatan, a Mayan Shaman named "Don Chabo" is sharing a meal with his daughter-in-law, Margot, and a visiting anthropologist. A young man, named "Yuum," approaches from the outside, and, standing at the window, asks: "Is Don Chabo seated?" Margot replies: "Go over there. He's drinking. Go over there inside." These are about as simple as sentences get.

And yet the meaning of these sentences is not so straightforward after all. For example, the people seated around the table are having a meal, so why does Margo say that Don Chabo is drinking? Furthermore, Margot's response implies that Don Chabo is drinking, despite the fact that he was, at that moment, gazing off into space with a roll in his hand. Indeed, in Mayan, it would have been equally true here to say Don Chabo was "drinking" had he been altogether done with (eating) his meal.

Margot's response implies, as well, that Don Chabo was "seated." Yet, it turns out, it would have been equally true to say he was seated had he been standing or even off somewhere else, even taking a bath in his own home.

Or, to take one final example, Margot uses the Mayan word for "there" that means "maximally distant from the speaker," the same word people in Yucatan use for relatives who live outside Yucatan, in other states in the Mexican Republic. She does this despite the fact that she is telling Yuum to go into her father-in-law's house, not 10 meters away from hers and within the same compound as her house.

How can it be that people can be drinking when they are eating or doing nothing at all? That they are seated when they are standing or taking a bath? That they are far distant from something 10 meters away?

Things work this way because Mayans (these Mayans, in any case), though they almost always take food with drink and vice versa, use the words "drink" and "eat" against a cultural model of meals in terms of which their morning and evening meals are "drinking" and their larger main meal in the midafternoon is "eating." Furthermore, to these Mayans, as long as the social engagement of mealtime is still going on, regardless of whether the "meal" itself is finished or not, a person is still "drinking" or "eating."

Many Mayans live in walled compounds that contain several houses. Their cultural models for house and home are, thus, rather different from (some of) ours. They use the word "seated" to mean that one is "at home" and available, regardless of where one is in the compound. Being "available" has, in addition, a special meaning for Shamans, since, of course, the whole business of Shamans brings to the fore a distinctive set of cultural models. To ask whether a Shaman is "available" is to use this word against these cultural models and is to ask, in part, whether he is available to engage in counseling.

Finally, Mayans have their own cultural models, as all of us do, of how physical and social space work and are related. Margot is excluded from her father-in-law's house, unless she has a specific reason to be there, for social reasons having to doing with Mayan cultural models of social relationships and spaces within homes. Thus, she uses the word for "far distant" due to social, rather than physical distance.

In this brief example, I have, in fact, given you very little of what you really need to know to fully understand these simple sentences (for example, why does Margot, rather than Don Chabo respond?). To really understand them, even to understand just their "literal meaning," one needs to understand how social hierarchies, gender, meals, social engagements, Shamanism, and a great deal more, work day-to-day in local settings among (certain of the) Mayans.

Hanks devotes dozens of pages of dense, scholarly prose to explicating what these sentences mean, not at any deep symbolic or thematic level, just at the "literal" level. He points out that when a husband asks his wife, early in the morning, in English, "D'the paper come today, sweetheart?" and she answers "It's right on the table," the situation is no less strange, complex, local, and cultural, however invisible all this complexity (our own) may be to us.

The moral that Hanks draws from even so simple sentences as these is this: meaning, even literal meaning, is wedded to *local, "on-site," social, and cultural practices*. To put the matter another way: meaning is not general and abstract, not something that resides in dictionaries, or even in general symbolic representations inside people's heads. Rather, it is *situated* in specific social and cultural practices, and is continually transformed in those practices. Or to put the matter in the terms we introduced in the last chapter: meaning is a matter of situated meanings, customized in, to, and for context, used always against a rich store of cultural knowledge (cultural models) that are themselves "activated" in, for, and by contexts (remember our example above of bedrooms).

This is, of course, as true of English as it is of Mayan, but, since we know our own local practices so thoroughly and unreflectively, the situated and local nature of meaning is largely invisible to us. It is easy for us to miss the specificity and localness of our own practices and think we have general, abstract, even universal meanings. We come to think, when we have confronted no other languages, that "sitting" is just sitting, "drinking" is just drinking, "over there" is just over there. In fact, the situated, social, and cultural nature of meaning often becomes visible to us only when we confront language-at-work in languages and cultures far distant from our own.

4.4 Cultural models in action: middle-class parenting

I want to briefly discuss two now classic examples from the literature of cultural models at work. Both examples demonstrate the connection between cultural models and social class, though in different ways. Thus, these examples, and others that follow below from my own research, begin our discussion of the social, cultural, and political issues that are implicated in the study of cultural models.

The first example is a study of middle-class parents in Cambridge, Massachusetts, in the United States (Harkness, Super, and Keefer 1992). When these parents talked about their children, two cultural models were highly salient. One was tied to the notion of "stages of development" through which children pass. The other was tied to the notion of the child's growing desire for "independence" as the central theme giving point and direction to these stages.

For example, consider how one mother talked about her son David:

> he's very definitely been in a stage, for the last three or four months, of wanting to help, everything I do, he wants to help. . . . And now, I would say in the last month, the intensity of wanting to do everything himself is . . . we're really into that stage. . . . I suppose they're all together . . . ya, I suppose they're two parts of the same thing. Independence, reaching out for independence. Anything he wants to do for himself, which is just about everything, that I move in and do for him, will result in a real tantrum.
>
> (ibid.: 165–6)

David's mother later gave as an example of his "wanting to do things for himself," an episode where she had opened the car door for him when he was having a hard time getting out of the car: "He was very upset, so we had to go back and . . . close the door" (p. 166). She also attributed David's recent dislike of being dressed or diapered to his growing sense of independence: ". . . he's getting to the point where it's insulting, and he doesn't want to be put on his back to have his diaper changed."

However, in the same interview, David's mother also mentioned another behavior pattern. To get David to sleep, she straps him into his car seat and pretends to be taking him for a drive. He almost immediately falls asleep, and then she returns home, leaving him in the car, with a blanket, to take a nap: "But he goes to sleep so peacefully, without any struggle, usually" (p. 167).

Though this latter pattern is a repeated daily routine, David's mother does not talk about this behavior as part of a "stage." Rather, she says, the behavior "just sort of evolved." This is somewhat remarkable. Being strapped into a car seat and taken for a ride that inevitably ends in a nap might be seen as inconsistent with David's need for "independence," just as having his diaper changed is, and thus equally cause for being "insulted."

Ironically, another pair of parents in the same study use their daughter's active resistance to being put in a car seat as an example of "this whole stage of development" and "the sort of independence thing she's into now," but in the same interview say "the thing that's interesting is that she allows you to clean her up, after changing her, a lot more easily than she used to. She used to hate to be cleaned up. She would twist and squirm."

So here too, parents appear to be inconsistent. They take the child's desire not to be manipulated into a car seat as a sign of a growing desire for "independence," but are not bothered by the fact that this desire doesn't seem to carry over to the similar event of having her diaper changed. And, oddly, this little girl exemplifies just the reverse pattern from David (who resents having his diaper changed, but willingly gets strapped into the car seat, even to take a nap).

Many parents, and many others in our culture, consider stages to be "real" things that are "inside" their children. Furthermore, they interpret these stages as signposts on the way to becoming an "independent" (and a rather "de-socialized") person. But, it appears, parents label behaviors part of a stage only when these behaviors represent new behaviors of a sort that both could be seen as negative or difficult and that require new sorts of responses from the parents.

Behaviors that are not problematic in the parent–child relationship – e.g. David yielding to naps in his car seat or the little girl yielding peacefully to being diapered – are not labeled as stages. Furthermore, the parents interpret these potentially negative behaviors which get labeled as stages in terms of the culturally valued notion of "independence," a notion that other cultures, even different social groups within our culture, may well view as socially disruptive or as "anti-social."

These notions of "stage" and "independence" are partially conscious and partially unconscious. These cultural models need not be fully in any parent or child's head, consciously or unconsciously, because they are available in the culture in which these parents live – through the media, through written materials, and through interaction with others in the society.

These parents, situated within their own social, cultural, and class-based Discourses, have a set of connected cultural models about child development, stages, interaction between parents and children, and independence.

Other social groups operate in terms of different cultural models. For example, some working-class families operate in terms of cultural models in which children are seen as inherently willful, independent, and selfish, and in need of socialization that leads not to more independence, but to collaboration with and caring about the needs of family and others (Philipsen 1975).

It is striking that the cultural models, in terms of which the Cambridge families operate, are quite similar to the "formal theories" found in child psychology and child rearing books. This should not really be surprising, however, since these are just the sorts of people that read and write such books. What we have to ask, however, is how much of psychology reflects the cultural models of upper-middle-class people because psychologists hold these models as part and parcel of their class and culture-bound experiences in the world, and not because they are "true" in any scientific sense?

4.5 Cultural models in conflict

My second example demonstrates that each of us can have allegiance to competing and conflicting cultural models. It also shows one way in which more powerful groups in society can influence less powerful groups through cultural models. The example comes from Claudia Strauss's studies (1992; see also Strauss and Quinn 1997: ch. 8) of working-class men in Rhode Island.

Consider for a moment a common American cultural model of "success" or "getting ahead," as discussed by D'Andrade (1984), a cultural model that is deeply embedded in U.S. society, in particular:

> It seems to be the case that Americans think that if one has ability, and if, because of competition or one's own strong drive, one works hard at achieving high goals, one will reach an outstanding level of accomplishment. And when one reaches this level one will be recognized as a success, which brings prestige and self-satisfaction.
>
> (ibid.: 95)

So pervasive is this cultural model in American culture that D'Andrade goes on to say: "Perhaps what is surprising is that anyone can resist the directive force of such a system – that there are incorrigibles" (ibid.: 98). However, people from different social groups within American society relate to this cultural model in quite different ways.

Claudia Strauss in her studies of working-class men in Rhode Island talking about their lives and work found that they accepted the above cultural model of success. For example, one working man said:

I believe if you put an effort into anything, you can get ahead. . . . If I want to succeed, I'll succeed. It has to be, come from within here. Nobody else is going to make you succeed but yourself . . . And, if anybody disagrees with that, there's something wrong with them.

(Strauss 1992: 202)

However, most of the men Strauss studied did not, in fact, act on the success model in terms of their career choices or in terms of how they carried out their daily lives. Unlike many white-collar professionals, these men did not choose to change jobs or regularly seek promotions. They did not regularly sacrifice their time with their families and their families' interests for their own career advancement or "self-development." These men recognized the success model as a set of values and, judging themselves by this model, concluded that they had not really been "successful," and thereby lowered their self-esteem.

The reason these men did not actually act on this model was due to the influence of another cultural model, a model which did effect their actual behaviors. This was the cultural model of "being a breadwinner." Unlike the individualism expressed in the success model, these workers, when they talked about their actual lives, assumed that the interests of the family came ahead of the interests of any individual in it, including themselves. For example, one worker said:

[The worker is discussing the workers' fight against the company's proposal mandating Sunday work] But when that changed and it was negotiated through a contract that you would work, so you had to change or keep losing that eight hours pay. With three children, I couldn't afford it. So I had to go with the flow and work the Sundays.

(Strauss 1992: 207)

This is in sharp contrast to the white-collar professionals studied in Bellah *et al.*'s classic book *Habits of the Heart* (1985), professionals who carried their individualism so far as to be unsure whether they had any substantive responsibility to their families if their families' interests stood in the way of their developing themselves as individuals. These Rhode Island workers accepted the breadwinner model not just as a set of values with which to judge themselves and others. They saw the model not as a matter of choice, but rather as inescapable facts of life (e.g. "had to change," "had to go with the flow"). Thus, the values connected to this model were much more effective in shaping their routine daily behaviors. In fact, this very distinction – between mere "values" and "hard reality" ("the facts") – is itself a particularly pervasive cultural model within Western society.

In contrast to these working-class men, many white-collar professionals work in environments where the daily behaviors of those around them conform to the success model more than daily behaviors on the factory floor conform to this model. For these professionals, then, their daily observations and social practices reinforce explicit ideological learning in regard to the cultural model for success. For them, in contrast to the working-class men Strauss studied, the success model, not the breadwinner model, is seen as "an inescapable fact of life," and, thus, for them, this model determines not just their self-esteem, but many of their actual behaviors.

The working-class men Strauss studied are, in a sense, "colonized" by the success model (we are all, in fact, "colonized" by a good many cultural models that have come to us without much reflection on our part about how well they fit our interests or serve us in the world). They use it, a model which actually fits the observations and behaviors of other groups in the society, to judge themselves and lower their self-esteem. But, as we have seen, since they fail to identify themselves as actors within that model, they cannot develop the very expertise that would allow and motivate them to practice it. In turn, they leave such expertise to the white-collar professionals, some of whom made the above worker work on Sunday against his own interests and wishes. On the other hand, many of these white-collar professionals fail to see that their very allegiance to the success model is connected to their failure to be substantive actors in their families or larger social and communal networks.

4.6 Different sorts and uses of cultural models

What Strauss's work leads us to see is that we need to distinguish between cultural models based on how they are put to use and on the effects they have on us. We can distinguish between, at least, the following sorts of cultural models in regard to these issues:

- *Espoused models*, that is models which we consciously espouse;
- *Evaluative models*, that is models which we use, consciously or unconsciously, to judge ourselves or others;
- *Models-in-(inter)action*, that is models that consciously or unconsciously guide our actions and interactions in the world.

Furthermore, cultural models can be about "appropriate" attitudes, viewpoints, beliefs, and values; "appropriate" ways of acting, interacting, participating, and participant structures; "appropriate" social, cultural, and institutional organizational structures; "appropriate" ways of talking, listening, writing, reading, and communicating; "appropriate" ways to feel or display emotion; "appropriate" ways in which real and fictional events, stories, and histories are organized and end, and so on and so forth.

Cultural models are complexly, though flexibly, organized. There are smaller models inside bigger ones. Each model triggers or is associated with others, in different ways in different settings and differently for different socioculturally defined groups of people. And, we can talk about "master models," that is sets of associated cultural models, or single models, that help shape and organize large and important aspects of experience for particular groups of people, as well as the sorts of Conversations we discussed in Chapter 2.

It is not uncommon that cultural models are signaled by metaphors (Lakoff 1987; Lakoff and Johnson 1980). Very often people are unaware of the full significance of these metaphors, which usually have come to be taken for granted. Sometimes these metaphors are connected to "master models" in the sense that the tacit theories they imply are used widely to organize a number of significant domains for a given culture or social group.

Consider, in this respect, Naomi Quinn's studies on how people talk about marriage and divorce (Quinn 1987; Strauss and Quinn 1997: Chs 6 and 7). Quinn finds that people organize a good deal of their thinking, acting, and interaction around marriage and divorce in terms of a small set of interlocked metaphors, e.g. "marriage is a form of effortful work like a job" or "marriage is an investment like investing money." For instance, consider the following remark by a woman, whom Quinn calls "Nan," talking about why she would not leave her marriage (Quinn 1987: 176):

Why in the world would you want to stop and not get the use out of all the years you've already spent together?

Notice that Nan makes a series of metaphorical equations here. She equates marriage with *time spent* in it. The phrase "time spent" here, then triggers the well-known metaphor in our culture: "time = money," so that time spent in marriage is being treated as an "investment" of time (like an investment of money). In terms of the investment metaphor, if we invest money/time, we are entitled to a "return." So, according to this model, it is silly not to wait long enough, having made an investment, to see it "pay off" and be able to "get the use out of" the time/money that has been invested (rather like a retirement fund!).

The whole idea of seeing things like effort and time as "investments" that will "pay off" is a master cultural model that is used widely across a number of significant domains. Here it is being used to talk about marriage, but the same model crops up in talk about careers, children, education, and so forth.

Metaphors are a rich source of cultural models, though, of course, most cultural models are not signaled by metaphors. Another example of a cultural model signaled by a set of metaphors is the way in which many people in our culture treat argumentation as a form of warfare: e.g. "she couldn't *defend* her argument," "I *defeated* his argument," "she *retreated from* her claims," "he wouldn't *give up* his claim," "she *marshaled* her evidence," etc. This can become a master model, as well, when people begin to extend it to think about personal, institutional, and political relationships, as many, in fact, do.

4.7 Cultural models can be partial and inconsistent

It should be clear by now that cultural models are deeply implicated in "politics." By "politics" I mean anything and anyplace (talk, texts, media, action, interaction, institutions) where "social goods" are at stake, things like power, status, or valued knowledge, positions, or possessions. Since cultural models embed assumptions about what is "appropriate," "typical," and/or "normal," they are political, through and through.

Cultural models, though they are theories (explanations), need not be complete, fully formed, or consistent. Their partiality and inconsistency are sometimes the result of the fact that one cultural model can incorporate different and conflicting social and cultural values, or values connected to groups to which some people who hold the model don't actually belong, or, at least, values that serve other people's interests better than their own. Sometimes it can be hard to tell whether a person holds two conflicting models (as in Claudia Strauss's work above) or one heterogeneous, conflicting one.

Ultimately, the partiality and inconsistency of cultural models reflect the fact that we have all had a great many diverse and conflicting experiences; we all belong to different, sometimes conflicting groups; and we are all influenced by a wide array of groups, texts, institutions, and media that may, in reality, reflect our "best interests" more or less poorly.

To get at some of these matters, let us look at some remarks made by a middle school Latina in the midst of an interview about her life, her attitudes towards family, school, and society, and her views on issues like racism and sexism. We will call this young woman "Marcella" (not her real name). Below, I reprint Marcella's remarks. In Chapter 6 I will discuss "lines and stanzas," but, for now, just treat the numbered lines and the stanzas in the text below as a way to make Marcella's themes clearer.

Interviewer: Uh huh. Um, why do you think there are relatively few African-American and Hispanic doctors?

Stanza 1
1 Because like white people get more education. [I: mmhm]
2 Like Hispanic people don't, don't, some of the Hispanic don't like go to college and stuff like that. [I: mm hm]

Stanza 2

3 And you know, just, the white people just like, they like to, they want a future,

4 You know, they, some, some Hispanic and stuff they, they just,

5 I'm Hispanic but I'm saying

6 So [I: mm hm] um, they just like, like to hang around,

7 They don't want to go to school, you know,

Stanza 3

8 So white people don't, don't think like that.

9 They want to get an education

10 They want to have, their [?life]

11 And they really don't care what people say,

Stanza 4

12 Like if they make fun of em. [I: mm hm]

13 Like gringos and stuff like that.

14 They don't, they don't care,

15 They just do their work

Stanza 5

16 And then, they see after, they're like, they're married and they have their professions and stuff, made, then, let's see who's gonna like, be better,

17 Maybe the Hispanic boy that said that you gonna, that like you're a nerd or something? [I: mm hm]

18 Probably in the streets looking for sh, for money and stuff like that. [I: mm hm] [?sick]

19 And you have a house, you have your profession, you got money, [I: mm hm]

Stanza 6

20 I, it's like I think like white people are smarter.

Interviewer: You think white people are smarter?

20 Yeah.

21 Cos I think like, you guys get more education than we do. [I: mm hm]

Interviewer: Why, I'm not sure why you're saying white people are smarter?

22 Because they get more education, they're smarter. [I: mm hm]

23 I don't know, they, –

Interviewer: Going to school makes them smarter? Or you mean, you know they're smarter because they go to school more?

Stanza 7

24 They're just, they're just smarter.

25 They, they, both, they go to school
26 And they, they, it's like they make an effort to be smart.
27 They make a effort, not,
28 Some, some white people and some Hispanics try to be more than something else, they try to be more than somebody else,

Stanza 8
29 But not I've seen the white people they want, they just want to be, they just wanna be smart, you know,
30 For so, when you go to college or something you know, you know how many points you have so you can make your career
31 You study [?all that] and you, I think, don't care about anybody else,
32 You just care about you, your profession,

Stanza 9
33 And then, you have your kids and you teach them the same thing. [I: uh huh]
34 You know, like you pass already and all that. [I: uh huh]
35 You have example for your kids and stuff.

Interviewer: Uh huh. What do you mean you don't care about anybody else?

Stanza 10
36 You, just, you know, like, oh you are, you're a nerd, you're a nerd cos you always do your homework
37 and you gonna stop doing your homework so they won't call you nerd no more. [I: uh huh]
38 You know, they they they don't, they don't care,
39 They just keep on going.

Interviewer: What is it about white people do you think that makes them like that?

Stanza 11
40 They're just smart. [slight laugh] [I: Uh huh]
41 I think they were born smart.
42 There's something like, their moms or something they give em a little piece of smart or something. [slight laugh] [I: laughs]
43 [?So they'll be smart]

One way to get at people's cultural models is ask "What must I assume this person (consciously or unconsciously) believes in order to make deep sense of what they are saying?," or, to put the question another way, "What 'theories' must the person (consciously or unconsciously) hold such that they are using just these situated meanings?"

Interestingly, when we ask these questions about Marcella's remarks, we see that she holds a cultural model quite close, in some respects, to a formal theory in sociology, namely the theory of the reproduction of cultural capital. This theory says that certain sorts of homes, usually middle-class homes, socialize their children early in life through practices that "resonate" with the practices of schools. At the same time, schools honor these practices, as if they were "natural," universal, and "normal," while ignoring the practices and values of other sorts of homes.

Thus, these advantaged children not only "take to" school well, "buying into" its values and practices, they also come to school ahead of the game and look (and are often treated as if they are) "gifted" or of "high ability." The "cultural capital" of the home translates into "value" in the school where it is "compounded" with "interest" and then passed on as an "inheritance" through the school-focused home-based socialization of the next generation. Thus, the "cultural capital" (that is, the values, attitudes, norms, beliefs, and practices, not just the economic "goods") of middle-class homes are "reproduced" (rewarded and sustained) by schools and renewed when the children, as adults, later socialize their own children at home.

In stanzas 8 and 9, Marcella comes close to her own version of the theory of the reproduction of cultural capital. But, it is clear from many different parts of her text that her cultural-model version of this theory is mixed with a tenet that "white people" are inherently smarter and more motivated than Hispanic people (see stanzas 1, 2, 3, 6, 7, 8, and 11 – e.g. stanza 11: "I think they were born smart"). This is a tenet that is, in fact, inconsistent with the formal theory of the reproduction of cultural capital (which is meant to explain why certain sorts of people are treated by schools as if they were smarter than others, when they are not inherently so).

Marcella seems also to hold a related cultural model in terms of which motivation and effort follow from being inherently "smarter": e.g. in stanza 7, she says, "They're just, they're just smarter And they, they, it's like they make an effort to be smart."

There is, then, a contradiction in Marcella's cultural model version of the reproduction of cultural capital. If home-based practices can account for the differential success of "white" people (see stanza 9), and if many of the attitudes, values, and practices that schools and certain middle-class homes reward are arbitrary (note Marcella's remarks in stanza 8: "you know how many points you have so you can make your career" and "you don't care about anybody else"), then we don't need to assume or appeal to the idea that "whites" are inherently smarter. Much as the working-class men in Claudia Strauss's studies were "colonized" by the way in which they used the "Success Model," so too, the "bite" of the theory of the reproduction of cultural capital in terms of which Marcella might indict the schools for their "conspiracy" with certain homes and not others, is mitigated by her attributing success as an inherent inborn property of "whites."

At the same time, it is clear that authentic education has much to work with in Marcella's own culturally-based theorizing. She has already hit upon, based on her own experiences, some of the ways in which families, race, class, and schools function politically in society. On this basis, school could certainly build her overt understanding and theorizing of history, society, politics, and institutions. That school has failed to do this for Marcella (and continues to as she now enters high school) is, of course, ironically part of the indictment inherent in the theory of the reproduction of cultural capital.

4.8 Cultural models as "recognition work"

Our last example of cultural models at work is meant to bring out the ways in which cultural models flow from our experiences and social positions in the world. Cultural models are not just based on our experiences in the world, they "project" onto that world, from where we "stand" (where we are socially positioned), certain viewpoints about what is right and wrong, and what can or cannot be done to solve problems in the world.

Consider the two texts printed below (we will consider these texts again in Chapter 7). One is from an interview with a female university professor in a post-industrial East coast city in the United States, a city with typical urban poverty, gang, and racial problems. The other text is from an interview with a female school teacher in the same city. It so happens that the university professor teaches in a college in the city where Marcella lives and the school teacher teaches in the middle school which Marcella attended.

These two women are talking about whether there are racial problems in their city and how they think about them. I cite only a small bit of each interview. I will attempt below to contextualize these bits in terms of the larger interviews from which they were taken (street and neighborhood names below are pseudonyms).

University professor:

Interviewer: . . . *How, do you see racism happening, in society, let's put it that way?*

Stanza 1
1 Um, well, I could answer on, on a variety of different levels. [I: uh huh]
2 Um, at the most macro level, um, I think that there's um, um,
3 I don't want to say this in a way that sounds like a conspiracy, [I: mm hm]
4 But I think um, that um, basically that the lives of people of color are are, are irrelevant to the society anymore. [I: mm hm]

5 Um, they're not needed for the economy because we have the third world to run away into for cheap labor, [I: uh huh]

Stanza 2

6 Um, and I think that, that the leadership, this country really doesn't care if they shoot each other off in in the ghettos, [I: uh huh]

7 Um, and, and so they let drugs into the ghettos, and they, um, they, let people shoot themselves, shoot each other, and they don't have, a police force that is really gonna, um, work , and they cut the programs that might alleviate some of the problems, and, um.

Stanza 3

8 So I think there's, that it's manifested at, at the most, structural level as, um, you know, a real hatred, of, of, of uh people of color. [I: uh huh]

9 And, and it's shown, in, the cutbacks and so forth

10 And, um, I think that um, that, it's, it's reflected in, in the fact that, they're, they're viewed as, expendable, [I: mm hm] by our leadership,

11 Um, and so I think, I see cutbacks in programs as just a, an example of, of a broader, [I: mm hm] you know, sense, that, that, from the point of view of, of those in power, people of color are expendable, [I: uh huh] and, and irrelevant. Um, –

Middle school teacher:

Interviewer: . . . *or maybe you in like leading the class would you ever tie that [i.e. social issues, JPG] into like present power relations or just individual experiences of racism in their lives or something like that.*

Stanza 1

1 Uh so [what] you you need to do about job hunting, you need to look the part. [I:mm hm]

2 You don't see anybody at any nice store dressed in jeans [I: uh huh],

3 They're not gonna have a job if they do that. [I: uh huh]

4 And a lot of the kids question that.

Stanza 2

5 uh I talk about housing,

6 We talk about the [????] we talk about a lot of the low income things,

7 I said "Hey wait a minute,"

8 I said, "Do you think the city's gonna take care of an area that you don't take care of yourself?" [I: uh huh]

Stanza 3

9 I said, "How [many of] you [have] been up Danbury Street?"

10 They raise their hands,

11   I say "How about Washington Ave,"
12   That's where those gigantic houses are,

Stanza 4

13   I said, "How many pieces of furniture are sitting in the front yard?" [I:mm hm] "Well, none."
14   I said "How much trash is lying around?" "None."
15   I said, "How many houses are spray painted?
16   How many of them have kicked in, you know have broken down cars in front of them? [I: uh huh]"

Stanza 5

17   I said, "They take care of their area,"
18   I said,"I'm not saying you kids do this,"
19   I said,"Look at Grand Avenue Valley, they burn the dumpsters.
20   That's your housing area [I: uh huh]
21   Do you know how fast that can *jump* into someone's apartment or whatever else?"

Stanza 6

22   I bring up the uh, they have in the paper, probably about two years ago, the uh police were being sued – uh the fire department were being sued by a family that had a girl with asthma,
23   And the kids had lit the dumpster outside of their bedroom window
24   And she had a severe asthma attack
25   And the fire department would not come in

Stanza 7

26   So they couldn't get the police escort.
27   The fire department used to only go in with a police escort/because the people living there would throw bottles and cans at them. [I: uh huh]

Stanza 8

28   And you know, again, the whole class would [???].
29   I don't understand this.
30   Here is someone who's coming in here –
31   Maybe the police I could understand because you feel like you're getting harassed by the police,
32   What has the fire department done to you that you're gonna throw bottles, rocks, cans at them [I: uh huh] and stop them from putting out a fire [I: uh huh] that could burn down your whole house. [I: uh huh]

Stanza 9

33   Why do you burn the grass? [I: mm hm]
34   There's grass here that every single summer as soon as it turns green they burn

35 And as soon as it grows back up they burn again.
36 Why do you do that?

Various cultural models are readily apparent in these remarks. The professor applies a widespread academic cultural model in terms of which actual behavior ("the appearances") follow from larger, deeper, more general, underlying, and hidden causes (Bechtel and Richardson 1993). The teacher applies a widespread cultural model in terms of which people's problems flow from their own behaviors as individuals, and it is through "correct" behavior and "proper" appearances that one achieves "success." It is also typical, at least of the city in which these women live, that the university academic codes questions about "racism" as about "people of color" (and this often means, for academics, a focus on African-Americans) and the teacher codes them as about class (many of the people she is referring to are white), though she never names class directly.

We can also look at these texts as attempts to get oneself and others to *recognize and relate* people and things like poverty, crime, fear, and segregated neighborhoods *in a certain way*. This amounts to taking people and things in the world and organizing them into a specific pattern that we then, take to be "out there." In reality, this pattern is a joint product of our experience in the world and the discursive work we do in communicating in specific settings.

Throughout her interview – and this is clearly a co-construction with the interviewer – the professor almost always wants (and is sustained by the interviewer in this effort) to recognize actors, events, activities, and practices in terms of economic and nation-state level politics. She wants to recognize "racial problems" as transcending her city and as a global affair, despite the fact that she could well point to many specific instances in her city (where racial problems very much have their own "spin").

Though the teacher is interviewed by the same interviewer, the interviewer and teacher co-construct a very different, much more local sort of recognition. In fact, in much other work in this city, and with teachers in other places, I have found that researchers and teachers alike always assume that teachers have only a "local voice" on such issues. Rarely are teachers invited into – or do they have access to – a "national voice." Even when invited to speak at national conferences, teachers usually speak as representatives of their local areas and their own experiences, while researchers speak as transcending locality and their own experiences.

In addition to her local focus, which is a co-construction with the interviewer, the teacher wants more specifically to recognize individual actors who, in fact, do not really belong to a "class" or "race," but whose individual behaviors ensure that they are poor and looked down upon by others, others who have no real obligation to help them, since they need to help themselves. I have found that many teachers in the city in which this teacher lives fiercely resist putting people, especially children, into "groups," and want to see them as individual actors who, if they are children, need nurturing, and if they are adults, need to take responsibility for themselves. Such teachers, in fact, actively work to "undo" the attempts of university academics to place people in social and cultural categories, especially children.

Thus, the university professor trades on cultural models that distance her from local circumstances, and, thus, too, from teachers like the one above, and students like Marcella, a student "of color," who live in her city. On the other hand, the teacher trades on cultural models that place her closer to local affairs, institutions, and students like Marcella. Note that neither one of these perspectives is inherently "right." In fact, in respect to a student like Marcella the professor's perspective is liable to be paralyzing and the teacher's will only encourage the tendency we have already seen that she has to "blame the victims," including herself.

4.9 Cultural models as tools of inquiry

As I did in the case of situated meanings in the last chapter, I have here spoken of cultural models realistically as existing in the mind and in the world of texts and social practices. But, in fact, I am primarily interested in their role as a "tool of inquiry." They lead us to ask, when confronted with a piece of talk, writing, action, or interaction, questions like these:

- What cultural models are relevant here? What must I, as an analyst, assume people feel, value, and believe, consciously or not, in order to talk (write), act, and/or interact this way?
- Are there differences here between the cultural models that are affecting espoused beliefs and those that are affecting actions and practices? What sorts of cultural models, if any, are being used here to make value judgments about oneself or others?
- How consistent are the relevant cultural models here? Are there competing or conflicting cultural models at play? Whose interests are the cultural models representing?
- What other cultural models are related to the ones most active here? Are there "master models" at work?
- What sorts of texts, media, experiences, interactions, and/or institutions could have given rise to these cultural models?
- How are the relevant cultural models here helping to reproduce, transform, or create social, cultural, institutional, and/or political relationships? What Discourses and Conversations are these cultural models helping to reproduce, transform, or create?

We always assume, until absolutely proven otherwise, that *everyone* has "good reasons" and makes "deep sense" in terms of their own socioculturally-specific ways of talking, listening (writing, reading), acting, interacting, valuing, believing, and feeling. Of course, we are all members of multiple cultures and Discourses and so the analytic task is often finding which of these, and with what blends, is operative in the communication. The assumption of "good reasons" and "deep sense" is foundational to discourse analysis. It is not only a moral principle. It is based, as well, on the viewpoint, amply demonstrated in work in cognitive science, applied linguistics, and in a variety of different approaches to discourse analysis, that humans are, as creatures, *sense makers par excellence*. Within their cultures and Discourses, they move to sense, the way certain plants move to light.

We obviously do not gain our evidence for cultural models by opening up people's heads. And we don't need to. Besides closely observing what they say and do, we look at the texts, media, social practices, social and institutional interactions, and diverse Discourses that influence them. As in the case of context and situated meanings in the last chapter, we can always gain more information. Thus, our conclusions are always tentative. However, here, too, we hope that eventually more information does not lead to substantive revision of our conclusions. This issue is related to the larger one of validity, an issue I take up in Chapter 5.

5 Discourse analysis

5.1 Situated meanings and cultural models revisited

In this chapter, I integrate the tools of inquiry we have discussed in the earlier chapters into an overall model of discourse analysis that stresses the six building tasks introduced at the opening of Chapter 2. I will also discuss, from the perspective on discourse analysis taken in this book, the role of transcripts in discourse analysis, what might constitute an "ideal" discourse analysis, and the nature of validity in discourse analysis.

In this section, I summarize the two types of meaning that I argued, in Chapters 3 and 4, attach to words and phrases in actual use: situated meanings and cultural models. After a brief review of these two notions, I will turn to a discussion of an important and related property of language, a property I will call "reflexivity." This is the "magical" property of language, which we discussed briefly at the outset of Chapter 2, in virtue of which language-in-use both creates and reflects the contexts in which it is used.

A situated meaning, as we saw in Chapter 3, is an image or pattern that we assemble "on the spot" as we communicate in a given context, based on our construal of that context and on our past experiences (Agar 1994; Barsalou 1991, 1992; Clark 1993; Clark 1996; Hofstadter 1997; Kress 1985, 1996; Kress and van Leeuwen 1996). In Chapter 3, I used the example of the following two utterances: "The coffee spilled, get a mop"; "The coffee spilled, get a broom" (p. 48). In the first case, triggered by the word "mop" in the context, you assemble a situated meaning something like "dark liquid we drink" for "coffee"; in the second case, triggered by the word "broom" and your experience of such matters, you assemble either a situated meaning something like "grains that we make our coffee from" or like "beans from which we grind coffee." Of course, in a real context, there are many more signals as how to go about assembling situated meanings for words and phrases.

Situated meanings don't simply reside in individual minds; very often they are *negotiated* between people in and through communicative social interaction (Billig 1987; Edwards and Potter 1992; Goffman 1981; Goodwin

1990). For example, in Chapter 2, I used the example of someone in a relationship saying "I think good relationships shouldn't take work." A good part of the conversation following such a remark might very well involve mutually negotiating (directly, or indirectly through inferencing) what "work" is going to mean for the people concerned, in this specific context, as well as in the larger context of their ongoing relationship. Furthermore, as conversations and indeed, relationships, develop, participants continually revise their situated meanings.

Words like "work" and "coffee" seem to have more general meanings than are apparent in the sorts of situated meanings we have discussed so far. This is because words are also associated with what, in Chapters 3 and 4, I called "cultural models." Cultural models are "storylines," families of connected images (like a mental movie), or (informal) "theories" shared by people belonging to specific social or cultural groups (D'Andrade 1995; D'Andrade and Strauss 1992; Holland and Quinn 1987; Strauss and Quinn 1997).

Cultural models "explain," relative to the standards of the group, why words have the various situated meanings they do and fuel their ability to grow more. Cultural models are usually not completely stored in any one person's head. Rather, they are distributed across the different sorts of "expertise" and viewpoints found in the group (Hutchins 1995; Shore 1996), much like a plot to a story or pieces of a puzzle that different people have different bits of and which they can potentially share in order to mutually develop the "big picture."

The cultural model connected to "coffee," for example, is, for some of us, something like: berries are picked (somewhere? from some sort of plant?) and then prepared (how?) as beans or grain to be made later into a drink, as well as into flavorings (how?) for other foods. Different types of coffee, drunk in different ways, have different social and cultural implications, for example, in terms of status. This is about all of the model I know, the rest of it (I trust) is distributed elsewhere in the society should I need it.

Cultural models link to each other in complex ways to create bigger and bigger storylines. Such linked networks of cultural models help organize the thinking and social practices of sociocultural groups. For example, taking a more consequential example than "coffee," as we saw in Chapter 4, some people use a cultural model for raising young children that runs something like this (Harkness, Super, and Keefer 1992): Children are born dependent on their parents and then they go through various stages during which they often engage in disruptive behaviors in pursuit of their growing desire for independence.

This cultural model, which integrates models for children, child-rearing, stages, development, and independence, as well as others, helps parents explain their children's behavior in terms of a value the group holds (e.g. independence). It is continually revised and developed (consciously and unconsciously) in interaction with others in the group, as well as through exposure to various books and other media. Other social groups view children differently (Philipsen 1975): for example, as beings who start out as too unsocialized and whose disruptive behaviors are not so much signs of their growing desire for independence as they are signals of their need for greater socialization within the family, i.e. for less independence (less "selfishness").

5.2 Reflexivity

When we think about how meaning is situated in actual contexts of use, we quickly face an important property of language, a property I will call "reflexivity" (Duranti and Goodwin 1992; Hanks 1996; Heritage 1984; Gumperz and Levinson 1996). This is the "magical" property of language with which we started Chapter 2. We can see this property clearly by considering even so simple a dialogue as: "How are ya?," "Fine," exchanged between colleagues in a office corridor. Why do they use *these* words in *this situation*? *Because* they take the situation they are in to be but a brief and mundane encounter between acquaintances, and these are the "appropriate" words to use in such a situation. But why do they take the situation to be *thus*? In part, *because* they are using just such words, and related behaviors, as they are. Had the exchange opened with "What's YOUR problem?," the situation would have been construed quite differently.

As we saw in Chapter 2, we face, then, a chicken and egg question: Which comes first? The situation or the language? This question reflects an important *reciprocity* between language and "reality": language simultaneously *reflects* reality ("the way things are") and *constructs* (*construes*) it to be a certain way. While "reciprocity" would be a good term for this property of language, the more commonly used term is "reflexivity" (in the sense of language and context being like two mirrors facing each other and constantly and endlessly reflecting their own images back and forth between each other).

5.3 Situations

Language then always simultaneously reflects and constructs the situation or context in which it is used (hereafter I will use the term "situation," rather than "context," because I want to define it in a particular way). But what do we mean by a "situation"? Situations, when they involve communicative social interaction, always involve the following inextricably connected components or aspects (Hymes 1974; Ochs 1996):

- A *semiotic* aspect, that is, the "sign systems," such as language, gestures, images, or other symbolic systems (Kress and van Leeuwen 1996), and the forms of knowledge, that are operative and important here and now. Different sign systems and different ways of knowing have, in turn, different implications for what is taken as the "real" world, and what is taken as probable and possible and impossible, here and now, since it is only through sign systems that we have access to "reality."

- An *activity* aspect, that is, the specific social activity or activities in which the participants are engaging; activities are, in turn, made up of a sequence of actions (Engestrom 1987, 1990; Leont'ev 1978; 1981; Wertsch 1998).
- A *material* aspect, that is, the place, time, bodies and objects present during interaction (Clark 1997; Latour 1991; Levinson 1996).
- A *political* aspect, that is, the distribution of "social goods" in the inter-action, such as, power, status, and anything else deemed a "social good" by the participants in terms of their cultural models and Discourses, e.g. beauty, intelligence, "street smarts," strength, possessions, race, gender, sexual orientation, etc. (Fairclough 1989, 1992, 1995; Gee 1996; Luke 1995).
- A *sociocultural* aspect, that is, the personal, social, and cultural know-ledge, feelings, values, identities, and relationships relevant in the inter-action, including, of course, sociocultural knowledge about sign systems, activities, the material world, and politics, i.e. all the other aspects above (Agar 1994; Barton and Hamilton 1998; Carbaugh 1996; Gee 1992, 1996; Hanks 1996; John-Steiner, Panofsky, and Smith 1994; Palmer 1996; Scollon and Scollon 1981; Sperber and Wilson 1989; Toolan 1996).

All these aspects together constitute a *system* (an interrelated network) within which each of the components or aspects simultaneously gives meaning to all the others and gets meaning from them. That is, we have another form of reflexivity here, as well. For a shorthand, let us call this system the "situation network."

Situations are never completely novel (indeed, if they were, we wouldn't understand them). Rather, they are repeated, with more or less variation, over time (that is, distinctive configurations or patterns of semiotic resources, activities, things, and political and sociocultural elements are repeated). Such repetition tends to "ritualize," "habitualize," or "freeze" situations to varying degrees, that is, to cause them to be repeated with less variation (Douglas 1986).

Such repetition (e.g. imagine the old style spelling bee or the traditional doctor–nurse–patient relationship around a hospital bed) is the life blood out of which *institutions*, such as distinctive types of schools, hospitals, busi-nesses, industries, government agencies, political parties, street gangs, academic disciplines, colleges or college classrooms, and so on and so forth through a nearly endless list, are created. Institutions, in turn, create forces (e.g. laws, disciplinary procedures, apprenticeships, etc.) that ensure the repetition and ritualization of the situations that sustain them. Studying the way in which situations produce and reproduce institutions, and are, in turn, sustained by them, is an important part of discourse analysis (Bernstein 1996; Bourdieu 1985; Foucault 1973, 1977; Gee, Hull, and Lankshear 1996; Lynch and Bogen 1996).

All of the elements in the situation network are like connected threads; if you pull on one you get all the others. Though discourse analysis usually focuses on the language (semiotic) aspect, it can start from any of these aspects of a situation and will, in the end, get right back to all the others. Let me give some brief examples of how all the aspects in the situation network are integrally intertwined.

Consider a small seminar room with a circular table in it, and blackboard on all sides. The room has a "front" and "back" when a teacher is standing at the "front" addressing students. What gives the room (a material thing) a "front" and a "back" (meanings/values) is a socioculturally distinctive activity, teaching of a certain sort, which some cultures engage in and others do not, an activity realized through socioculturally distinctive forms of language and certain sorts of sociocultural knowledge, attitudes, and identities. Furthermore, the "front"–"back" dimension of the room reflects the traditional political alignments of teachers as "authorities" and students as subservient. Thus, the room, the activity, the talk, socio-cultural identities, and political relations all mean together, giving and taking meaning from each other.

When a committee meets in the same room around the circular table, the room now has no front or back (or, we might say, the room is oriented less strongly in a front–back dimension than when a teacher is lecturing in the room), but the table has a "head" positioned wherever the "chair" sits. When a student discussion group, with no "chair," meets around the same table, then front, back, and head all disappear. In both these cases, language, activity, sociocultural identities, and political relationships are different from the teaching situation with which we started. Here we see how the material world takes on meanings that emerge from the interaction of that world with human activity, language, sociocultural knowledge, atti-tudes, and identities, and political relationships. But we can say the same of each of the other aspects in the situation network.

Take language, a semiotic system, for another example: consider that "fine" in response to "How are you?" means something quite different when uttered as part of the activity of a mundane corridor interaction between colleagues than when uttered as part of a medical exam between a doctor and a patient. Or take the sociocultural aspect: consider that when the doctor asks me in an offhand way during "chit chat" in an office visit how many languages I know, she is activating my identity as a linguist (from her perspective of what linguists are), but when she asks me if I am having trouble recalling common words, as she looks over my CAT scan, she is activating my identity as a patient. To enact "chit chat" as against "medical exam" (activities) or different situated sociocultural

identities (linguist as against patient), I have to use characteristic and different sorts of language (and vice versa).

Or, finally, consider the political aspect. When the young woman we saw
in Chapter 2 says to her parents, "Well, when I thought about it, I don't
know, it seemed to me that Gregory should be the most offensive," and
to her boyfriend, "What an ass that guy was, you know, her boyfriend,"
she is responding to the differential status of her parents and her boyfriend
in terms of age and other variables. But she is also using language to create,
or reproduce, these power relationships (one of deference to her parents
and solidarity with her boyfriend) here and now.

5.4 Six building tasks

Discourse analysis focuses on the thread of language (and related semiotic
systems) used in the situation network. Any piece of language, oral or
written, is composed of a set of grammatical *cues* or *clues* (Gumperz 1982)
that help listeners or readers (in negotiation and collaboration with others
in an interaction) to *build* six things (in one sense of the word, these
six things are interlinked "representations," that is, "re-presentings").
I want to stress that utterances are made up of cues or clues as to how to
move back and forth between language and context (situations), not signals
of fixed and decontextualized meanings. These cues or clues are part and
parcel of what we called, in Chapter 2, "grammar one" and "grammar
two" (p. 29).

Language, then, always contains cues or clues that guide us (either as
interpreters on the scene or as analysts) in the six sorts of building tasks
listed below (these were briefly discussed in Chapter 2). These building
tasks involve us in using language (and other semiotic systems) to construe
the situation network in certain ways and not others. They are carried out
all at once and together. And, they are carried out in negotiation and
collaboration with others in interaction, with due regard for other related
oral and written texts and situations we have encountered before.

Even when we are silently reading, these building tasks are carried out in
negotiation and collaboration with the writer in various guises such as the
"actual writer," "assumed writer," and the narrator, as well as in collaboration with other, related texts we have read, sociocultural knowledge we
bring to the text, and discussions we have had with other people. That is,
these building tasks can be seen simultaneously as cognitive achievements,
interactional achievements, and inter-textual achievements.

The six building tasks, the tasks through which we use language to
construct and/or construe the situation network, at a given time and place,
in a certain way, are:

1 *Semiotic building*, that is, using cues or clues to assemble situated
   meanings about what semiotic (communicative) systems, systems of

knowledge, and ways of knowing, are here and now relevant and activated.

2 *World building*, that is, using cues or clues to assemble situated meanings about what is here and now (taken as) "reality," what is here and now (taken as) present and absent, concrete and abstract, "real" and "unreal," probable, possible, and impossible.

3 *Activity building*, that is, using cues or clues to assemble situated meanings about what activity or activities are going on, composed of what specific actions.

4 *Socioculturally-situated identity and relationship building*, that is, using cues or clues to assemble situated meanings about what identities and relationships are relevant to the interaction, with their concomitant attitudes, values, ways of feeling, ways of knowing and believing, as well as ways of acting and interacting.

5 *Political building*, that is, using cues or clues to construct the nature and relevance of various "social goods," such as status and power, and anything else taken as a "social good" here and now (e.g. beauty, humor, verbalness, specialist knowledge, a fancy car, etc.).

6 *Connection building*, that is, using cues or clues to make assumptions about how the past and future of an interaction, verbally and nonverbally, are connected to the present moment and to each other – after all, interactions always have some degree of continuous coherence.

Different grammatical devices contribute differently to these six tasks and many devices contribute to more than one at the same time. All together these six building tasks spell out the work of the semiotic aspect of the situation network, with special reference here to language. That is, they are the work that we do with language (and other semiotic systems, such as gestures or images) to construct or construe a situation in certain ways and not others.

Cues or clues in the language we use (different sorts of cues and clues in different social languages) help assemble or trigger specific situated meanings through which the six building tasks are accomplished. In turn, these situated meanings activate certain cultural models, and not other ones. Finally, the social languages, situated meanings, and cultural models at play allow people to enact and recognize different Discourses at work (i.e. to see each other and various things in the world as certain "kinds of people" and certain "kinds of things" engaged in certain "kinds of activities").

5.5 Social languages revisited

What is important to discourse analysis are not languages at the level of English and Navaho. All languages, whether English or Navaho, are, as we argued in Chapter 2, composed of many different *social languages*

(Bakhtin 1981, 1986). Physicists engaged in experiments don't speak and write like street-gang members engaged in initiating a new member, and neither of these speak or write like "new capitalist" entrepreneurs engaged in "empowering front-line workers." Each social language uses somewhat different and characteristic grammatical resources to carry out our six building tasks.

All of us control many different social languages and switch among them in different contexts. In that sense, no one is monolingual. But, also, all of us fail to have mastery of some social languages that use the grammatical resources of our "native language," and, thus, in that sense, we are not (any of us) "native speakers" of the full gamut of social languages which compose "our" language.

It is important, as well, to note that very often social languages are not "pure," but, rather, people mix ("hybridize") them in complex ways for specific purposes. It is sometimes quite hard to know whether it is best to say whether someone is switching from one social language to another ("code switching") or actually mixing two of them to assemble, for a given context, a transformed (even novel) social language (which may, of course, eventually come to be seen as a "pure" and different social language in its own right, when people forget that it arose as a mixture). It is, of course, more important, in a discourse analysis, to recognize this matter than to settle it. People can even mix or switch between different social languages that are drawn from different languages at the level of things like English and Navaho. In Chapter 2 I gave a variety of examples of different social languages at work building and being built through actual situations.

It is social languages which contain the cues or clues that guide the six building tasks listed earlier. Different social languages contain different sorts of cues or clues, that is, they use grammar in different ways as a resource for the six building tasks. For example, consider again the young woman above who said to her parents, "Well, when I thought about it, I don't know, it seemed to me that Gregory should be the most offensive," and to her boyfriend, "What an ass that guy was, you know, her boyfriend," when she was talking about the same character in the same story. These utterances are in two different social languages.

In the first case, when the young woman is speaking to her parents, the following sort of *pattern* of grammatical features is indicative of a particular social language: preliminary clause about having been reflective ("when I thought about it"); mitigators ("I don't know," "seemed to me"); complex subordinating syntax (*when*-clause, *it-seems-that* construction); repeated references to self ("I," "me") as careful claimer/knower; Latinate vocabulary ("offensive"); complex modality ("should be"). This social language contains cues and clues for deference, respect, school-based learning, reflection, attention to knowledge and claims, and so forth.

In the second case, when the young woman is speaking to her boyfriend, the following sort of pattern of grammatical features is indicative of another sort of social language: Exclamation ("What an ass "); informal vocabulary ("ass," "guy"); right dislocation ("her boyfriend"); attention to hearer ("you know"); directly making claims with no mitigators or attention to self as claimer. This social language contains cues or clues for solidarity, informality, participatory communication, attention to shared values, and a focus on the social world and not the self.

Such patterns are part and parcel of what we called "grammar two" in Chapter 2 (p. 29). Interpreters (listeners or readers) who are members of the Discourses whose social languages these are recognize (however unconsciously) the patterns in the same rapid and intuitive way they recognize the situated meanings of words.

5.6 Units and transcription

With ever more sophisticated recording and computer equipment, it is possible to get incredibly detailed records of speech that include small pauses, slight hesitations, subtle changes in sound, pitch, rate, and loudness, as well as close synchronizations of overlaps between speakers (see Edwards and Lampert 1993; Schiffrin 1994: Appendix 2). It is tempting to believe that such detailed records represent some pure, objective, and unanalyzed "reality." In fact, they do no such thing. Speech always has far more detail in it than any recording or transcription system could ever capture (or that the human ear can hear).

A discourse analysis is based on the details of speech (and gaze and gesture and action) or writing that are arguably deemed *relevant* in the situation *and* that are relevant to the arguments the analyst is attempting to make. A discourse analysis is not based on *all* the physical features present, not even all those that might, in some conceivable context, be meaningful, or might be meaningful in analyses with different purposes. Such judgments of relevance (what goes into a transcript and what does not) are ultimately theoretical judgments, that is, based on the analyst's theories of how language, situations, and interactions work in general and in the specific situation being analyzed (Mishler 1991; Ochs 1979). In this sense, a transcript is a theoretical entity. It does not stand outside an analysis, but, rather, is part of it.

Any speech data can be transcribed in more or less detailed ways such that we get a continuum of possible transcripts ranging from very detailed (what linguists call "narrow") transcripts to much less detailed (what linguists call "broad") ones. While it is certainly wise to begin one's analysis by transcribing for more detail than may in the end be relevant, ultimately it is the purposes of the analyst that determine how narrow or broad the transcript must be. The validity of an analysis is not a matter of how detailed one's transcript is. It is a matter of how the transcript works together with all the other elements of the analysis to create a "trustworthy" analysis (for which, see Section 5.8 on p. 94).

There is not space here to go into the linguistic details of transcripts (for details, see Edwards and Lampert 1993; Schiffrin 1994: Appendix 2). Instead, I will simply give one example of how "minor" details can take on "major" importance in interaction, and, thus, must, in those instances, be included in transcripts. Consider the interaction below between a Anglo-American female researcher ("R") and a fourth grade African-American girl ("S" for student) with whom the researcher is discussing light as part of a school science education project. This student comes from a very poor home and her schooling has been continuously disrupted by having to move in order to find housing. The researcher is about to start an interaction with the student in which the student will be asked to reason about light by manipulating and thinking about a light box and how a light beam focused by the box interacts with different plastic shapes, including a prism (which causes the light to break into a rainbow of colors).

The following transcript uses notational devices to name features of speech which we have not yet discussed, but which we will discuss in Chapter 6. For now, it is enough to know that each line of the transcript represents a tone unit, that is a set of words said with one uniform intonational contour (that is, said as if they "go together" – see Chapter 6). A double slash ("//") indicates that the tone unit is said with a "final contour," that is, a rising or falling pitch of the voice that sounds "final," as if a piece of information is "closed off" and "finished" (the fall or rise in pitch is realized over the underlined words and any words that follow them, see Brazil, Coulthard, and Johns 1980 for many more details). A tone unit that has no double slash is said on a "non-final contour," a shorter rising or falling contour that sounds as if there is more information to come.

I have organized the text below into "stanzas," a language unit that we will discuss in Chapter 6. Stanzas are "clumps" of tone units that deal with a unitary topic or perspective, and which appear (from various linguistic details) to have been planned together. In this case, the stanzas are interactively produced. Words that are underlined carry the major stress in their tone unit (as we will see in Chapter 6, stress in English is marked by bumping or gliding the pitch of the voice up or down or increasing loudness or both). Capitalized words are emphatic (said with extra stress). Two periods ("..") indicates a hearable pause. Two dots following a vowel ("die:d") indicate that the vowel is elongated (drawn out). "Low pitch" means that the preceding unit was said on overall low pitch. This transcript is certainly nowhere as narrow as it could be, though it includes some degree of linguistic detail.

Stanza 1
1 R: Where does the <u>light</u> come from
2 R: when it's <u>outside</u>? //

3   s: <u>Sun</u> (low pitch) //
4   r: From the <u>sun</u> (low pitch) // .. hum

Stanza 2
5   s: Cause the <u>sun</u> comes up
6   s: <u>REALLY</u> early //
7   r: um .. And that's <u>when</u> we get light (low pitch) //

Stanza 3
8   s: And that's how the, the the me .. my .. <u>me and my class</u>
9   s: is talkin' about <u>dinosau:rs</u>
10   s: and how they <u>die:d</u> //
11   s: And we <u>found out</u> ..
12   s: some things . about how they <u>die:d</u> //
13   r: Oh <u>really</u> //

Start of Stanza 4
14   r: Does that have to do with <u>LIGHT</u>? //
(interaction continues)

After a long interaction from which this bit is taken, the researcher felt that the child often strayed from the topic and was difficult to understand. However, it can be argued, from the above data, that the researcher "co-constructed" (contributed to) these topic changes and lack of understanding.

Children in school are used to a distinctive school activity in which an adult asks them a question (to which the adult already knows the answer, but to which the answer is not supposed to be obvious), the child answers, and the adults responds in some way that can be taken as evaluating whether the child's answer was "acceptable" or not (Sinclair and Coulthard 1975).

There is also a common and related practice in schools in which the teacher asks one or more obvious and rather "everyday" questions in order to elicit items that will subsequently be treated in much more abstract ways than they typically are in "everyday" (lifeworld) interaction (Keith Stenning, personal communication). A science teacher might ask "What is this?" of a ruler. Receiving the answer "a ruler," she might ask "What do we do with rulers?" Having elicited an answer like "measure things," the teacher may very well go on to treat measuring devices and measurement in quite abstract ways. In the interaction above, the researcher appears to want to elicit some everyday information about light in order to subsequently get the child to treat light in terms of abstract notions like "light sources," "directions," "reflection," and "refraction," that is, much more abstractly than specific things like the sun. There is ample evidence from what we otherwise know about the student being discussed here that she is, in all likelihood, unfamiliar with and unpracticed in this sort of (on the face of it rather odd) school-based practice.

In the above interaction, the researcher starts with a question to which the student responds with the word "sun" said on a low pitch and with a final falling contour. This way of answering indicates (in many dialects of English) that the respondent takes the answer to be obvious (this already constitutes a problem with the question–answer-evaluation activity).

The researcher's response is said in exactly the same way as the child's (low pitch, final falling contour) – and in just the position that a student is liable to expect an evaluation – indicating that she, too, takes the answer to be obvious. The student might well be mystified, then, as to why the question was asked.

In lines 5 and 6 the student adds tone units that are said on a higher pitch than the previous ones. Furthermore, line 6 contains an emphatic "really." This way of saying lines 5 and 6 indicates that the student takes this information to be new or significant information. She may well have added this information in a search for some response that would render the initial question something other than a request for obvious information and in a search for some more energetic response from the researcher, one that would let the student know she was "on the right track" in the interaction.

However, the student once again gets a response from the researcher (low pitch, falling final contour) that indicates the researcher takes the student's contribution, again, to be obvious. The student, then, in line 8, launches off on yet another contribution that is, once again, said in a way that indicates she is trying to state new or significant information that will draw a response of interest from the researcher.

The student also uses a technique that is common to some African-American children (Gee 1985). She states background information first before stating her main topic (light), though her "found out/some things" clearly implies, in this context, that these things will have to do with light (which they do – she has studied how a meteor blocked out sun-light and helped destroy the dinosaurs). The researcher, listening for a more foregrounded connection to light, stops the student and, with emphasis on "light," clearly indicates that she is skeptical that the student's contribution is going to be about light, a skepticism that is, from the student's per-spective, not only unmerited, but actually surprising and a bit insulting (as subsequent interaction shows).

Here the "devil" is, indeed, in the details: aspects of the school-based "known question–answer–evaluation" activity, different assumptions about how information is introduced and connected, as well as details of pitch and emphasis (as well as a good many other such details) all work together to lead to misunderstanding. This misunderstanding is quite con-sequential when the adult authority figure attributes the misunderstanding to the student and not to the details of language and diversity (most certainly including the researcher's own language and diversity).

One may wonder why the researcher asked the questions she did and responded as she did. To make a long story short, the research project was based on the idea that giving children too much explicit information or overt challenging responses would restrict their creativity and "sense making," especially with minority students who may not interpret such overt instruction and challenging the same way the instructor does. Ironically, a situation set up to elicit the "best" from the child by leaving her as "free" as possible, led to her being construed as not making sense, when, in fact, she was making sense at several levels in a deeply paradoxical setting created by the researchers.

Note, then, how the details of the transcript are rendered relevant in the analysis and how the transcript is as detailed as it needs to be, no more, no less (other details in the transcript could well have been brought into the analysis). Of course, it is always open to a critic to claim that details we have left out *are* relevant. But some details will always have to be left out (e.g. should we mark just how much vowels are adapted to final consonants? just how much pitch declines across a tone unit?) and, thus, such a criticism cannot mean that we must attempt to put in all the details. The burden simply falls on the critic to show that details we have left out are relevant by adding them in and changing the analysis (thus, discourse analysts must always be willing to share their data).

5.7 An "ideal" discourse analysis

Before discussing, in the next section, what constitutes validity for a discourse analysis, let me summarize the components of an "ideal" discourse analysis. Actual analyses, of course, usually develop in detail only a small part of the full picture. However, any discourse analysis needs, at least, to give some consideration, if only as background, to the whole picture. Essentially a discourse analysis involves asking questions about how language, at a given time and place, is used to construe the aspects of the situation network as realized at that time and place and how the aspects of the situation network simultaneously give meaning to that language (remember reflexivity). A discourse analysis involves, then, asking questions about the six building tasks we listed on pp. 85–6.

Below, I sketch out some of these questions using the categories we have discussed in this chapter:

Questions to ask about building tasks

Semiotic building

1 What sign systems are relevant (and irrelevant) in the situation (e.g. speech, writing, images, and gestures)? How are they made relevant (and irrelevant), and in what ways?
2 What systems of knowledge and ways of knowing are relevant (and irrelevant) in the situation? How are they made relevant (and irrelevant), and in what ways?
3 What social languages are relevant (and irrelevant) in the situation? How are they made relevant (and irrelevant), and in what ways?

World building

4 What are the situated meanings of some of the words and phrases that seem important in the situation?
5 What situated meanings and values seem to be attached to places, times, bodies, objects, artifacts, and institutions relevant in this situation?
6 What cultural models and networks of models (master models) seem to be at play in connecting and integrating these situated meanings to each other?
7 What institutions and/or Discourses are being (re-)produced in this situation and how are they being stabilized or transformed in the act?

Activity building

8 What is the larger or main activity (or set of activities) going on in the situation?
9 What sub-activities compose this activity (or these activities)?
10 What actions (down to the level of things like "requests for reasons") compose these sub-activities and activities?

Socioculturally-situated identity and relationship building

11 What relationships and identities (roles, positions), with their concomitant personal, social, and cultural knowledge and beliefs (cognition), feelings (affect), and values, seem to be relevant to the situation?
12 How are these relationships and identities stabilized or transformed in the situation?
13 In terms of identities, activities, and relationships, what Discourses are relevant (and irrelevant) in the situation? How are they made relevant (and irrelevant), and in what ways?

Political building

14   What social goods (e.g. status, power, aspects of gender, race, and class, or more narrowly defined social networks and identities) are relevant (and irrelevant) in this situation? How are they made relevant (and irrelevant), and in what ways?
15   How are these social goods connected to the cultural models and Discourses operative in the situation?

Connection building

16   What sorts of connections – looking backward and/or forward – are made within and across utterances and large stretches of the interaction?
17   What sorts of connections are made to previous or future interactions, to other people, ideas, texts, things, institutions, and Discourses outside the current situation (this has to do with "intertextuality" and "inter-Discursivity")?
18   How do connections of both the sort in 16 and 17 help (together with situated meanings and cultural models) to constitute "coherence" – and what sort of "coherence" – in the situation?

5.8 Validity

Throughout this book I have held off discussing the question of what constitutes validity for a discourse analysis. This question could not be answered until enough of the "tools of inquiry" used in a discourse analysis had been laid out. However, now we are ready to deal with the issue of validity, an issue that has continually vexed so-called "qualitative research" (but see my remarks in the Introduction to this book).

Validity is not constituted by arguing that a discourse analysis "reflects reality" in any simple way (Carspecken 1996; Mishler 1990). And this is so for two reasons: First, humans *construct* their realities, though what is "out there" beyond human control places serious constraints on this construction (so "reality" is not "only" constructed). Second, just as language is always reflexively related to situations so that both make each other meaningful, so, too, a discourse analysis, being itself composed in language, is reflexively related to the "language-plus-situation" it is about. The analyst interprets his or her data in a certain way and that data so interpreted, in turn, renders the analysis meaningful in certain ways and not others.

These two considerations do not mean that discourse analyses are "subjective," that they are just the analyst's "opinion." I take validity to be something that different analyses can have more or less of, i.e. some analyses are more or less valid than others. Furthermore, validity is never "once and for all." All analyses are open to further discussion and dispute, and their status can go up or down with time as work goes on in the field.

Validity for discourse analysis is based on the following four elements:

1 *Convergence:* A discourse analysis is more, rather than less valid (i.e. "trustworthy"), the more the answers to the previous eighteen questions *converge* in the way they support the analysis or, to put the matter the other way round, the more the analysis offers *compatible* and *convincing* answers to many or all of them.

2 *Agreement:* Answers to the eighteen questions are more convincing the more "native speakers" of the social languages in the data and "members" of the Discourses implicated in the data agree that the analysis reflects how such social languages actually can function in such settings. The native speakers do not need to know why or how their social languages so function, just that they can. Answers to the eighteen questions are more convincing the more other discourse analysts (who accept our basic theoretical assumptions and tools), or other sorts of research (e.g. ethnographic research), tend to support our conclusions.

3 *Coverage:* The analysis is more valid the more it can be applied to related sorts of data. This includes being able to make sense of what has come before and after the situation being analyzed and being able to predict the sorts of things that might happen in related sorts of situations.

4 *Linguistic details:* The analysis is more valid the more it is tightly tied to details of linguistic structure. All human languages have evolved, biologically and culturally, to serve an array of different communicative functions. For this reason, the grammar of any social language is composed of specific forms that are "designed" to carry out specific functions, though any form can usually carry out more than one function. Part of what makes a discourse analysis valid, then, is that the analyst is able to argue that the communicative functions being uncovered in the analysis are linked to grammatical devices that manifestly can and do serve these functions, according to the judgments of "native speakers" of the social languages involved and the analyses of linguists.

Why does this constitute validity? Because it is *highly improbable* that a good many answers to eighteen different questions, the perspectives of different "inside" and "outside" observers, additional data sets, and the judgments of "native speakers" and/or linguists *will* converge unless there is good reason to trust the analysis. This, of course, does not mean the analysis is true or correct in every respect. Empirical science is social and accumulative in that investigators build on each other's work in ways that, in the long run, we hope, improves it. It does mean, however, that a "valid" analysis explains things that any future investigation of the same data, or related data, will have to take seriously into account.

Validity is social, not individual. A given piece of discourse work will have a major point or theme, or a small set of them. These are the work's hypotheses. Authors will normally argue for the validity of their analyses by arguing that some aspects of convergence, agreement, coverage, and linguistic details are met in their analysis. But no piece of work can, or should, ask all possible questions, seek all possible sources of agreement, cover all the data conceivably related to the data under analysis, or seek to deal with every possibly relevant linguistic detail.

A discourse analysis argues that certain data support a given theme or point (hypothesis). In many cases, for the individual piece of work, convergence and linguistic details are the most immediately important aspect of validity – that is, showing that answers to a number of questions like our eighteen questions (pp. 92–4) and linguistic details converge to support the analysis. It is important, as well, that these questions come from a consideration of different building tasks, not just one, and that a number of different linguistic details support the conclusions drawn. It is important, too, that the researcher openly acknowledges if any answers to these questions or any linguistic details support opposing conclusions. Various aspects of agreement and coverage are also important in different ways in different sorts of studies (sometimes through citations to, and discussion of, the literature).

The individual piece of work is, then, of course juxtaposed to earlier and later work in the field. This juxtaposition allows further aspects of convergence, agreement, coverage, and linguistics to be socially judged and adjudicated. Validity is as much, or more, in those social judgments and adjudications, as it is in an individual piece of work.

5.9 Starting to do discourse analyses

In the next chapter I will deal with some aspects of how language is planned and produced and with some ways that a discourse analyst can start to organize his or her thinking about a piece of language. In Chapter 7 I turn to an example of discourse analysis. The example will deal with teenagers making sense of their selves, lives, and society in interviews. It is here that my warning in the Introduction to this book must be most heeded: the method I have developed in this book is not intended as a set of "rules" to be followed "step-by-step." In turn, the example in Chapter 7 is not meant as a "recipe" or "how to" manual. Rather, it is meant merely to show some of the tools we have discussed in this book put to use, not in and for themselves, but to speak to particular themes, points, and issues. This example, then, is meant as a "thinking device" to encourage others to engage in their own discourse-related reflections. Many other examples could have been used, and other examples would have used the tools in somewhat different ways.

What I would suggest for "beginners" who are pursuing their first discourse analyses is this: Pick a piece of data (a big or small interaction, narrative or other extended piece of language, an interview, or a written text, for example) that both interests you and that you believe will speak to or illuminate an important issue or question. If the data is speech, transcribe it as closely as you can, but with an eye to the features you think will be most important for the issue or question in which you are interested. Start with a reasonable amount of your data (you don't need to use it all) and use more of it as the need arises (if it does).

Pick some key words and phrases in the data, or related families of them, and ask what *situated meanings* these words and phrases seem to have in your data, given what you know about the overall context in which the data occurred. Think about what cultural models these situated meanings appear to implicate. Think about the social languages and Discourses that appear to be relevant, in whatever ways, to your data. If it is easier to think about what Conversations (see Chapter 2) are relevant to your data, then do that.

As you think about social languages, Discourses, and Conversations, you are thinking about what and how social activities and socially-situated identities are being enacted and/or recognized in your data (by participants and/or yourself as analyst). As you think about all these things, look closely at your data, ask yourself what linguistic details appear to be important for how situated meanings, cultural models, social activities, socially-situated identities, social languages, and Discourses are being "designed," enacted, or recognized in your data.

After some initial reflections on these matters, or as a way to engage in these reflections, ask yourself the eighteen questions listed in section 5.7 (pp. 92–4) (and any other questions you can think of), taking notes and reflecting on your answers to these questions, guided by the theme or question with which you started, but paying attention to any others that seem to emerge. Pay particular attention to where answers to several different questions seem to converge on the same point or theme (whether or not these are related to the original theme, interest, or question that started you off). Some questions under some building tasks may not be relevant or may not yield illuminating answers for the data you have picked.

As you think about the points or themes that emerge from asking the eighteen questions, either relate them to the theme or question with which you started or revise that theme or question. Then, organize your analysis so that the material you have developed (the answers to the questions you have asked about the building tasks and the reflections you have made on them) speaks to, argues for, and illuminates the final main point(s), theme(s), or issue(s) you have chosen to address in your paper.

Be sure you appeal to a variety of linguistic details in your analysis and try to address different building tasks (and their related questions) to begin to achieve some degree of validity in regard to convergence. You can, if appropriate, try to extend your analysis to other parts of your data or new sources of related data (or to data in the literature) to begin to achieve some degree of validity in regard to coverage. You can use interviews with participants (keeping in mind that they are not always conscious of what they mean and do), citations from related literature, and collaboration with others to begin to achieve some degree of validity in regard to agreement.

Note

This book is an introduction to one particular approach to discourse analysis and I have made no attempt to compare and contrast this approach to others. For introductions to other approaches, see van Dijk (1985) and Schiffrin (1994). Two volumes edited by van Dijk (1997a, b) contain articles on a wide variety of approaches to, aspects of, and topics in discourse analysis. "Conversational analysis" is a specialized approach to discourse analysis centered in sociology and is discussed in van Dijk 1997b (see the paper by Pomerantz and Fehr, pp. 64–91); see also, Goodwin and Heritage (1990); Ochs, Schegloff, and Thompson (1996), and Psathas (1995). Malone (1997) does a good job of combining conversational analysis and symbolic interactionism. Macdonnell (1986) and Mills (1997) are short introductions to discourse with a focus on feminist, poststructuralist, and postmodern work. Fairclough's (1989, 1992, 1995) "critical discourse analysis," though drawing on somewhat different tools of inquiry and a somewhat different linguistic tradition, none the less bears important similarities to the approach sketched in this book. Lemke (1995) and Kress (1985; Kress and van Leeuwen 1996) are both important approaches to discourse based on "social semiotics." Hicks (1995) overviews some approaches to discourse analysis as they apply to teaching and learning. Luke (1995) is a good discussion of issues of discourse, politics, and education. Judith Green and David Bloome have developed a distinctive approach to discourse in classrooms (see Bloome 1987; Bloome and Egan-Robertson 1993; Green and Dixon 1993; Green and Harker 1988; Green and Bloome 1997; Santa Barbara Discourse Group 1992; see also Gee and Green 1998). Duranti (1997); Duranti and Goodwin (1992); Gumperz and Levinson (1996); and Levinson (1983) are good overviews of larger approaches to language that incorporate discourse analysis.

6 Processing and organizing language

6.1 Speech in produced in small spurts

This chapter deals with a few aspects of how speech is produced and what this has to do with the sorts of meanings we speakers hope to convey and we hearers (always actively and creatively) try to "recover." We will deal here with a few technical details about the structure of sentences and of discourse. However, these details are not important in and of themselves. What is important is that the discourse analyst looks for patterns and links within and across utterances in order to form hypotheses about how meaning is being constructed and organized. What grammatical terminology we choose to use is less important than the patterns we find and the hypotheses we form and test.

Notions like "situated meanings," "cultural models," and "Discourses" will take a back seat here. In this chapter we are primarily concerned with some initial ways into a text. We are concerned with ways in which the analyst can start to organize his or her thinking about a piece of language. Of course these initial insights must quickly lead to thinking about situated meanings, cultural models, and Discourses. In turn, ideas about these will influence and, at times, change how the analyst thinks about the linguistic patterns in a text. Discourse analysis is a reciprocal and cyclical process in which we shuttle back and forth between the structure (form, design) of a piece of language and the situated meanings it is attempting to build about the world, identities, and relationships.

Thanks to the way the human brain and vocal system are built, speech, in all languages, is produced in small spurts (Chafe 1979, 1980, 1994). Unless we pay close attention, we don't usually hear these little spurts, because the ear puts them together and gives us the illusion of speech being an unbroken and continuous stream. In English, these spurts are often, though not always, one "clause" long.

In a rough and ready way we can define a "clause" here as any verb and the elements that "cluster" with it (see the appendix for more on grammar). So in a sentence like "Mary left the party because she was tired," we have two clauses, "Mary left the party" and "because she was tired." The sentence "Mary left the party" contains only one clause. In a sentence like "Mary intended to leave the party," we also have two clauses, "Mary intended" and "to leave the party" (where "Mary" is understood as the subject of "to leave"). Here the second clause ("to leave the party") is embedded in the first clause ("Mary intended") as the direct object of the verb "intend." These two clauses are so tightly bound together that they would most often be said as a single spurt.

In the example below, taken from a story told by a seven-year-old child, each spurt is one clause long, except 1b and 1e where the child has detached parts of clauses to be spurts on their own (of course, children's speech units tend to be shorter than adults):

1a there was a hook
1b on the top of the stairway
1c an' my father was pickin me up
1d an' I got stuck on the hook
1e up there
1f an' I hadn't had breakfast
1g he wouldn't take me down
1h until I finished all my breakfast
1i cause I didn't like oatmeal either

To understand how these spurts work in English (they work differently in different languages), we need to discuss a set of closely interrelated linguistic concepts: function words, content words, information, stress, intonation, lines, and stanzas. We will start with the distinction between function words and content words.

6.2 Function words and content words

Content words (sometimes also called "lexical words") belong to the major parts of speech: nouns, verbs, and adjectives. These categories are said to be "open categories" in the sense that they each have a large number of members and languages readily add new members to these categories through borrowing from other languages or the invention of new words.

Function words (also sometimes called "grammatical words") belong to smaller categories, categories which are said to be "closed categories" in the sense that each category has relatively few members and languages are resistant to borrowing or inventing anew such words (though they sometimes do). Such categories as determiners (e.g. "the," "a/n," "this/that," "these/those" – these are also sometimes called "articles"), pronouns (e.g. "he/him," "she/her," "it," "himself," "herself"), prepositions (e.g. "in," "on," "to," "of"), and quantifiers (e.g. "some," "many," "all," "none") are function word categories.

Function words show how the content words in a phrase, clause, or sentence relate to each other, or how pieces of information fit into the overall on-going communication. For example, the definite determiner "the" signals that the information following it is already "known" to the speaker and hearer. Pronouns signal that their referents have been previously mentioned, or are readily identifiable in the context of communication or on the basis of the speaker and hearer's mutual knowledge. Prepositions link nouns and noun phrases to other words (e.g. in "lots of luck," *of* links *luck* to *lots*; in "ideas in my mind," *in* links *my mind* to *ideas*; and in "look at the girl," *at* links "the girl" to the verb "look"). I have not yet mentioned adverbs. Adverbs are messy and complicated. Very often they function in a way that is mid-way between a function word and a content word.

Since function words show how content words relate to each other, they can help us make guesses about what categories (e.g. nouns or verbs) of content words accompany them and what these words mean. To see this consider the first stanza of Lewis Carroll's poem "Jabberwocky":

> Twas bryllyg, and the slythy toves
> Did gyre and gymble in the wabe:
> All mimsy were the borogoves;
> And the mome raths outgrabe.

I have underlined the function words. I have also underlined the plural affix ("es" and "s") since it functions just like a function word, though it is not a separate word. In this poem, Carroll uses real English function words, but nonsense content words (how do we know they are content words? By how they are placed in relation to the function words). Despite the fact that half the "words" in this text are nonsense, any speaker of English can use the function words to unravel the grammar of the sentences and to make good guesses about what content word categories (noun, verb, adjective) the nonsense content words belong to. The speaker of English can even make some good guesses about what the nonsense words might mean or what they might refer to. Thus, we readily interpret the stanza as a description of an outdoor scene with creatures of various sorts frolicking or moving about.

6.3 Information

Since function words carry less of the real content of the communication (their job being to signal the grammar of the sentence), we can say that they tend to be *informationally less salient* than content words. While they are certainly helpful, they are often dispensable, as anyone who has written a telegram knows.

Thus, let us make a distinction between two types of information in a sentence. First, information that is relatively new and relatively unpredictable I will call "informationally salient." The actual specific meaning of any content word in a sentence is unpredictable without knowing exactly what the content word means. In the Carroll poem, we vaguely know that "toves" are probably active little animate creatures, but we have no idea what exactly they are. Thus, content words are usually informationally more salient than function words.

Second, information that is given, assumed already known, or predictable, I will call "informationally less salient." Very often even if you have not heard a function word you could pretty well predict where it should have been and what word exactly it would have been. For example, if you heard "Boy has lots ideas," you could predict that "the" is missing in front of "boy," and "of" between "lots" and "ideas." If, however, you heard "That man has lots of," you could not predict what content word should come after "of" (though "of" signals it will be a noun or a noun phrase). Thus, function words are usually informationally less salient than content words.

In general, then, the content word–function word distinction is a distinction between two types of information. However, beyond this gross dichotomy, the distinction between information that is more or less salient is one that can only be drawn in the actual context of communication. We turn to this matter now.

6.4 Stress and intonation

Information saliency in English is marked by *stress*. In turn the different stress patterns in a spurt of speech set up its *intonational contour*. To see what these terms mean, consider the little dialogue below:

1   Speaker A: Have you read any good books lately?
    Speaker B: Well, I read a shocking book recently.
                 [Goes on to describe the book]

How speaker B crafts her response is partially set up by the remark made by speaker A, which here represents part of the context in which B's response occurs. Let's think a moment about how the sentence uttered by B might have been said. English speakers mark the information saliency of a word by how much *stress* they give the word.

Stress is a *psychological concept, not a physical one*. English speakers can (unconsciously) use and hear several different degrees of stress in a speech spurt, but this is not physically marked in any uniform and consistent way. Stress is physically marked by a combination of increased loudness, increased length, and by changing the pitch of one's voice (raising or lowering the pitch, or gliding up or down in pitch) on a word's primary ("accented") syllable. Any one or two of these can be used to trade off for the others in a quite complicated way.

In any case, English speakers unconsciously use and recognize stress, and it can be brought to conscious awareness with a little practice (some people are better than others at bringing stress differences to consciousness awareness, though we can all unconsciously use and recognize it). A word with more stress than another word sounds more salient (it often sounds louder, though it may not really be louder, but just be longer or have a pitch change on it, both of which will make English speakers think it sounds louder).

So let's return to speaker B's response and assume it was said as one spurt of speech. Its first word, "well," can be said with little stress, on a relatively low pitch and/or with little loudness, since it carries no content, but simply links speaker B's turn to speaker A's. This is not to say that words like "well" are not important in other ways; such words, in fact, have interesting discourse functions in helping to link and package information across sentences. Since "well" is the first word of speaker B's spurt of speech, and starts her turn, it will be said on a pitch that is taken to be close to the "basic pitch" at which speaker B will be speaking (perhaps, kicked up a bit from B's basic pitch and, too, from where speaker A left off, to mark B's turn as beginning).

"I" is completely predictable in the context of the question speaker A has asked, and it is a function word. Thus, it is not very salient informationally and will receive little stress, just enough loudness to get it said and with a pitch close to the basic pitch speaker B has chosen (for this spurt or related run of spurts as she keeps speaking). The content word "read" is predictable because it has already occurred in speaker A's preceding question. So, too, for the word "book" later in B's remark. Both of these words will have a fairly low degree of stress. They will have more than the function words "well," "I," and "a," since as content words they do carry content, but certainly much less than the word "shocking" which carries new and non-redundant information. The indefinite article "a," of course, is informationally very unsalient and will get little stress. The speaker will mark what stress words like "read" and "book" have by bumping the pitch of her voice up or down a bit from the "basic pitch" she has established or is establishing and/or by increasing loudness a bit relative to words like "I" and "a."

On the other hand, the word "shocking" is the most unpredictable, informationally salient, new information in the sentence. The speaker will mark this saliency by giving this word the most stress in the sentence. Such a word or phrase, which carries the greatest degree of stress in a sentence (or a given spurt of speech) is marked not just by bumping the pitch of the voice up or down a bit in pitch and/or by increasing loudness, but by a real *pitch movement* (called a "glide").

The speaker begins to glide the pitch of her voice up or down (or even up-then-down or down-then-up) on the word "shocking," allowing the pitch movement to continue to glide up or down (whichever she has chosen) on the words that follow it, here "book" and "recently." Of course, what sort of pitch movement the speaker chooses, that is, whether up, down, up-then-down, or down-then-up, has a meaning (for example, the speaker's pitch glide rises in certain sorts of questions and falls in certain sorts of statements). We are not now concerned, however, with these meaning differences.

The pitch glide which begins on the word "shocking" marks "shocking" as the *focus* of the *intonation unit*. An "intonation unit" is all the words that precede a pitch glide and the words following it over which the glide continues to move (fall or rise). The next intonation unit begins when the glide is finished. The speaker often hesitates a bit between intonation units (usually we pay no attention to these hesitations) and then steps the pitch up or down a bit from the basic pitch of the last intonation unit on the first word of the next unit (regardless of whether it is a content word or not) to "key" the hearer that a new intonation unit is beginning.

In B's response to A, the content word "recently" is fairly redundant (not too salient) because, while it has not been mentioned in A's question, it is certainly implied by A's use of the word "lately." Thus, it receives about as much stress, or, perhaps a little more, than the content words "read" and "book." The speaker may increase her loudness a bit on "recently" and/or bump the pitch of her voice up or down a bit on its main syllable (i.e. "cent") as her pitch continues basically to glide up or down over "recently" as part of (and the ending of) the pitch glide started on the word "shocking."

Below, I give a visual representation of how speaker B might have said his utterance:

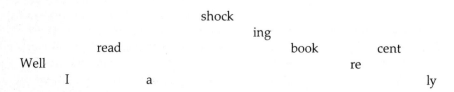

There are, of course, other ways to have said this utterances, ways which carry other nuances of meaning.

There is one last important feature of English intonation to cover here. In English, if the intonation focus (the pitch glide) is placed on the last content word of a phrase (say, on "flower" in the phrase "the pretty red flower"), then the salient, new information is taken to be either just this word *or* the material in the phrase as a whole (thus, either just "flower" or the whole phrase "the pretty red flower"). Of course, the context will usually determine which is the case. If the intonation focus (pitch glide) is placed on a word other than the last word in the phrase, then that word is unequivocally taken to be the salient, new information (e.g. if the intonation focus is on "red" in "the pretty red flower," then the salient, new information is taken to be just "red"). In our example above, "shocking" is not the last word in its phrase (it is an adjective in a noun phrase "a shocking book") and, thus, is unequivocally the new, salient information.

An interesting situation arises when the intonation focus (pitch glide) is placed in the last (content) word in a sentence. Then, we cannot tell whether the salient, new information the speaker is trying to indicate is *just* that word or also other words that precede it and go with it in the phrase or phrases to which it belongs. So in an utterance like "This summer, Mary finished fifteen assigned books," if the speaker starts her glide on "books," the new salient information she intends to mark may be just "books" (answering a question like "Mary finished fifteen assigned whats?"), or "assigned books" ("Mary finished fifteen assigned whats?"), or "fifteen assigned books" ("What has Mary finished?"), since "books" is part of the noun phrase "fifteen assigned books." The new salient information could even be "finished fifteen assigned books," since these words together constitute a verb phrase ending with, and containing, the word "book" ("What has Mary done?"). In fact, since "books" is the last word of the sentence, everything in the sentence could be taken to be new and salient ("What happened?"). Of course, in actual contexts it becomes clearer what is and what is not new and salient information.

Ultimately, the context in which an utterance is uttered, together with the assumptions that the speaker makes about the hearer's knowledge, usually determines the degrees of informational saliency for each word and phrase in a sentence. Speakers, however, can also choose to downplay or play up the information saliency or importance of a word or phrase and ignore aspects of the context or what they assume the hearer to know and not know already. This is part of how speakers actively create or manipulate contexts, rather than just simply respond to them. Of course, if speakers take this too far, they can end up saying things that sound odd and "out of context."

In a given context, even a function word's information might become important, and then the function word would have a greater degree of stress. For example, consider the context below:

2 A: Did Mary shoot her husband?
   B: No, she shot YOUR husband!

In this context, the information carried by "your" is unpredictable, new, and salient. Thus, it gets stressed (in fact, it gets extra stress because it is contrastive – *yours* not *hers* – and surprising). In fact, in 2B, given its context

(2A), it will be the focus of the intonation unit. When speakers want to contrast or emphasize something, they can use extra stress (marked by more dramatic pitch changes and/or loudness) – this is sometimes called "emphatic stress."

6.5 Lines

Each small spurt out of which speech is composed usually has one salient piece of new information in it that serves as the focus of the intonation contour on the spurt (e.g. "shocking" in dialogue 1 and "your" in dialogue 2). There is often a pause, slight hesitation, or slight break in tempo after each spurt.

Speaking metaphorically, we can think of the mind as functioning like the eye (Chafe 1980, 1994). To take an example, consider a large piece of information that I want to communicate to you, such as what happened on my summer vacation. This information is stored in my head (in my long-term memory). When I want to speak about my summer vacation, my "mind's eye" (the active attention of my consciousness) can only focus on one small piece of the overall information about my summer vacation at a time.

Analogously, when my eye looks at a large scene, a landscape or a painting for example, it can only focus or fixate on one fairly small piece of visual information at a time. The eye rapidly moves over the whole scene, stopping and starting here and there, one small focus or fixation at a time (watch someone's eye as they look over a picture, a page of print, or at a scene in the world). The "mind's eye" also focuses on one fairly small piece of information at a time, encodes it into language, and puts it out of the mouth as a small spurt of speech. Each small chunk in speech represents one such focus of the mind's eye, and usually contains only one main piece of salient information.

Such chunks (what I have heretofore been referring to as "spurts") have sometimes been called "idea units" when people want to stress their informational function, and "tone units" when people want to stress their intonational properties (Chafe 1979, 1980, 1994; Halliday 1989). I will refer to them here, for reasons that will become apparent later, as "lines" (Gee 1986).

To see lines operating, consider the example below, taken from the opening of a story told by a seven-year-old African-American girl (we saw some of these lines at the outset of this chapter). Each line is numbered separately. Within each one, the word or phrase with the most stress and carrying the major pitch movement (i.e. the focus of the intonation contour), and which carries the new and most salient information, is underlined (in cases where more than one word is underlined, the last word in the phrase was where the pitch glide occurred and I am judging from context how much of the phrase is salient information):

3a   last yesterday
3b   when my father
3c   in the morning
3d   an' he . . .
3e   there was a hook
3f   on the top of the stairway
3g   an' my father was pickin me up
   ("pick up" is verb + particle pair, a single lexical unit whose parts can be
   separated; the pitch glide starts on "pick")
3h   an' I got stuck on the hook
3i   up there
3j   an' I hadn't had breakfast
3k   he wouldn't take me down
   ("take down" is also a verb + particle pair)
3l   until I finished all my breakfast
3m   cause I didn't like oatmeal either

Notice that each underlined word or phrase (minus its function words, which are necessary glue to hold the phrase together) contains new information. The first line (3a) tells us when the events of the story happened (in this child's language "last yesterday" means "in the recent past"). The second line (3b) introduces the father, a major character in the story to follow. The third line (3c) tells us when the first event of the story (getting stuck on a hook) took place. The fourth line (3d) is a speech dysfluency showing us the child planning what to say (all speech has such dysfluencies). The fifth line (3e) introduces the hook; the sixth line (3f) tells us where the hook is. The seventh line (3g) introduces the action that leads to getting stuck. Thanks to having been mentioned previously in 3b, the father is now old information and thus "my father" in 3g has little stress. Therefore, "my father," now being old information, can be part of the line "my father was pickin' me up," which contains only one piece of new information (the action of picking up). The eighth line (3h) gives the result of the previous one, that is, that the narrator gets stuck.

The rest of the lines work in the same way, that is, one salient piece of information at a time. Adults, of course, can have somewhat longer lines (thanks to their increased ability to encode the focuses of their consciousness into language), but not all that much longer.

Notice, too, that once the child gets going and enough information has been built up (and thus, some of it has become old information), then each line tends to be one clause long. After line 3f all the lines are a single clause, except for 3i. And as the child continues beyond the point I have cited, more and more of her lines are a single clause. Most, but not all, lines in all speech are one clause long, though styles of speaking differ in interesting ways in this regard, with some styles having more single-clause lines than others.

When readers read written texts, they have to "say" the sentences of the text in their "minds." To do this, they must choose how to break them down into lines (which, thanks to the luxury of saying-in-the-mind, rather than having to actually produce and say them anew, can be somewhat longer than they would be in actual speech). Such choices are part of "imposing" a meaning (interpretation) on a text and different choices lead to different interpretations. Writers can, to a greater or lesser degree, try to guide this process, but they cannot completely determine it.

For example, consider the two sentences below, which I have taken at random from the beginning of a journal article by David Middleton entitled "The social organization of conversational remembering: Experience as individual and collective concerns." I have put slashes between where I, on my first "silent reading," placed line boundaries:

> My topic is the social organization of remembering / in conversation.
> My particular concern is to examine / how people deal with experience
> of the past / as both individually and collectively relevant.
> (Middleton 1997: 71)

I find myself treating "in conversation" as a separate line in the first sentence – perhaps, because remembering can be socially organized in many ways, of which conversation is but one, though the one in which Middleton is interested. The way in which I have parsed the second sentence above into lines treats Middleton's main topic, announced in his first sentence ("the social organization of remembering in conversation," and referred back to by "my particular concern [in this topic] is to examine"), as having two parts: "how people deal with experience of the past" (one line) and "as both individually and collectively relevant" (another line). That is, he is going to deal a) with memory and b) with memory as both an individual and collective phenomena. Note that this bi-partite division is announced in the title of Middleton's article, where the colon separates the two themes. Lines reflect the information structure of a text, whether that text is oral or written.

6.6 Stanzas

The information embraced within a single line of speech is, of course, most often too small to handle all that the speaker wants to say. It is necessary usually to let several focuses of consciousness (which lines represent) scan a body of information larger than a single focus. This is to say that the speaker has larger chunks than single focuses of consciousness in mind, and that several such focuses may constitute a single unitary larger block of information.

Consider again the beginning of the young girl's story in the last section. These focuses of consciousness (lines) constituted the opening or setting of her story, the background material one needs to know in order to situate and contextualize the main action of the story that follows. That is, these lines constitute a larger unitary block of information (the setting) within the story as a whole. However, within this block of information, there are smaller sub-blocks: the little girl devotes several lines to one topic (namely, getting stuck) and several other lines to another topic (namely, having breakfast). I will call such sets of lines devoted to a single topic, event, image, perspective, or theme a *stanza* (Gee 1986, 1991; Scollon and Scollon 1981; Hymes 1981, 1996).

Below, I lay out the opening of the little girl's story in terms of its lines and stanzas:

Setting of story:

Stanza 1 (getting stuck):
4a last yesterday
4b when my father
4c in the morning
4d an' he . . .
4e there was a hook
4f on the top of the stairway
4g an' my father was pickin me up
4h an' I got stuck on the hook
4i up there

Stanza 2 (having breakfast):
4j an' I hadn't had breakfast
4k he wouldn't take me down
4l until I finished all my breakfast
4m cause I didn't like oatmeal either

Each stanza is a group of lines about one important event, happening, or state of affairs at one time and place, or it focuses on a specific character, theme, image, topic, or perspective. When the time, place, character, event, or perspective changes, we get a new stanza. I use the term "stanza" here because these units are somewhat like stanzas in poetry.

Connected speech is like a set of boxes within boxes. The focuses of consciousness (lines), most of which are single clauses, are grouped together as one larger, unitary body of information, like the setting for a story. This larger body of information is itself composed of stanzas, each one of which takes a single perspective on an event, state of affairs, or character. Presumably this distribution of information has something to do with how the information is stored in the speaker's head, though speakers can actively make decisions about how to group or regroup information as they plan their speech.

6.7 Macrostructure

Larger pieces of information, like a story about my summer vacation, an argument for higher taxes, or a description of a plan for redistributing wealth, have their own characteristic, higher-level organizations (Labov 1972b; Labov and Waletzky 1967; van Dijk and Kintsch 1980). That is, such large bodies of information have characteristic parts much like the body has parts (the face, trunk, hands, legs, etc.). These parts are the largest parts out of which the body or the information is composed. They each have their own smaller parts (ultimately body parts are composed of skin, bones and muscles, and the parts out of which a body of information is composed are ultimately composed themselves of stanzas and lines). The setting of the child's story we have been discussing is a piece of the larger organization of her story. It is a "body part" of her story.

Below, I reprint this child's story as whole. Each larger "body part" of the story is numbered with a Roman numeral and labeled in bold capitals (**SETTING, CATALYST, CRISIS, EVALUATION, RESOLUTION,** and **CODA**). These larger "body parts" of the story as a whole can be called its "macrostructure," as opposed to its lines and stanzas which constitute its "microstructure."

In order to see the patterning in the little girl's story all the more clearly, I do something a bit different in the way I represent lines and stanzas. I remove from the girl's story the various sorts of speech hesitations and dysfluencies that are part and parcel of all speech (and that tell us something about how planning is going on in the speaker's head). I also place the little girl's lines back into clauses when they are not full clauses (save for "last yesterday" which is a temporal adverb with scope over most of the story). What I have produced here, then, are what I will call *idealized lines* (Gee 1991).

Idealized lines are useful when we are interested in discovering meaningful patterns in people's speech and in getting at their basic themes and how they are organized. Using them does not mean that we have totally ignored the more superficial patterns of the actual speech. In fact, we can use hesitations, pauses, dysfluencies, and non-clause lines as indicators of how planning is working, where stanza boundaries exist, and how the speaker views her information at a micro-level. In actual analyses we always shuttle back and forth between the actual lines and idealized lines.

I. SETTING

Stanza 1
1   Last yesterday in the morning
2   there was a hook on the top of the stairway
3   an' my father was pickin' me up
4   an I got stuck on the hook up there

Stanza 2

5   an' I hadn't had breakfast
6   he wouldn't take me down
7   until I finished all my breakfast
8   cause I didn't like oatmeal either

II. CATALYST

Stanza 3

9   an' then my puppy came
10 he was asleep
11 he tried to get up
12 an' he ripped my pants
13 an' he dropped the oatmeal all over him

Stanza 4

14 an' my father came
15 an he said "did you eat all the oatmeal?"
16 he said "where's the bowl?"
17 I said "I think the dog took it"
18 "Well I think I'll have t'make another bowl"

III. CRISIS

Stanza 5

19 an' so I didn't leave till seven
20 an' I took the bus
21 an' my puppy he always be following me
22 my father said "he – you can't go"

Stanza 6

23 an' he followed me all the way to the bus stop
24 an' I hadda go all the way back
25 by that time it was seven thirty
26 an' then he kept followin' me back and forth
27 an' I hadda keep comin' back

IV. EVALUATION

Stanza 7

28 an' he always be followin' me
29 when I go anywhere
30 he wants to go to the store

31   an' only he could not go to places where we could go
32   like to the stores he could go
33   but he have to be chained up

V. RESOLUTION

Stanza 8
34   an' we took him to he emergency
35   an' see what was wrong with him
36   an' he got a shot
37   an' then he was crying

Stanza 9
38   an' last yesterday, an' now they put him asleep
39   an' he's still in the hospital
40   an' the doctor said he got a shot because
41   he was nervous about my home that I had

VI. CODA

Stanza 10
42   an' he could still stay but
43   he thought he wasn't gonna be able to let him go

This girl's story has a higher-order structure made up of a SETTING, which sets the scene in terms of time, space, and characters; a CATALYST, which sets a problem; a CRISIS, which builds the problem to the point of requiring a resolution; an EVALUATION, which is material that makes clear why the story is interesting and tellable; a RESOLUTION, which solves the problem set by the story; and a CODA, which closes the story. Each part of the story (except the evaluation and coda) is composed of two stanzas.

In some ways this is the structure of all stories, regardless of what culture or age group is telling them. However, there are also aspects of story structure that are specific to one cultural group and not another. For example, devoting a block of information to an evaluation prior to a story's resolution is more common among some African-American (young) children than it is with some other groups of children. Adults tend to spread such evaluation material throughout the story or to place it at the beginning, though African-American adults engage in a good deal of "performance" features, which are a type of evaluation, and tend to use evaluation material to "key" a hearer into the point of the story, rather than to hit them over the head with the point bluntly indicated. Of course, such cultural information is never true in any very exclusive way: there are many varieties of African-American culture, as there are of any culture (and some African-Americans are in no variety of African-culture, but in some other variety of culture or cultures). And other groups do similar or overlapping sorts of things.

Another aspect of this story that is more specific to African-American culture, though also in a non-exclusive way, is the large amount of parallelism found in the way language is patterned within the stanzas. Note, to take one example of many, how stanza 3 says "an' then my puppy came" and then gives four things about the puppy, and then stanza 4 says "an' my father came" and then says four things (all of them speech) about the humans involved. This parallel treatment of the father and the puppy forces the hearer to see the story as, in part, about the conflict between the puppy as a young and exuberant creature and the adult world (home and father) as a place of order and discipline. As a seven-year-old child, the teller of the story is herself caught in the conflict between her own urges to go free and her duty to go to school and ultimately enter the adult world.

Notice that the part of the story labeled evaluation makes clear that the essential problem with the puppy is that he wants to freely *go* places where he cannot go, just as, we may assume, a child often wants to go where she is not allowed to go and must go where she doesn't want to go. In line 21, the child says "My puppy he always be following me," and repeats this in the evaluation. This "naked *be*" is a form in African-American Vernacular English that means an action is habitual (regularly happens). Here it indicates that the puppy's urge to follow and go with the girl is not just a once or sometime thing, but a regular and recurrent event that follows from the nature of the puppy. It is a problem that must be resolved.

The resolution of the conflict between the puppy and the adult world takes place at a hospital where a doctor (an adult) gives the puppy a shot and puts him to "sleep." Thus, the adult world dictates that in the conflict between home and puppy, the adult norms must win. The child is working through her own very real conflicts as to why she can't have her puppy and, at a deeper level, why she must be socialized into the adult world of order, duty, and discipline (by the way, the hook in the first stanza is just a dramatic device – the child is simply trying to say that her parents require discipline in the home; she is not, by any means, accusing anyone of mistreatment – for a fuller analysis of this story, see Gee (1985). The girl may also mean in Stanza 2 that the father would not get her down until she agreed to go finish her breakfast). This, in fact, is the basic function of narrative: narrative is the way we make deep sense of problems that bother us.

Linguists and psychologists have proposed many other approaches to the higher-order structure of stories and other connected sorts of language (exposition, argument, description). But they all agree that such connected blocks of information are stored in the mind in terms of various "body parts" and that, in telling or writing such information, we often organize the information in terms of these parts, though of course we can actively rearrange the information as we produce it and we often discover structure in information as we produce it.

6.8 Macro-lines

So far I have used a young child's story as my source of examples of lines and stanzas. Lines and stanzas are often quite easy to find in children's language. With adults, complex syntactic structures within and across sentences sometimes make it harder to find the boundaries of lines and stanzas. Adults sometimes use the syntactic resources of their language to get lines and stanzas to integrate tightly with each other, to meld rather smoothly together. Indeed, in such language the beginning of a stanza is often constructed to link back to the last stanza and the end of the stanza to link forward to the next, with the "heart" of the stanza in the middle.

And, of course, adults often have much more complex language than children. It is often said that, in speech, there are no such things as "sentences," that the sentence as a linguistic unit is a creature of writing only. I do not believe this is true. What is true is that sentences in speech are much more loosely constructed, much less tightly packaged or integrated, than in writing. None the less, people often use the syntactic resources of English to tie together two or more lines into something akin to a sentence. I will call these "sentences" of speech, *macro-lines*, referring to what we have so far called "lines" (i.e. intonational units, idea units, tone groups) as "micro-lines" when I need to distinguish the two.

Let me give an example of what I mean by "macro-lines." The example is part of a much longer stretch of speech from a woman in her twenties suffering from schizophrenia. As part of a battery of tests, this woman (who is, like many schizophrenics, poor and not well educated) was placed in a small room with a doctor in a white coat and told to talk freely for a set amount of time, the doctor giving her no responses or "feedback cues" the whole time.

This "language sample" was used to judge whether she showed any communication disorders connected with her mental state. Not surprisingly (given the limitations of collecting data in this way) the doctors (with little sophistication in linguistics) concluded the woman's text was "disturbed" and not fully coherent. In fact, I have argued elsewhere (Gee 1991) that the text is wonderfully coherent and a typical, if striking, example of human narrative sense making.

Below I reprint just the first two stanzas of this young woman's long series of narratives. Below, each unit on a numbered line (e.g. "1a" and "1b") is a micro-line. I include unfinished (cut off) micro-lines as separate micro-lines. I underline the focus of each micro-line. Each unit that has a single number (e.g. "1" or "2") is a macro-line (thus, 1a and 1b together constitute a macro-line):

Stanza 1 (Play in thunderstorms)

1a Well when I was <u>little</u>
1b the <u>most exciting</u> thing that we used to do is
2a There used to be <u>thunderstorms</u>
2b on the <u>beach</u> that <u>we</u> lived on
3   And we <u>walked</u> down to <u>meet</u> the thunderstorms
4a And we'd turn around and <u>run home</u>
4b <u>running away</u> from the
4c running away from the <u>thunderstorms</u>

Stanza 2 (Play in waves from storms)

5a That was most <u>exciting</u>
5b one of the most <u>exciting</u> times we ever had
5c was doing <u>things</u> like that
6   Besides having like –
7a When there was hurricanes or <u>storms</u> on the ocean
7b The <u>waves</u>
7c they would get really <u>big</u>
8   And we'd go down and <u>play</u> in the waves when they got big

Consider stanza 1 (the grammatical details to follow in the next few paragraphs are not important in and of themselves – the point is simply to ask oneself how various intonation units or micro-lines are related to each other). Line 1a is a *when*-clause that is syntactically subordinated to 1b as its main clause. So 1a and 1b together constitute a sentence. Lines 2a and 2b are clearly part of one sentence, since 2b is an argument of the verb ("to be") in 2a. Line 3 is a two clause sentence ("we walked down" and "to meet the thunderstorms") that has been said as a single intonation unit (micro-line). Line 4b is an incomplete micro-line that is said completely in 4c. Line 4c is a participial clause (an *-ing* clause) that is subordinated to 4a as its main clause.

Now turn to stanza 2. Line 5a is an incomplete micro-line. Line 5b is the subject of the predicate in 5c, the two together making up a single sentence (5b contains the phrase "one of the most exciting times" and the relative clause "we ever had"). Line 6 is a false start that does not get continued. Line 7a is a *when*-clause that is subordinated to 7b/c as its main clause. In 7b, the speaker has made "the waves," the subject of the sentence "The waves would get so big," a separate micro-line and then repeated this subject as a pronoun in the full sentence in the next micro-line ("they would get really big"). This pattern, common in speech, is called "left dislocation." Line 8 is a single sentence with two clauses in it ("we'd go down and play in the waves" and "when they got big"). The speaker could have chosen to say this sentence as two micro-lines (intonation units), rather than one.

In many oral texts, it is possible, then, to identify "sentences" (macro-lines) by asking how various micro-lines (intonation units) are syntactically connected to each other, though the connection may be rather loose. In any case, the whole point of macro-lines is get the analyst to think about how syntax is used to stitch intonation units (micro-lines) together.

Let me give one more example of macro-lines. My example comes from the first formal meeting of a project sponsored by an educational research institute. The meeting was attended by a researcher from the institute, several undergraduate and graduate students and research assistants, six elementary school teachers, a university professor, and two curriculum consultants. The purpose of the meeting was to start a joint institute–university–schools project on teaching history in elementary schools in the town in which the meeting was being held. The text below comes from the opening remarks of the researcher from the institute who was leading the meeting and the project (for a full analysis, see Gee 1993):

1a   I'm sort of taking up a <u>part</u> of
1b   coordinating this <u>project</u>
1c   bringing the two schools <u>together</u>
1d   and trying to <u>organize</u>
1e   well what we're going to <u>do</u> in these meetings
2a   what it <u>means</u>
2b   for teachers and researchers and historians and curriculum <u>people</u>
2c   to come on and try to organize a <u>team</u>
2d   and students interested in <u>history</u> and other things
2e   to try to organize a team to get a <u>piece</u> of curriculum
2f   essentially up and running and working in the <u>schools</u>

Line 1b is, of course, the object of the preposition in 1a. Lines 1c and 1d are coordinate clauses (two clauses connected by "and") that are subordinated to the main clause in 1a/b. Line 1e represents the complement of the verb "organize" in 1d (note that thanks to "well" it is only quite loosely integrated with 1d).

All of 2 is a recast of 1e. Since all of 2 can also be seen as an appositive on the sentence in 1, 1 and 2 could just as easily be seen as one macro-line and all labeled "1." Line 2b is part of the material that goes with the verb "means." Line 2c is a predicate (verb phrase) whose subject is in 2b. Line 2d is also loosely understandable as a clause conjoined to "a team" ("to organize a team and students interested in . . ."), and, thus, along with "team," it is a direct object to the verb "organize" in 2c. Line 2e recasts and adds to 2c. Finally, 2f is a complement to the verb "to get" in 2e (the syntax here is: "to get (verb) the curriculum (object) up and running and working (complement)").

This is a perfect example of how loosely integrated sentences often are in speech. None the less, the syntactic resources of the language are used to link micro-lines together and thereby to indicate some clues as to how the hearer can integrate and link up information across intonation units (micro-lines).

In many respects the speaker often discovers or modifies some of these links as she is speaking. For various reasons, having to do with personality and social and institutional relationships, it turns out the speaker of the text above did not want to be the person responsible for running meetings in the future or even the rest of this first meeting. Thus, having said that she is trying to organize "well what we're going to do in these meetings," she, then, recasts this throughout all of 2 as trying to organize not meetings, but "what it means" for all the participants to "try to organize" (themselves as) a team to get certain work done. Of course, "what it means" does not really fit semantically with the verb "organize" in 1d, despite the fact that it is recasting, and, thus, loosely taking on the role of the direct object of this verb in 1e.

This is a good example of how syntax, meaning, and organization are an emergent phenomena "on line" as we speak and interact with each other in real time. There is a good deal more in the details of this text (e.g. "taking up a part of coordinating this project," rather than just "coordinating this project," or "try to organize a team," rather than "organize a team") through which we could uncover the workings of individual, social, and institutional factors, or which we could relate to what we may know or suspect about such factors from other sources of evidence.

6.9 Tools of inquiry

Lines, macro-lines, stanzas, and macrostructure are important because they represent how speakers marry structure and meaning. They show us how speakers carve up or organize their meanings.

At the same time, the way in which we analysts break up a text in terms of these units represents our hypothesis about how meaning is shaped in the text. It depicts our analysis of the patterning of meaning in the text. As such, these units are also our tools of inquiry.

We ask ourselves where we think lines, macro-lines, stanzas, and macrostructural units exist in the text, based on intonational, syntactic, and discourse features in the language we are analyzing, and what we know about the speaker's possible meanings, from whatever other sources (e.g. the larger context, other texts, interviews, ethnographic information, etc.). We make these structural decisions based partly on our emerging ideas about the overall themes and meaning of the text. We then use the structures (e.g. lines and stanzas) that are emerging in our analysis to look more deeply into the text and make new guesses about themes and meaning. We may come to think that some of the units we have demarcated are wrong, based on a deeper inspection of the intonation, syntax, and discourse features of the text, as well as on the basis of the deeper meanings we are coming to believe and argue that the text has.

In the end, a line and stanza representation of a text, like the one given for the seven-year-old's story about her puppy (pp. 110–12), simultaneously serves two functions. First, it represents what we believe are the patterns in terms of which the speaker has shaped her meanings "on line" as she spoke. Second, it represents a picture of our analysis, that is, of the meanings we are attributing to the text. As analysts, we must tie back to this representation all the situated meanings, themes, images, perspectives, and cultural models we are attributing to the text and its context.

7 An example of discourse analysis

7.1 Interview data as an example

This chapter will deal with data in an attempt to exemplify some of the tools of inquiry discussed in this book. As I pointed out in Chapter 5, actual discourse analyses will rarely, if ever, fully realize the ideal model sketched there. Real analyses concentrate more on some of the building tasks we have discussed than on others; they use some tools of inquiry more thoroughly than they do others. Since discourse analysis, like all science, is a social enterprise, we hope and trust the gaps in our own work will be filled in by others.

In this chapter, I do not attempt any full discourse analysis. Furthermore, I do not want to suggest that there is any "lock step" method to be followed in doing a discourse analysis. Thus, I use data here simply to give some examples relevant to a number of points raised in earlier chapters. I hope that my remarks are suggestive in helping others to think about their own data.

The data I use here comes from extended interviews with middle-school teenagers conducted by my research team. Our interviews take a specific form. In the first part, we ask teenagers questions about their lives, homes, communities, interests, and schools. We call this the "life part" of the interview. In the second part, the teens are asked to offer more "academic-like" explanations and opinions about societal issues such as racism and sexism. We call this the "society part" of the interview. In addition, we "shadow" the teenagers in their lives in school, at home, in their communities, and with their peer groups, as well as collect data about those schools, homes, and communities.

Each teenager is interviewed by a different research assistant on our project who is familiar with the teenager and his or her environment. The teens all view the interviewer as a school-based (indeed, college-based) person. And, in fact, we are interested in whether, and how, each teenager will accommodate to this identity. We have also interviewed, in a similar way, some of the teenagers' teachers and some university academics to see how they talk about similar issues.

I will concentrate here on two sets of our interviews. One set are interviews with teenagers from what I will call "working-class families." They all live in a post-industrial urban area in Massachusetts (U.S.) where traditional working-class jobs are fast disappearing. The other set are interviews with teenagers from what I will call "upper-middle-class" families. These teens attend elite public schools in Massachusetts suburban communities and all have parents one or both of whom are doctors, lawyers, or university professors.

I do not focus on two contrasting groups because I think any simple binary distinction exists here. There are clearly multiple and complex continua at play. None the less, this particular contrast is an important starting place in today's "new capitalist," high-tech, global world (Gee, Hull, and Lankshear 1996). Across much of the developed world, young people from traditional working-class communities face a future with a severe shortage of good working-class jobs. They often attend troubled schools with limited resources, schools that engage in what, from the point of view of current school reform efforts, are less efficacious ways of teaching. On the other hand, many students in wealthy suburbs and ex-urban "edge cities" (Kaplan 1998) live in communities and attend schools that, unlike those available to less well-off urban students, often give them "cultural capital" for an information-driven global world (Bourdieu 1985, 1998).

It has been argued that our new global capitalism is fast turning these two groups into separate "cultures" composed of people who share little or no "co-citizenship" (Reich 1992; Kaplan 1998; Kanter 1995). The wealthier group is coming progressively to feel more affiliation with similar elites across the world and less responsibility for the less well-off in their own country (Reich 1992). And, of course, such affiliations are both the product and cause of shared cultural models, social languages, and Discourses. The same phenomenon is happening across much of the globe.

Our "social class" labels ("working class" and "upper middle class") have no more import than what the last paragraph has tried to convey. In fact, discourse analysts often look at two contrasting groups not to set up a binary contrast, but in order to get ideas about what the poles of a continuum may look like. We can get ideas that can then inform the collection of new data out of which emerges a much more nuanced and complex picture.

7.2 Co-constructing socioculturally-situated identities

I want to start with a consideration of the way socially-situated identities are mutually co-constructed (co-built) and what this has to do with situated meanings, social languages, cultural models, and Discourses. We will also see here a connection between building socially-situated identities and building different socially-situated activities.

Socially-situated identities are mutually co-constructed in interviews, just as much as they are in everyday conversations. For example, consider the following brief extracts from our interviews (we looked at these extracts in Chapter 4, as well, pp. 74–7). The first one is from a college academic (an anthropologist) who teaches at a prestigious college in the town where our working-class teens live. The other is from a middle-school teacher who has had a number of our working-class teenagers in her classes. In these extracts, each numbered line is what I referred to in Chapter 6 as a "macro-line" (p. 114). If one macro-line is interrupted by another one, I use a notation like "2a" and "2b" to connect the two separated parts of the discontinuous macro-line.

College professor (female)

Interviewer: . . . How, do you see racism happening, in society, let's put it that way.

1   Um, well, I could answer on, on a variety of different levels. [I: uh huh]
2a   Um, at the most macro level, um, I think that there's um, um,
3   I don't want to say this in a way that sounds like a conspiracy, [I: mm hm]
2b   But I think um, that um, basically that the lives of people of color are are, are irrelevant to the society anymore. [I: mm hm]
4   Um, they're not needed for the economy because we have the third world to run away into for cheap labor, [I: uh huh]

Middle school teacher (female)

Interviewer: I'm just curious whether eighth graders will tie that [consideration of social issues in their social studies class, JPG] into their, or maybe you in like leading the class would you ever tie that into like present power relations or just individual experiences of racism in their lives or something like that.

. . .
1   uh I talk about housing,
2   We talk about the [????] we talk about a lot of the low income things,
3   I said "Hey wait a minute,"
4   I said, "Do you think the city's gonna take care of an area that you don't take care of yourself?" [I: uh huh]
5   I said, "How [many of] you [have] been up Danbury Street?"
6   They raise their hands,
7   I say "How about Washington Ave.,"
8   That's where those gigantic houses are,
9   I said, "How many pieces of furniture are sitting in the front yard?" [I: mm hm] "Well, none."

10   I said "How much trash is lying around? None."
11   I said, "How many houses are spray painted? How many of them have
doors kicked in, you know have broken down cars in front of them?"

Throughout her interview, the professor treats actors, events, activities, practices, and Discourses in terms of economic and nation-state level politics. She treats "racial problems" as transcending her city and as a global affair, despite the fact that she could well point to specific instances in her city. However, this "global voice" is co-constructed with the interviewer who very often couches both her main questions (which concern the same basic topics in each interview) and her follow up questions in much more "theoretical," "abstract," and "global" terms than she does those to the middle-school teacher.

Though the middle-school teacher is interviewed by the same interviewer, the interviewer and teacher co-construct a very different, much more local sort of socially-situated identity and voice for the teacher. In fact, researchers and teachers alike usually assume that school teachers, unlike college academics, have only a "local voice." Rarely are teachers invited to speak in more global and national ways about racial, literacy, or schooling issues.

Even these short extracts can lead us to some hypotheses about different cultural models being used by the middle-school teacher and the university academic. The professor seems to apply a widespread academic cultural model in terms of which actual behavior ("the appearances") follow from larger, deeper, more general, underlying, and hidden causes. The teacher seems to apply a widespread cultural model in terms of which people's problems flow from their own behaviors as individuals, not from larger institutional, political, and social relationships among groups.

Any close inspection of the college professor's language and the middle-school teacher's would show that they are using different linguistic resources to enact two different social languages. The college professor uses more academic-like lexical items (e.g. "variety," "levels," "macro," "conspiracy," "people of color," "irrelevant," "the economy," "the third world," "cheap labor") and more complex syntax (e.g. "At the most macro level, I think there's . . ." or "They're not needed for the economy because we have the third world to run away into for cheap labor"), as well as a clear argumentative structure, to speak in a global and abstract way that distances her from individuals and local realities.

The middle-school teacher uses less academic-like lexical items (e.g. "the low income things," "gigantic houses," "trash," "broken down cars") and somewhat less complex syntax (e.g. there are no instances of syntactic subordination between clauses in the above extract, save for the relative clause in macro-line 4), together with enacting dialogues in which she plays both the teacher and student parts. She speaks in a way that is dramatic, personal, and directly situated in her local experience.

We can see here, then, the ways in which the middle-school teacher and the college professor each use a distinctive social language and a distinctive set of cultural models to situate the meanings of their words within two different and distinctive Discourses. The middle-school teacher speaks out of "teacher Discourse," inflected, of course, with the concrete realities of her school and community. The college academic, on the other hand, speaks out of a recognizable academic Discourse, again, of course, inflected by her own discipline and institution (note, by the way, how I have here myself constructed a more global identity for the academic by talking about "disciplines" and "institutions" and a more local one for the teacher by talking about "school" and "community").

Let me just quickly mention here something about activity building in regard to the aforementioned extracts. If one looks at the whole interviews, I believe there is evidence that the interviewer–interviewees are involved in somewhat different social activities in their respective interviews. In the interview with the college professor, the interviewer (an advanced doctoral student from another university in the same city, interested in society and culture) and interviewee share a good deal of situated meanings and cultural models. Their interview is akin to a collaborative discussion, in which they readily enact their mutual affiliation in their language. In the interview with the middle-school teacher, the interviewer appears much more to be extracting "esoteric" information from the interviewee from an "outside" perspective. I only suggest this difference in how the interviews are built as distinctive social activities as a hypothesis for which we would need to gather more evidence from the whole interviews.

If we did find substantive evidence for this hypothesis (and, if I had more space, I believe I could lay out such evidence), we would have to conclude that the "data" from the university academic may very well "mean" something quite different than the "data" from the middle-school teacher. There is a sense, perhaps, in which in the interview with the college professor, the interviewer and interviewee are using a social language in which they are both quite fluent. On the other hand, the middle-school teacher is often speaking in a social language in which she, but not the interviewer, is fluent, however much the interviewer may aid and abet her in using this social language. For example, the tactic of enacting both parts of a teacher–student dialogue is one that I have often heard and recorded from school teachers in this teacher's city. I have never heard the interviewer or any college teacher use this tactic, though we college professors all teach in classrooms. And, in fact, no instance of such a speech tactic occurs in our interviews with college professors in this city.

7.3 Building socially-situated identities and building different worlds

Let me start this section by stating a hypothesis we have drawn from our interviews with middle-school teenagers, and then looking at some of the data that we believe support this hypothesis. In looking at our data, we have tentatively reached the following conclusion: The working-class teens in our interviews use language to fashion their identities in a way that is closely attached to a world of "everyday" social and dialogic inter-action (what Habermas 1984 calls "the lifeworld"). The upper-middle-class teens in our interviews use language to construct their identities in a way that detaches itself from "everyday" social interaction and orients more towards their personal biographical trajectories through an "achieve-ment space" defined by the (deeply aligned) norms of their families, schools, and powerful institutions in our society. In addition, the upper-middle-class teens often seem to use the abstract language of rational argu-mentation to "cloak" (or "defer") their quite personal interests and fears, while the working-class teens much more commonly use a personalized narrative language to encode their values, interests, and themes (a differ-ence, perhaps, not unlike that between the college professor and the middle-school teacher).

One way, among many, to begin to get at how the working-class and upper-middle-class teenagers build different socially-situated identities in language is to look at when they refer to themselves by speaking in the first-person as "I." Let us call such statements "I-statements" (e.g. "I think that the lives of people of color are irrelevant to the society" in the extract from the college professor on p. 121). We can categorize dif-ferent I-statements in terms of the type of predicate that accompanies "I," that is, in terms of what sort of thing the teenager says about himself or herself. We will consider the following kinds of I-statements:

- "cognitive statements" where the teenager talks about thinking and knowing (e.g. "I think . . . ," "I know . . . ," "I guess . . .");
- "affective statements" where the teenager talks about desiring and liking (e.g. "I want . . . ," "I like . . .");
- "state and action statements" where the teenager talks about his or her states or actions (e.g. "I am mature," "I hit him back," "I paid the bill");
- "ability and constraint statements" where the teenager talks about being able or having to do things (e.g. "I can't say anything to them," "I have to do my paper route"); and
- a category of what I will call "achievement statements" about activities, desires, or efforts that relate to "mainstream" achievement, accomplish-ment, or distinction (e.g. "I challenge myself," "I want to go to MIT or Harvard").

Table 7.1 Distribution of I-predicates in interviews

	Working class			Upper middle class			
	Sandra	Jeremy	Maria	Brian	Emily	Ted	Karin
Category A							
Affective	32	21	28	7/5	8	12	13
Ability-constraint	7	7	7	5/6	1	4	2
State-action	39	49	40	44/36	24	18	7
Sub-total (A)	78	77	75	57/48	33	28	22
Category B							
Cognitive	22	23	23	28/34	54	50	65
Achieve	0	0.5	2	15/18	13	22	13
Sub-total (B)	22	23	25	43/52	67	72	78

These categories are, obviously, not randomly chosen. We have picked categories that our overall consideration of all the interviews lead us to believe might be important and interesting. Table 7.1 shows, for seven of our teenagers, the distribution of different types of I-statements in terms of the percentage of each type out of the total number of I-statements the interviewee used in his or her whole interview (e.g. Table 7.1 shows that 32 percent of all Sandra's I-statements were "affective statements," such as "I don't like them"). For the time being ignore the fact that there are two sets of numbers for Brian – we will explain why this is so in a later section. The numbers in Table 7.1 are not meant to be "significant" in themselves. In fact, discourse analysis, as I have construed it in this book, is not primarily about counting things. We use such numbers simply to guide us in terms of hypotheses that we can investigate through close scrutiny of the actual details and content of the teenagers' talk.

In Table 7.1, I have sub-totaled the scores for "affective," "ability-constraint," and "state-action" I-statements, on the one hand, and the scores for "cognitive" and "achievement" I-statements, on the other. I will call the first combination "Category A" and the second "Category B." When we make such combinations, we find something interesting and suggestive. The working-class teens are high in Category A and low in Category B, while the upper-middle-class teens are low in A and high in B. Why should this be so? It is, I would argue, our first indication that the working-class teens fashion themselves in language as immersed in a social, affective, dialogic world of interaction and our upper-middle-class teens in a world of information, knowledge, argumentation, and achievements built out of these.

What the teens actually say in each category is more important than how many times they say certain sorts of things. In this and other studies (e.g. Gee and Crawford 1998) we have found that working-class and upper-middle-class teenagers talk about quite different things when they speak in the first person, even when they are using the same I-statement category (e.g. "cognitive" or "affective"). For example, consider a few typical examples of cognitive I-statements and affective I-statements from the "life part" of Sandra's and Maria's (working class) and Emily's and Karin's (upper middle class) interviews:

Cognitive I-statements

Sandra (working class):
I think it is good [her relationship with her boyfriend];
I think I should move out [of the house];
I didn't think it was funny [something she had done that made others laugh].

Maria (working class)
I guess they broke the rules;
I think I'm so much like a grown up;
I don't think they'd let me.

Emily (upper middle class):
I think it's okay for now [living in her current town];
I think I have more of a chance of getting into college;
I think she's the coolest person in the whole world [a trip leader she admired].

Karin (upper middle class)
I think they [her parents] want me to be successful;
I think of that as successful;
I don't really know anyone who doesn't understand me.

Affect/desire

Sandra (working class)
Like I wanted to say, "Kinda kinda not. How could you kinda kinda not?";
I don't want to sit next to her, I don't want her huggin me or something;
(They [her friends] give me the answer) I want to hear.

Maria (working class)
I like hanging around with my aunt;
I like hanging around with big people;
I want to get out of my house.

Emily (upper middle class)
Now I want to go to Europe;
I want to go to MIT [Massachusetts Institute of Technology, JPG];
I like backpacking and outdoor stuff.

Karin (upper middle class)
I don't really care what other people think of me;
I feel pretty accomplished;
I'd like to be comfortable with my work [what she will do in the future].

The working-class teens' cognitive statements (here and throughout our data) almost always assume a background of dialogue and interaction. For example, Sandra makes clear elsewhere in her interview that other people don't like her boyfriend and that there is a debate about who should move out of the house. Or, to take another example, when Maria says, "I think I'm so much like a grown up," she has made it completely clear that this is a response to an ongoing struggle with her parents who will not give her the independence she wants.

The upper-middle-class teens' cognitive statements are explanatory claims within an explicit or assumed argumentative structure, rather than directly dialogic and interactional. We can point out, as well, that the upper-middle-class teens are very often focused on direct or implied assessment and evaluation of self and others. For example, when Emily says, "I think it's okay for now [living in her current town]," nothing in her interview suggests that this is in reaction to anything anyone else has said or thought. It is simply her assessment of her own autobiographical trajectory towards her own goals for success. When Karin says, "I think they want me to be successful," nothing in her interview suggests that this is in response to any doubts or debates about the matter. Karin, in fact, repeatedly says how supported and well understood she is by her parents.

If we consider the teenagers' affective I-statements (examples above) and I-statements about their actions (not given above), we see that the upper-middle-class teens very often talk about relationships and activities in ways that seem to have a direct or indirect reference outside of themselves to achievement, success, and/or distinction in the adult world and in their futures. The working-class teens, on the other hand, seem to talk about activities and relationships in and of themselves and without such a side-long glance at their implications for the future. For example, considering two of our upper-middle-class teens, Emily's interview makes it clear that going to Europe and backpacking (see her affective I-statements), and other similar activities mentioned throughout her interview, are like items on a résumé that will help towards getting into a prestigious college like MIT; Karin's remarks, here and throughout her interview, are heavily focused on what her present desires, feelings, and activities portend for the future in terms of achievement and success.

To see this point about activities further, consider a representative sample of Maria's (working class) and Karin's (upper middle class) I-statements that refer to actions (some of Karin's actions are actually classified in the category of achievement I-statements). I list actions involving speech separately below:

Karin (upper middle class)

Action

I went a lot over the summer
   (to Boston)
I go to the Community center
I've met people with different racial
   ethnicity
I play a lot of sports
I go to gymnastics two nights a
   week
I did well at that

I go sometimes to Faneuil Hall
On weekends I hang around with
   friends
I go to school
I do soccer and gymnastics and
   tennis
I do tennis in Holiston
I always make sure that I do it
   [homework]

Speech

I'd say an event that changed my
   life (was) . . .
I'd say over half of the people
but I've heard many . . .

I usually let them know
I heard (about Rodney King)
I'm not saying that they didn't
   choose that

Maria (working class)

Actions

I look at her
I see (teenagers) walking places
when I do something right
I'll do the dishes
I go up to this one kid
I would help her cook

I see something pretty
after I come from New York
I wash the dishes
I watch (the videos)
I did my project on AIDS
I go crying to her

Speech

I talk to her a lot
I always tell her
I ask on Monday
I ask and they'll say no
I was like "I'm going to kill myself"
I'm like "why did I do that"

I'm like "I don't want to"
I ask once a week
I'm going to ask
I'll just go "fine"
I was like "what am I doing?
I don't talk to her as much

It is clear that Karin's actions and activities are often tied to institutions and personal achievements, Maria's are not. In fact, the closest Maria comes to activities that appear to refer outside themselves to institutions or achievements is her remark that "I did my project on AIDS." Interestingly, she introduces this as a way to talk about her relationship with and attitude toward her younger sister, whom she considers much less mature than herself ("Last year I did my project on AIDS . . . we had condoms on our board and my sister used to be like all yelling and she was all laughing").

When Karin talks about speech events, her verbs of saying are, in many cases, "cognitive," that is, estimates or claims (e.g. "I'd say over half the people . . . ," "I'd let them know" – most of Karin's few speech events are in the society section of her interview and part of arguments she is making to a fictionalized audience). Maria devotes far more of her interview to depicting herself as a speaker and her speech events are much more interactional and dialogical (even when speaking to herself she is responding to what has happened in an interaction).

One other indication that the working-class teens are more focused on the world of interaction than the upper-middle-class teens is the fact that they narrativize far more than the upper-middle-class teenagers. The percentage of lines in each teenager's transcript that are involved in a narrative are given in Table 7.2 ("line" here means "micro-lines" in the "lines and stanzas" sense, basically "clauses" or "tone units," see Chapter 6, p. 114):

Table 7.2 Percentage of lines in each transcript that are involved in a narrative

Sandra	Jeremy	Maria	Brian	Emily	Ted	Karin
57%	35%	36%	19%	17%	12%	8%

Let me conclude this section by briefly summarizing the differences I have pointed to, thus far. The upper-middle-class teenagers are focused on knowledge claims, assessment, evaluation, their movement through achievement space, and the relationship between the present and the future. The working-class teens are focused on social, physical, and dialogic interactions.

It is important to see, as well, that these teenagers not only build different socially-situated identities in language, they also build different worlds. They make the material world and the world of institutions mean different things. We see some indication above of what would emerge yet more strongly if we had the space to consider the interviews in full: the upper-middle-class teenagers' interviews express, directly and indirectly, an alignment (and trust) among family, school, community, adult, and teen in terms of norms, values, and goals. The working-class teens express, directly and indirectly, much less alignment (indeed, in many cases active disalignment) among family, school, community, adult, and teen in terms of norms, values, and goals. More importantly, the world for the upper-middle-class teens (as they construct it in these interviews) is a space where families, schools, and institutions create trajectories of achievement leading from their homes through prestigious schools to successful lives (in terms of things like status and careers). The world for the working-class teens (as they construct it in these interviews) is a space where schools and other institutions impinge much less directly on the world of the family, peer group, and "everyday" social interaction.

7.4 Social languages

Speaking in the first-person ("I") is only one of many ways in which people build identities in and through language. But, no matter how they do so, building different identities in language always implicates different social languages, since it is in and through different social languages, as they are embedded in different Discourses, that we enact, perform, and recognize different socially-situated identities.

In fact, we have already pointed out that the working-class teenagers engage in narrative much more than the upper-middle-class teenagers do. And this is part of the difference between the distinctive social languages the teenagers are using in these interviews. Of course, in reality, each teen uses different social languages at different points of the interview. Nonetheless, we can see the narrative difference as connecting to specific, but different social languages that are dominant in the working-class as against the upper-middle-class interviews. The opposite side of this narrative difference is the fact that our upper-middle-class teens engage in a great deal more of what we might call "viewpoint and argument giving" ("argument" here is used in the sense of a set of grounded claims, not in the sense of a dispute). Such viewpoint and argument giving recruits a quite different and distinctive form of language.

Since our interviews had a second part (what we called above the "society part") that was based on more abstract, academic-like questions, we might have expected that all of our interviewees would, especially in this part of the interview, have engaged in a lot of fairly impersonal or abstract viewpoint and argument giving. This is, in fact, true for the upper-middle-class teens, but not for the working-class teens. In fact, our expectation that "viewpoint and argument giving" will be accomplished through fairly impersonal and abstract language turns out simply to be a prejudice stemming from our own academic Discourses. The working-class teens often discuss social and personal events and feelings in the society part of the interview, just as they do in the life part. At the same time, the upper-middle-class teens by no means restrict their more impersonal "viewpoint and argument giving" to the society part of the interview, but engage in such talk in the life part, as well. I will argue below that the upper-middle-class teens' "viewpoint and argument giving" actually does often reflect personal motifs or themes, but in a fairly "impersonal" language.

Thus, we find that the upper-middle-class teenagers devote far more of their interviews, in both parts, to stating their viewpoints and constructing arguments for them in relatively distanced and impersonal ways. For example, consider two of our upper-middle-class teens: Brian devotes 39 percent of the lines in his interview to stating viewpoints and constructing arguments, and Karin devotes 44 percent of hers to these tasks. Such talk, though it does occur in our interviews with the working-class teenagers, is vanishingly rare in these interviews.

However, a deeper look at the interviews seems to show, I believe, that when the upper-middle-class teens are engaged in "viewpoint/argument" talk, they are often rhetorically clothing their own very personal interests and concerns in a more distanced language than the working-class teenagers typically use. At the very least, they are probably very much aware of the connections between their "distanced arguments" and their personal interests, values, and favored themes or motifs. For example, consider first Jeremy (working class) and Brian (upper middle class) on racism, and then a piece of talk from Karin (upper middle class). To save space, here and below I run transcript lines together and print texts continuously:

Jeremy

Interviewer: . . . *Is there racism [in society]?*
. . . like colored people I don't, I don't like. I don't like Spanish people most of 'em, but I like, I like some of 'em. Because like if you, it seems with them, like they get all the welfare and stuff. Well, well white people get it too and everything but, I just – And then they think they're bad and they're like – They should speak English too, just like stuff like that.

Brian

Interviewer: *Why do you think there are relatively few Hispanic and African-American doctors?*
. . . well, they're probably discriminated against, but, but it's not really as bad as – as people think it is, or that it once was. Because, uh, I was watching this thing on TV about this guy that's trying to – How colleges and and some schools have made a limit on how many white students they can have there, and a limit – and they've increased the limits on how many Black and Hispanic students they have to have. So, a bunch of white people [rising intonation] are getting – even if they have better grades than the Black or Hispanic student, the Black or Hispanic student gets in because they're Black or Hispanic so. So, I think that that kinda plays an effect into it.

Karin

Interviewer: . . . *just say that it's a really really poor neighborhood um or a ghetto school, and, um, do you feel like somebody who goes to school there would have a chance, um, to succeed or become what they want to become?*
Not as good as they would in a good school system. It depends on – I know that they probably don't. If they don't have enough money, they might not have enough to put into the school system and not- may not be able to pay the teachers and, um, the good supplies and the textbooks and everything. So maybe they wouldn't – they probably wouldn't have the same chance. But, I believe that every person has equal chances, um, to become what they want to be.

Jeremy (working class) personalizes his response and subordinates his argumentative "facts" to his by no means distanced viewpoint on minorities. Brian does not, at first, seem to personalize his response in the same way. However, in an interview replete with worries about "making it" in terms of going to a top college and having a successful career, there is little doubt that Brian's response is quite personal nonetheless (note also the rising emphatic intonation on "a bunch of white people"). While he most certainly could have stated his concerns as directly related to his own fears of affirmative action negatively impacting on his plans and desires, he chose not to.

Karin (upper middle class), after having spent a good deal of time discussing how good her school is and how important this fact is to her future, is then asked about the connection between poor schools and success. She first offers an argument, consistent with her views on her own school and future, that such schools will lower children's chances of success. However, she then contradicts her own argument when she says that she believes that every person has equal chances to become what they want to be. Given the fact that Karin spends a great deal of her interview talking about her hopes and fears for a successful future, it is easy to interpret her remark "they probably wouldn't have the same chance" as meaning the "the same chance as ME." Karin's "distanced" argument has come too close to rendering the grounds of "worth" and "distinction" (of the sort she seeks) a matter of "chance," or, worse yet, injustice.

In fact, the upper-middle-class teenagers (as they all say in their interviews) have little actual experience with cultural diversity, too little to talk about it in the personal way in which Jeremy and Maria do. Bernstein (1974) would say that Jeremy and Maria are speaking in a "restricted code." But, ironically, this is so because their experience of social and cultural diversity is *not restricted* and the upper-middle-class teens' experience is. In fact, the upper-middle-class teens' language appears to be more "elaborated" in large part because they distance themselves from "everyday" social interaction, mediate almost everything they say through their relationship to, and fears about, achievement and success, and sometimes "cloak" or "defer" their "material interests" with abstract argumentative talk in which they fail to directly mention their own personal interests and concerns.

7.5 Connection building

When we look at how our teenagers use language to build connections across their sentences, stanzas, and larger portions of their texts, we discover linguistic details that further reflect the different social language they are using. For example, consider how the two groups use the word "because" (or "'cause").

"Because" (in all genres of talk) can be used to connect two clauses and name a causal relationship. For example, consider two examples from Brian's interview, one from a narrative and one from an argument: "I was like the most hated kid in the grade, *because* I was such a spaz" or "We were actually the bad guys in that situation , *because* we made treaties with them and we broke the treaties." I will call this the "causal use" of "because." "Because" also has a more discourse-based use to introduce a new stanza, event, or episode. For example, consider an example from Kevin's interview: "And we go play that, like, it's like an army game, it's almost like Jailbreak. *Cause* there's this place we call Indian caves . . .".

Table 7.3 below shows the distribution of the "causal use" of "(be)cause" across the seven teenagers in Table 7.1 on p. 125:

Table 7.3 Percentage of "causal uses" of "(be)cause" out of all uses of "(be)cause"

Sandra	Kevin	Maria	Brian	Emily	Ted	Karin
49%	44%	39%	89%	76%	84%	89%

We see a very similar thing if we consider the connecting word "so," a word that has as one of its uses connecting one clause as the "result" of the state of affairs named in another clause (e.g. from Brian's interview: "I owed BMG like sixty dollars **so** I just paid them off," where paying is the result of owing). If we compare Brian (upper middle class) and Kevin (working class), we find that Brian uses a "so" in this sort of use once per 109 words in his interview. Kevin uses "so" this way only once per 545 words (and, ironically, the interviewer uses many more "so's" to Kevin than a different interviewer does to Brian).

These differences suggest that whether or not the upper-middle-class teens are talking "viewpoint and argument talk," narrativizing, or engaging in some other sort of talk, they take a more syntactic and less discourse-based view of information, stressing "logical" relations over more thematic, discourse-level connections. These differences represent linguistic aspects of the different social languages the teens are using and the different ways in which they are building connections among the situated meanings they are building.

I do not, however, want to suggest that connection building only involves linguistic items like "because" and "so." When we talk, we build connections at all levels of our language. We connect clauses and sentences in certain ways; we connect stanzas, episodes, and arguments in certain ways; and we connect larger themes in certain ways. Furthermore, what doesn't get connected is just as important as what does. To make this clear, let me give an example of a *dis*connection at a thematic level.

Consider our interview with Emily, an upper-middle-class girl. In her interview, Emily several times tells of correcting people for racist and homophobic remarks. Furthermore, she condemns the students in her school for ignoring the small number of African-Americans who are bussed in. However, much later in her interview, when Emily is asked directly about racism (in the "society part" of the interview), she says: "I think like I mean I think it is a problem, but I don't think it's, that big of a problem, like," and gives no indication she has seen any instances of racism, though she could readily have appealed to her earlier remarks.

What this indicates, I would argue, is that earlier in her interview, when Emily is discussing racist remarks, she is really speaking, not to the theme of racism, but to a different theme. The theme in the earlier part of her interview seems to be that she herself is less "sheltered" and more worldly-wise than the other kids in her current town, kids many of whom, she very well knows, count as having more "potential" and being more "successful" than those who lived in her previous town. The actual fact of racism enters in only as fodder for her assessment of her fellow upper-middle-class peers. In the "society part" of her interview one of her themes is the unfairness of, and lack of a real need for, affirmative action. Emily fails (we might say "actively fails") to connect her two themes. Failing to connect things is as much a meaningful device as is connecting them.

Here we see that sense making is "local" and in the service of "themes," not necessarily globally consistent across large stretches of discourse. This is often true of human sense making (and academic Discourses are, by no means, exempt, Selzer 1993). Meanings are situated in the specific contexts we are building here and now in our interactions with others.

7.6 Building meaning in narrative

Narratives are important sense-making devices. People often encode into narratives the problems that concern them and their attempts to make sense or resolve these problems. We turn now to how situated meanings and cultural models work in narratives to build socially-situated identities. We talk yet more about narratives in the next section, as well. We can get a start here if we turn, at last, to why there are two sets of numbers listed for Brian in Table 7.1 on p. 125. The first set of numbers is for Brian's interview as a whole. The second set is the numbers Brian receives when we remove the only extended narrative in his interview. We have seen already that the upper-middle-class teens narrativize much less than the working-class teens. The difference in Brian's numbers is illuminating when we see that his single extended narrative, without which his interview patterns yet closer to those of his fellow upper-middle-class teens, is precisely about moving from being an "outsider" to being an "insider" among those very teens.

Below, I print Brian's narrative, followed by some of the interviewer's follow up questions and Brian's answers. I have highlighted in bold Brian's repeated use of the habitual aspect marker "used to." Since it will not play a role in our analysis, I do not place Brian's interview into its lines and stanzas (we will use lines and stanzas in an analysis in the next section):

Interviewer: ... *did anything happen that changed your life significantly?*
Oh um, when I was in like fifth and sixth grade, I **used to** take like hyper-spasms at recess. Like I **used to** get like mad and run around like a freak. And I was like the most hated kid in the grade, because I was such a spaz and I **used to** run around, and I **used to** be like – I **used to** be like – Like I'd play tetherball at recess. So whenever like I lost, and somebody like cheated, I **used to** get so mad
I **used to** run around and everybody **used to** gather around like laughing at me and stuff. But then – but then like – then after awhile, I just like realized why the hell am I doing this, everybody hates me, so then I stopped. And then – and then, it's not really any problem now. I'm just kind of – I dunno.

Interviewer: *Did it kind of come to a head, where like it went really bad one time, and it was after that you just realized that –*
No, not really, I just – in fifth grade I was pretty bad, but in sixth grade I just slowly, slowed down. And then in seventh grade I didn't have any and then I haven't had any this year.

Interviewer: *So, did you feel like it was cause you just – you hate losing? I mean when – I mean you were younger and –*
No, no, the thing I hate is, I hate unfairness in games, and I just really hate it.

Interviewer: *If somebody cheats?*
Yeah and I got so mad, because whenever I played, they knew that I would take like, hyper-spasms, so they all gathered around and then when I – and then when I tried to hit the ball, they would like grab my shirt or something. So I was like [burned???].

Like many narratives that attempt to make deep sense of very real concerns, Brian's narrative is not "logically" consistent (Gee 1990). In deep narratives, people do not focus on logical consistency, rather, they focus on the theme they are attempting to instantiate and develop. Brian describes himself as a pariah ("hyper-spasms," "get mad and run around like a freak," "most hated kid," "a spaz"). His repeated use of the habitual aspect marker "used to" stresses that his pariah behavior and status were an enduring and ingrained trait, part of his "habitus" in Bourdieu's (1998) terms ("habitus" means one's habitual way of being in the world as an embodied social being). He was driven to a state of frenzy by "cheating" or "unfairness in games."

Brian's "redemption" is described as a moment of sudden, personal, individual, rational realization. All at once, based on his personal effort, he "stopped" (note that the "unfairness" need not have stopped). But when the interviewer asks if, indeed, Brian's transformation was so sudden, he indicates that it was not (it appears to have taken a year or two).

We have seen that Brian, in his interview, is, like our other upper-middle-class teenagers, deeply invested in assessment of self and others, the connection between today's activities and tomorrow's success, and movement through "achievement space." Brian's narrative is his "origin" story, how he transformed himself through his own individual efforts and through rational calculation into an "acceptable" and "worthy" person (with the "right" *habitus*). Such "redemptive moments" are, in fact, typical of many male autobiographical stories in Western culture (Freccero 1986). In stressing individual effort and rationality overcoming emotion, Brian is enacting classic values of U.S. middle-class, capitalist culture.

At the same time, the "old Brian" (the one that "used to") learns that one cannot show too much emotion in the face of competition, even in the face of unfair competition. In middle-class, Anglo-centered culture, the person who shows heightened emotion, or too much emotion, "loses" (Kochman 1981). And, yet, if one has learned to let go of one's anger at unfairness in competition, it is not likely that the larger inequities of our society (things such as racism, classism, and sexism) will engender much passion in Brian, and, indeed, they do not in his interview. Brian's transformation story – his only extended narrative – is, then, too, the story of an upper-middle-class child rationalizing (in several senses of the word) his assumption of an upper-middle-class *habitus* (Bourdieu 1985, 1998), a process that actually took extended norming and socialization.

7.7 A case study

I want to close this discussion by considering just a single case. While I have backgrounded semiotic building and political building above, they will both play important roles in the following analysis. The girl who we will meet is "Sandra" (not her real name), one of our working-class teenagers. Sandra is an active and resilient participant in her environments, with no "special" problems untypical of those environments, though those environments present plenty of very real problems for teenagers like Sandra. The interviewer was a middle-class white female graduate student earning a Ph.D. in psychology. She was known to Sandra to be interested in teenage girls' lives at home and at school.

My main concern with Sandra's interview will be to analyze one of the many narratives she tells. But I want to set the analysis of this narrative in the larger context of Sandra's whole interview. I want to stress the ways in which an analysis of the rest of the interview and of the narrative can mutually support each other, helping us to achieve some degree of validity in terms of criteria like coverage and convergence (as well as linguistic detail, as we draw on a variety of different aspects of language).

We will start our analysis of Sandra's interview by considering the whole interview and reflecting on each of the six building tasks we discussed in Chapter 5 (pp. 85–6). One way to do this is to start with "Connection Building." In particular, we look across the whole interview for themes, motifs, or images that co-locate (correlate) with each other, that is, themes, images, or motifs that seem to "go together." Such related themes connect diverse parts of the interview together and give it a certain overall coherence and texture.

There are three related motifs that run through Sandra's interview. In each of these cases, Sandra uses many words and phrases that appear to share certain aspects of situated meaning with each other. Below, I list some examples of each of these under the labels "Disconnection," "Not caring," and "Language and laughter." It is apparent that "Not caring" is also a form of disconnection, and many of the "Language and laughter" examples involve affective language, nonsense, noise, or laughter as ways to disconnect from authority and hurtful (judgmental) language. These three motifs constitute connected threads that run throughout Sandra's interview:

Motif 1

Disconnection: Examples: Sandra's boyfriend is blamed for things, but "like nothing happens, he don't get punished"; Sandra tells her father to "shove it," but "I don't get punished" (there is "no point since they are getting a divorce"); Sandra's best friend is punished by her father "for nothing"; her best friend's father makes her friend clean up a mess she didn't make; Sandra's boyfriend refuses to clean up a mess he made, but goes on to clean up the whole yard unasked; Sandra is "always in trouble for what she didn't do"; drunken neighbors give her too much money for baby-sitting; Sandra "forgets to forget" a baby-sitting appointment that had been canceled and shows up anyway, and the people go out anyway; Sandra emotionally "freaks out" at night, but doesn't really know why; Sandra wants no relationship with her parents because too good a relationship would be "weird"; Sandra was "supposed to have been a boy," but the adoption agency failed to tell her parents she was a girl; Sandra's mother punishes her sister without knowing what really happened; a friend tells her one of her favorite dresses is ugly and offers to take it to the Salvation Army only to keep it for herself; Sandra's grandmother is the "thing she holds onto," but "she is kinda flaky lately"; Sandra's friends laugh at her at a party, but she can't understand what's so funny, she doesn't "get it at all."

Motif 2

Not caring: Examples: Sandra's boyfriend swears and smokes and his "mom doesn't care"; he smokes weed and "nobody cares"; he was "on house arrest and he went out anyway"; Sandra and her friends blame her boyfriend for everything, but "he don't care"; Sandra "doesn't care" that "nobody likes him [her boyfriend]," nor that her father "hates" him [her boyfriend]; Sandra's best friend is adopted, but "she doesn't care"; Sandra's best friend writes on mirrors "and she doesn't care"; if people say she's a "slut," "it doesn't bother her."

Motif 3

Language and laughter: Examples: Sandra's sister's fiancé says he hates her and then gives her a diamond ring; Sandra's sister's fiancé threatens her, but he "is only fooling around"; Sandra blurts out "shut up, you fart smellers" at a wedding party when people are looking at her and she doesn't know what to say; Sandra often says things like "pool pilter" instead of "pool filter"; people she cares about give her "the answer I want to hear, that sounds right, with my problem"; Sandra's grandmother says "weird funny" things to make her laugh, like "I smell you" rather than "I love you"; Sandra's oldest sister says something good "and then ruins it"; Sandra's best friend's mother is "cool" and "we talk to her" because she "buys cigarettes for people" and "she won't say nothin'"; if someone says something to hurt her feelings, Sandra shakes until "someone says something to make me feel better"; Sandra's boyfriend and grandmother hold her to make her feel better, but her mother "says stupid things"; when Sandra confronts a white girl who "thinks she's black" and who has insulted Sandra, the girl puts her fist to Sandra's face and says "Talk to the hand, my face don't understand" and Sandra replies "If your hand had a mouth I'd talk to it"; Sandra likes her boyfriend because he's "funny" and "makes me laugh"; her best friend makes her laugh when she does funny stuff she doesn't realize she's doing; her best friend makes her laugh by making funny noises; her best friend makes her laugh by pretending to smoke in a way she really doesn't.

There are various things we could do with these motifs, in terms of worries about the validity of our analysis. For example, we could get "inter-judge reliability" in regard to the words and phrases within these themes, or in regard to similar or different themes independent judges might come up with. While there is certainly nothing wrong with this, my interest in these themes is in using them to begin to form hypotheses about some of Sandra's situated meanings and cultural models, hypotheses that I can then check by further consultation of this and other data.

Ultimately, the validity of the analysis will reside in how the ideas we can generate from the above data help to illuminate other data (coverage), data that we hope will lead us to similar conclusions (convergence). I will also appeal, below, to the details of linguistic structure, and I have had a number of other discourse analysts go over this data with me, checking my conclusions with them and being sure that they do not see important motifs I have missed (agreement). Remember, validity is never "once and for all." Other people working on our data, or similar data, will discover things that either support, revise, or challenge our own conclusions. Validity is social.

I am now going to make observations about each of our building tasks in regard to the above motifs. From these observations I seek ultimately to draw hypotheses that I can check against other data:

Semiotic building

In Motif 3, in particular, Sandra seems to disavow the *representational* function between words and the world, the very language function that others (e.g. schools) take to underlie the sorts of connections that Motifs 1 and 2 deny and undercut. By "representational function," I mean the idea that language connects directly and straightforwardly ("objectively") to the world "out there" ("re-presents" it), and that this has little to do with how people feel, what their needs are, or what their personal opinions, based on their own lived experiences, are. Sandra sees words said only because they are "true" or are "facts" backed up by some authority figure (e.g. her sister, her mother, her father, or, by extension, her teacher) as "stupid" and as a way to "ruin" things.

In turn, Sandra celebrates the social, bonding, and affective functions of language. Language that is silly or funny, but that "feels right" and that is intended to make one feel good is the only truly efficacious language. Sandra wants to relate only to those who tell her "the answer I want to hear, that sounds right, with my problem"; she wants a relationship with an adult only if they "won't say nothin'" (i.e. engage in judgmental language or tell on her) or if they speak "silly," but endearing talk to her, like her grandmother.

World building

In Motif 1, Sandra paints a social world in which disconnections and reversals are salient: between words and deeds, causes and effects, happenings and knowledge about them, and presumed relationships (e.g. between parents and children). We will see further below that the world she constructs is a heavily local and social one, and a world that does not "cohere" together in very significant ways.

Activity building

We have said above that Sandra's interview is replete with disconnections in events and relationships, and with a language of authority and judgment that has no "uptake." However, it contains a refusal to acknowledge understanding of or, often, control over events, even events in which laughter or socialization takes place. Here we see the darker side of Sandra's disavowal of the representational "knowledge bearing" function of language (e.g. "And they all just started laughing. I'm like 'What'd I do?'"; "I just don't get it"; "There's something happened that day, and it concerned me, and I won't understand it").

Activities in Sandra's interview are constructed as full of laugher, nonsense, and resistance to adult authority as they involve peers or sympathetic adults (e.g. her grandmother), and as full of a lack of caring, disconnection, and threat when connected to adults seeking to leverage authority and control (her parents, her older sister, her sister's fiancé). Sandra constructs herself as participating in activities as a full social participant, but without a great deal of understanding or control.

Socioculturally-situated identity and relationship building

We said above that in Motif 1, Sandra paints a social world in which disconnections and reversals are salient, including disconnections in social relationships (e.g. between parents and children). In Motif 2, she indicates an affective disconnection (lack of caring) about these disconnections, both on the part of "authority" figures (who might enforce such connections) and on the part of herself and her peers (who, in fact, "don't care" about adult standards in regard to such things anyway). Sandra constructs quite different relationships with peers and sympathetic adults than she does with other people connected to authority. Furthermore, for Sandra, "good" relationships are based on language and interaction centered in bonding and response to emotional needs, not on giving people "facts" and telling them the "truth."

Political building

Across all her motifs Sandra disavows "authority," whether adult control or the authority of asocial "factual" language, both in terms of how her world is and in terms of her ways of being in that world. This disavowal is coupled with a celebration of social interaction outside of or opposed to such authority.

Sandra's interview is replete with laughter and silliness that deflect authority and "fact"; it is replete, also, with a language of authority and judgment that has no "uptake."

Connection building

We started here. Each motif creates discourse connections across the interview. Furthermore, all three motifs are similar in certain respects and, therefore, create even higher-order connections in the interview, giving it a certain overall texture and "feel."

There are a number of hypotheses that we could draw from the above data, as a guide to further investigation. One of these is this:

Hypothesis:

> Sandra disavows – is disinterested in and untrusting of – knowledge and language as the grounds of judgment, "fact," and coherence. She sees such language as the preserve of "authority" figures whom she distrusts. In contradistinction to such language, Sandra celebrates language that is used for social bonding and which speaks to people's emotional needs. Another way to put this is: Sandra disavows "authoritative representation" (whether adult control or the authority of asocial "factual" language), both in terms of how her world is and in terms of her ways of being in that world. This disavowal is coupled with a celebration of social interaction outside of or opposed to such authoritative representation.

An example that captures this basic theme well is Sandra's response to the interviewer's question "Is there someone . . . who you feel really doesn't understand you?" Sandra breaks into a long story about taking a drive with her sister after she had been punished by her mother, where her sister clearly wanted to offer Sandra "authoritative" advice and to know "facts" about her life (e.g. in regard to boys and safe sex) outside of any ongoing social interaction ("She's never talked to me like that before"). While there are other parts of Sandra's interview where she talks freely about sex with her friends, her response here is "Wow! That's weird."

The understanding Sandra wants from her sister – or anyone else, for that matter – is based on words that consider her affective (not cognitive)

perspective, that are part and parcel of ongoing egalitarian social interaction, and that are used to heal and bond. Words outside such a context,
"authoritative words," make "no sense." Thus, she says of her sister:
". . . she'll give me a right answer, like the answer that I want to hear, . . .
but then we'll keep talking about it, and it will make no more sense, no
more sense."

However, my main interest here is to see how our data and ideas about
Sandra's motifs can illuminate and get illuminated by a close look at one of
her narratives. Turning to one of Sandra's narratives allows us to get much
closer to the details of her actual language and "voice."

At the beginning of her interview, Sandra brings up her boyfriend, and
the interviewer asks "What kind of boyfriend is he?" Sandra responds
with what sounds like a series of only loosely connected stories. However,
Sandra's approach to narrative is classically "oral" (Gee 1985; Havelock
1986; Ong 1982). Once we carefully consider the features of such storytelling, it becomes apparent that Sandra's seemingly multiple stories constitute one tightly organized unified story.

Sandra's story is reprinted below, labeling its sub-stories and sub-sub-
stories in terms that will become clear in the analysis to follow (The story
is printed in terms of its ideal lines – see Chapter 6, p. 110 – and stanzas,
see Gee 1991):

Story: the return of the table

FRAME

Stanza 1
1 [Sighs] He's nice.
2 He's, he's, he like he's okay, like
3 I don't know how to explain it.
4 Like, say that you're depressed, he'd just cheer ya up somehow.
5 He would, he'd make ya laugh or somethin
6 And you can't stop laughin, it's so funny

Sub-story 1: breaking things

Sub-sub-story 1: breaking the fan

EXPOSITION

Stanza 2
7 Like he does these, like today his mom hit the, she she, he was, he was,
    he was arguing with his mom,
8 He swears at his mom and stuff like that,
9 He's like that kind of a person
10 And his mom don't care.

Stanza 3
11 He smokes,
12 His mom don't care or nothin,
13 He smokes weed and everything and nobody cares.
14 Cos they can't stop him,
15 He's gonna do it any way
16 Like on house arrest he went out anyway.

START OF SUB-SUB-STORY 1 PROPER

Stanza 4 [Started]
17 So they're like so yesterday he was arguing
18 And she held a rake
19 And she went like that to hit him in the back of the butt,

Stanza 5 [Expository aside]
20 Like she don't hit him,
21 She wouldn't hit him
22 She just taps him with things,
23 She won't actually like actually hit him

Stanza 4 [Continued]
24 She just puts the rake like fool around wit' him,
25 Like go like that,
26 Like he does to her.

Stanza 6
27 Like he was, and like she was holding the rake up like this
28 And he pushed her
29 And the rake toppled over the um, fan.
30 It went kkrrhhh, like that.
31 And he started laughing,

Stanza 7 [Expository aside]
32 And when he laughs, everybody else laughs
33 Cos the way he laughs is funny,
34 It's like hahahahah!
35 He like laughs like a girl kind of a thing.
36 He's funny.

Stanza 8
37 And then his mother goes, "What are you doing Mike?"
38 And she's like going, "What are you doing? Why are you laughing?"
39 And she goes, "Oh my god it broke, it broke!"
40 And she's gettin all, she's gettin all mad the fan's broken
41 And she trips over the rake,

Stanza 9

42 And she goes into the room
43 And she's like, "Don't laugh, don't laugh,"
44 And he keeps laughin.
45 It's just so funny.

Sub-sub-story 2: breaking the table

EXPOSITION

Stanza 10

46 And he'll knock down the table
47 And he'll, like we'll play a game,
48 It's me, Kelly and him and Kelly's boyfriend,
49 It's just kinda fun
50 Cos it's just weird,

Stanza 11

51 We like don't get in trouble,
52 Like he gets blamed for it,
53 Like nothing happens.
54 He don't get punished.

Stanza 12

55 So we always blame him for everything.
56 He don't care,
57 He says, "go ahead, yeah, it doesn't matter."

START OF SUB-SUB-STORY 2 PROPER

Stanza 13

58 So we were pulling the table
59 And he was supposed to sit on it, jump on it and sit on it
60 And he didn't,
61 He missed

Stanza 14

62 And the table went blopp! over
63 And it broke.
64 Like it's like a glass patio thing
65 And it went bbchhh! All over everywhere.

Stanza 15

66 He's like, "Oh no!"
67 Well Kel's like, Kelly goes, "What happened, What happened? What did you do now Mike?"
68 He goes, "I broke the table,"
69 She's like "[sigh]," like that.

Sub-story 2: money from window falling on hand

Stanza 16
70 He just got money from his lawyers
71 Because he slit, he slit his wrists last year,
72 Not on purpose,
73 He did it with, like the window fell down on him,

Stanza 17
74 Well, anyway, it came down and sliced his hand like right um here
75 And has a scar there
76 And um, it was bleeding
77 So they had to rush him to the hospital,
78 It wouldn't stop,
79 He had stitches.

Stanza 18
80 And they said that he could sue,
81 And they got five grand.
82 So they just got it two weeks ago
83 So he just bought her new table.

FRAME

Stanza 19
84 He's okay.
85 He's, he's nice in a caring,
86 He's like really sweet

Sandra organizes her oral text in terms of "the principle of the echo," that is, later parts of the text echo or mirror earlier ones, a key device in oral storytelling in many cultures (Havelock 1986; Ong 1982). This lends – to switch to a visual metaphor – a "Chinese boxes" shape to her text. Below, in Figure 7.1, the structure of Sandra's oral text is outlined, notating but a few of its most salient echoing features (for some readers, Figure 7.1 may be distracting until they have read the analysis of Sandra's story – feel free to skip it, if that is the case, and come back to it later):

FRAME: S1: Boyfriend is nice

```
 _____
| STORY: Replacing the table
|  _____
|  | SUB-STORY 1: Breaking things
|  |  _____
|  |  | SUB-SUB-STORY 1: Breaking the fan
|  |  |
|  |  | S2–3:     Exposition: Boyfriend does things, nobody cares
|  |  |
|  |  | S4:       Mother fooling around with boyfriend leads to:
|  |  |
|  |  | S6:       Fan falls and makes noise: kkrrhhh
|  |  |           Boyfriend laughs
|  |  |
|  |  | S7:       Boyfriend laughs
|  |  |           Boyfriend makes noise: hahahahah!
|  |  |
|  |  | S8:       Mother asks: "What are you doing Mike?"
|  |  |
|  |  | S9:       Mother tells boyfriend not to laugh
|  |  |           Boyfriend keeps laughing
|  |  |_____
|  |   _____
|  |  | SUB-SUB-STORY 2: Breaking the table
|  |  |
|  |  | S10–12: Exposition: Boyfriend does things, doesn't get in trouble
|  |  |
|  |  | S13:      Boyfriend fooling around with the girls leads to:
|  |  |
|  |  | S14:      Table falls and makes noise: blopp! bbchhh!
|  |  |
|  |  | S15:      Sheena asks "What did you do now, Mike?"
|  |  |           Sheena makes a noise: sigh
|  |  |_____
|  |_____
|   _____
|  | SUB-STORY 2: Boyfriend gets money from window falling on his hand
|  |_____
|
| END OF STORY: Boyfriend replaces table ("So he just bought her new table")
```

FRAME: S19: BOYFRIEND IS NICE

Figure 7.1 Outline of Sandra's story with some "echoes" noted

Sandra's whole oral text is bracketed by a repeated frame: the boyfriend is nice. The main story is composed of two sub-stories. The first ("sub-story 1") is about losses caused by the boyfriend accidentally breaking things. The second ("sub-story 2") is about the boyfriend gaining money because a thing (i.e. a window) has accidentally "broken" him (i.e. injuring his wrists). This "inverse accident" leads to one of the "lost" things being restored (i.e. the table), yet another sort of inversion. And, of course, "restoration" of a "lack/loss" is a classic narrative closing device in oral-based cultures (Propp 1968). The first sub-story ("sub-story 1") is itself composed of two stories. The first ("sub-sub-story 1") is about the breaking of the fan; the second ("sub-sub-story 2") is about the breaking of the table.

There are large amounts of parallelism between the two breaking narratives (the fan and the table). Both begin with expository stanzas saying that the boyfriend's actions always go unpunished. These stanzas are followed, in both cases, by "fooling around" involving the boyfriend. Then, in each case, an object falls and makes a noise. The accident leads, in the first case, to the boyfriend being asked "What are you doing?," and, in the second, to his being asked "What did you do now?" These questions both go unanswered. The fan story closes with the mother issuing a verbal command to the boyfriend to stop laughing, a command which goes unheeded. The table story closes with the boyfriend's sister issuing no verbal command, but merely an unverbalized sigh. The boyfriend's laughter in the first story is echoed by his sister's sigh in the second.

These two breaking stories are both about "accidents" involving the boyfriend that lead to loss (fan, table). They are followed by a story (sub-story 2) about another accident involving the boyfriend – only this accident is not play, but a serious injury; a person rather than a thing breaks; and the accident leads not to loss, but to gain (money) and restoration (the table). In the fan story, the boyfriend will not heed his mother when she asks him to stop laughing. In the window story, the boyfriend restores the table to the mother without being asked to do so. Such "reversals" and "inversions," are, of course, powerful integrative or connection devices. Additionally, this sort of parallel structuring lends a certain "equivalence" logic to the text. Different stanzas are equated either through direct similarity or reversals, a looser sort of similarity.

One of my interests, as a linguist, in Sandra's story is this: it is now well known that many African-American children, teenagers, and adults can tell extremely well formed "oral-style" stories (which, by no means, implies they are not perfectly literate, as well) – though this style of storytelling is not usually "successful" in school, especially in the early years and outside of "expressive" exercises (Michaels 1981). These stories share aspects of the style of Western oral-culture "classics" like Biblical stories and Homer's epics (not to mention a great many non-Western oral-culture "classics"), as well as aspects of literature such as some poetry and the prose of "modernist" writers like James Joyce and Virginia Woolf (Gee 1985, 1992,

1996). They also incorporate some features unique to African-American culture, as well as features rooted in African cultures.

We know much less – next to nothing – about the "natural occurring" (i.e. non school-based) narrative abilities of white working-class people, especially children and teenagers. What little has been said is pretty negative (e.g. Heath 1983). I would hope that Sandra tempts a reassessment.

Sandra's story encapsulates many of the themes and motifs we have discussed earlier in this section: disconnection (no direct consequences to boyfriend's acts; table restored unasked); disavowal of authoritative language as efficacious (the mother's command goes unheeded, her question and the sister's go unanswered; the sister/peer only sighs); a world of laughter, noise, and physical and social action interaction; a world of accidents and play, not facts, connections, and knowledge; a world in which what counts is the affect (e.g. laughter) you effect in others.

We can see that the sorts of hypotheses we drew from our study of Sandra's motifs (one of which I listed above), hypotheses which are illuminated by, and draw further support from a study of Sandra's first-person statements (not discussed here), help, in turn, to illuminate the deeper sense of Sandra's narrative. At the same time, our analysis of that narrative gives us further support for the sorts of hypotheses we can draw from Sandra's motifs. What we are gaining here, then, is coverage (ideas inspired by one part of the data extend to and illuminate other parts) and convergence (ideas from new parts of the data-base continue to support ideas that we have collected from other parts of the data-base). Furthermore, we have begun to support our ideas with a variety of different linguistic details in the data (linguistics).

Ultimately, what we see is that Sandra thematizes an opposition between "authoritative representation" and "sympathetic social interaction" as part and parcel of her "identity work." Since the realm of "authoritative representation" is quite likely to be associated with schools, Sandra's very identity work will (and, in fact, does) work against her affiliation with school, unless the school comes to know, understand, and adapt to her language and identities.

Appendix
Grammar in communication

This appendix is meant to give a quick overview of the role of grammar in communication. For those new to discourse analysis, it is often useful to ask quite specific questions about the grammar of a text as a way to begin to generate ideas about how meanings are being built in the text. Grammar is the set of devices that speakers and writers use to design or shape or craft (however we want to put it) their sentences and texts for effective communication.

In this brief overview, I will use as a source of examples the short excerpt from Paul Gagnon's book *Democracy's Untold Story: What World History Textbooks Neglect* (1987: 65–71) that we discussed in the Introduction. I reprint it below:

> Also secure, by 1689, was the principle of representative government, as tested against the two criteria for valid constitutions proposed in the previous chapter. As to the first criterion, there was a genuine balance of power in English society, expressing itself in the Whig and Tory parties. As narrowly confined to the privileged classes as these were, they nonetheless represented different factions and tendencies. Elections meant real choice among separate, contending parties and personalities.

A.1 Clauses and participants: the experiential function of language

From the point of view of how we process language when we speak and write, the most crucial unit is the *clause* (Halliday 1994; Levelt 1989). Clauses mediate between lower-order units (words and phrases) and higher-order ones (sentences). There are many different ways to define what a clause is. Here I will use the term in such a way that in any sentence there are as many clauses as there are verbs. A clause is made up of a verb and a set of what I will call "participants." By "participants" I mean the nouns or noun phrases that name people and things playing *roles* in the action, event, process, or state of affairs named by a verb.

When we look at the verb and participants in a clause we are primarily concerned with the content of the clause, what it says about or how it represents the world outside language itself. Halliday (1994) refers to this as the *experiential function* of language, that is, its function to represent experience.

Let me give some examples of sentences broken down into their component clauses. I place each clause in brackets and underline the verb in the clause. Note that some clauses are inside other ones – we will discuss this further below:

1   Mary loves the child.
    [Mary loves the child] (there is only one clause in this sentence)
2   Mary loves the child and the child loves Mary.
    [Mary loves the child] and [the child loves Mary]
3   Mary thinks that the child loves her.
    [Mary thinks [that the child loves her]]
4   Mary wants the child to love her.
    [Mary wants [the child to love her]]
5   Mary wants to love the child.
    [Mary wants [to love the child]]
6   That the child loves Mary amazes her.
    [[That the child loves Mary] amazes her]
7   Giving the child money is fun, as long as it lasts.
    [[Giving the child money] is fun], [as long as it lasts]

In sentence 1 above "Mary" names the person who plays the role of the *lover* and "the child" names the person who plays the role of the *lovee* in the state of affairs named by the verb "love." A verb can be accompanied by several participants. In the sentence "Mary tapped John on the head with a hammer" (one clause long, since there is only one verb, namely "tapped"), "Mary" names the *tapper*, or to put the matter more generally, the actor; "John" names the *tappee*, or, again, to put the matter more generally, the patient or undergoer; "on the head" names the *location of tapping*; and "with a hammer" names the *instrument of tapping*. The actor, patient, location, and instrument are all participants in the action named by the verb "tap."

In addition to a verb and participants, a clause can contain "satellites" that specify more general information about the action, event, or state of affairs. For example, in the sentence "Yesterday, in the park, Mary tapped John on the head with a hammer," "yesterday" and "in the park" name the general time and place when and where the event of tapping John on the head with a hammer took place. Such words and phrases can often be placed at the front or back of the sentence and sometimes in between the other phrases in the sentence (as in "Mary, yesterday, tapped John on the head with a hammer, in the park"). Adverbs and adverbial phrases typically play the role of satellites, as in "Regrettably, the big girl crushed the small box" or "The big girl, regrettably, crushed the small box."

Sometimes a verb has as one of the participants in the action, event, process, or state of affairs it names, not a noun (like "Mary"), or a noun phrase (like "the child"), but another clause. This is the case in examples 3–6 above. For example, in 3, "Mary" names the participant playing the role of the *thinker* (or, more generally, the experiencer) and the whole clause "that the child loves her" is the *thing being thought*. In example 4, "Mary" is the *wanter* (or, again, if we want a more general label, the experiencer) and the truncated clause "to love the child" (missing the *lover* because it is assumed to be "Mary") is the *thing wanted*. When a whole clause (which, of course, contains its own verb) is a participant of the state of affairs named by another verb, I place the participant clause in brackets and put it inside the brackets of the clause where it plays the role of a participant (e.g. [Mary thinks [that the child loves her]]).

So far we have used terms like the "tapper" and the "tappee" for the roles participants play in a clause like "Mary tapped John." Linguists, however, have used several different systems to name these roles in more general ways. We have seen some much more general labels above, when we used terms like "actor" and "patient." Thus, in a sentence like "The big girl crushed the small box with a rock" we might say that "the big girl" names the actor, "the small box" names the patient, and "a rock" names the instrument. In a sentence like "The big girl gave a book to the small boy" we might say that "the big girl" names, once again, the actor (and also the source), "a book" names the thing transferred, and "the small boy" names the recipient or beneficiary. In "The big girl loved the small boy," we might say that "the big girl" names the experiencer and "the small boy" names the patient or, perhaps, we could say the goal.

The names we use for participant roles are less important than asking what participants speakers and writers choose to include or exclude from their clauses and how they choose to name them. In this respect, consider the sentence below from Gagnon's text:

8 As narrowly confined to the privileged classes as these were, they none the less represented different factions and tendencies.

Here Gagnon is essentially saying "The Whig and Tory parties (= they) represented different factions and tendencies." The verb "represent" is ambiguous in this sentence. In one sense, the verb "represent" goes with two participants. One participant is the person that represents or speaks for others. The other participant is the people being represented or spoken for. Thus, in a sentence like "Bill Smith represents the people of Townsville in Parliament," "Bill Smith" names the person doing the representing (the member of Parliament) and "the people of Townsville" names the people being represented (and, of course, "in Parliament" names a location, where the people are represented).

In its other sense, the verb "represent" goes with two different sorts of participants. One participant names a person or thing that stands for, symbolizes, or instantiates something and the other participant names what the person or thing stands for, symbolizes, or instantiates. For example, consider the sentence: "Corrupt politicians represent the death of democracy." Here "corrupt politicians" names people who symbolize or instantiate something and "the death of democracy" names what they symbolize or instantiate.

Gagnon's sentence could have either meaning. Perhaps, he means that the Whig and Tory parties represented, in the sense of "spoke for" or were representatives of, different factions and tendencies of (some of) the English people. Or, perhaps, he means that Whig and Tory parties themselves symbolized or instantiated different factions, tendencies, or belief-systems (i.e. Whigs and Tories were really different from each other and believed different things). It is most likely that Gagnon means the latter, at least on my reading of the text.

But exactly what Gagnon means here is less important than how he manages to heavily background the whole issue of exactly what people are spoken for or represented by the Whigs and Tories. Even if Gagnon means that the Whigs and Tories represented other people, we still have no idea exactly who these other people are. Gagnon leaves out who or what the factions and tendencies are factions and tendencies of. It certainly can't be "factions of the population as a whole," because most people at the time had no vote or representation. If, on the other hand, Gagnon's sentence means, as it probably does, that the Whigs and Tories themselves can be viewed as different factions and tendencies, then whoever they represented ("spoke for") is left out altogether.

Either way, Gagnon seems to want to avoid really discussing what it means to talk about political "representation" and "democracy" in a situation where only "the privileged classes" (and how big are these?, who are these people exactly?) are included in the process. Gagnon does make the concession that the Whigs and Tories were narrowly confined to the privileged classes, but he does not tell us who "elected" them and whose interest (beyond their own) they represented.

In addition to asking about what participants are included and excluded from the clauses in a text, and how they are named, we can also ask about what sorts of verbs have been chosen in the various clauses in a text. For example, in the short passage above, Gagnon uses several verbs that basically have a "semiotic" meaning, that is, verbs that deal with what things symbolize or mean, e.g. "test," "represent," and "mean." This certainly gives the passage the "feel" that Gagnon is judiciously weighing what the "historical facts" really "mean." An historical text that used lots of action verbs (e.g. "The Whigs and Tories debated each other fiercely") would have had a very different "feel."

In discourse analysis, then, one can ask of the clauses in a text questions like: What types of verbs are being used? What participants are included and excluded? How are participants named? How would other ways of formulating the clauses lead to the inclusion or exclusion of different participants?

A.2 Grammatical relations: the interpersonal function

When you design an utterance you plan it clause by clause. As we have just seen, for any clause, you must pick a verb and the participants in the action, event, process, or state of affairs named by a verb. Say I pick the verb "crush." The action this verb names requires a participant that will name an actor (a hitter) and a patient (something or someone being hit). So say I pick the noun phrase "The big girl" to name the actor and the noun phrase "the small box" to name the patient. The verb "crush" allows, but does not require, a participant that names an instrument (a thing used to crush someone or something with). Say I choose to include the instrument in my clause and I pick the noun phrase "a rock."

Now I have to choose how to assign the participants in the action, process, event, or state of affairs the verb names to grammatical relations (subject, object, prepositional complement). I can do this in a variety of different ways. In some cases, I can leave out one or more of the participants if I assume they can otherwise be identified from the conversation or I do not want to mention them. Below I label subjects and objects. Any participant that is accompanied by a preposition is a prepositional complement:

9a The big girl (subject) crushed the small box (object) with a rock.
9b The small box (subject) was crushed with a rock by the big girl.
9c The small box (subject) was crushed by the girl. (Leave out the instrument "a rock.")
9d The small box (subject) was crushed with a rock. (Leave out the actor "the big girl.")
9e The small box (subject) was crushed. (Leave out the actor "the big girl" and the instrument "a rock.")
9f A rock (subject) crushed the small box (object). (Have to leave out the actor "the big girl.")

Grammatical relations like "subject" and "object" are part of what Halliday (1994) calls the *interpersonal function* of language. The interpersonal function involves designing your sentences so as to shape how your hearers or readers can interact and negotiate with you over meaning. The participant I choose as "subject" of a clause is the "topic" of that clause. If my hearers or readers want to negotiate over, or contest, my utterance, they must do so in terms of claiming or counter-claiming things about the sub-ject I have chosen. Thus, if you want to argue with 9a, you have to ask ques-tions about, or make counter-claims in regard to, the big girl. On the other hand, if you want to argue with 9b, you have to ask questions about, or make counterclaims in regard to, the small box.

The participant I choose as direct object is viewed as more directly involved in the action, process, or state named by the verb than are pre-positional complements. Thus, if I say "The big girl crushed the small box with a rock," I am viewing the small box as directly involved and affected by the crushing, and the rock as less so. If, on the other hand, I say "The big girl pushed a rock onto the small box," I am viewing the rock as more centrally involved with the action of the verb (here "pushing") and the box as less so (the box is now treated just as the location where the rock ends up).

In English, verbs come in two basic forms: finite and non-finite. A finite verb either carries a marker of tense, present or past, meaning that the state of affairs named by the verb is either co-present with, or exists at the same time as, the act of speaking or in the past of the act of speaking. For example in "The big girl crushes the small box," the "es" on "crushes" marks it as present tense, or in "The big girl crushed the small box," the "ed" on "crushed" marks it as past tense. A finite verb can also be lacking a marker of tense, but be accompanied instead by a modal helping verb, as in "The big girl might hit the small boy." A modal verb is one of a series of helping verbs (i.e. may/might; will/would; shall/should; can/could; must) that name things having to do with possibility, probability, obliga-tion, intention, the future, ability, and so forth. Tense can sometimes be marked on a helping verb, rather than the main verb, as in "The big girl does/did crush the small box," "The big girl is/was crushing the small box," or "The big girl has/had crushed the small box." Non-finite verbs lack tense or an accompanying modal helping verb. They are often accom-panied by the word "to," as in "The big girl intended to crush the small box," where "to crush" is a non-finite form of the verb "crush."

The finiteness marking on or accompanying a verb (tense marking or modality) is also part of the interpersonal function of language and also determines how one can negotiate over an utterance I have made. The finiteness marking orients a hearer or reader to the degree and type of validity a speaker or reader takes his or her claim to have. If I say "The big girl crushed the small box" you must ask questions about, or make counter-claims about, the event of crushing as past, done with, and treated as a discrete event in the past, possibly sequenced with other such events (e.g. "The big girl crushed the small box and then ran out of the room"). If I say "The big girl was crushing the small box" you must ask questions about, or make counter-claims about, the event of crushing as something that is seen as an event that unfolded in time in the past, possibly in relation to the timing of other events (e.g. "The big girl was crushing the small box, when I came into the room"). If I say "The big girl might crush the small box" you must ask questions about, or make counter-claims about, this claim as something that is possible, but not certain to happen.

Consider, in respect to the role of grammatical relations, Gagnon's sentence on p. 151, part of which is repeated below:

10 They (i.e. the Whig and Tory parties) nonetheless represented different factions and tendencies.

Here Gagnon has chosen "the Whig and Tory parties" (in the guise of the pronoun "they") as the subject of his sentence. His comment on this subject is "nonetheless represented different factions and tendencies." If you want to negotiate with Gagnon over his claim, you have to ask questions about, or make counter-claims about, "the Whig and Tory parties," for example, "Who was in these parties?" or "What did Whigs and Tories believe?"

If Gagnon had written the sentence as "Different factions and tendencies were represented in the Whig and Tory parties," then his sentence would have been about – and invited questions about – different factions and tendencies. In fact, to have written his sentence this way and make it fit with the rest of his text, he would have had to have re-written the rest of his paragraph as something like:

As to the first criterion, there was a genuine balance of power in English society, expressing itself in different factions and tendencies. As narrowly confined to the privileged classes as representation was, these different factions and tendencies were represented in the Whig and Tory parties. Elections meant real choice among separate, contending parties and personalities.

Written as above, Gagnon's paragraph becomes almost contradictory: we immediately see the paradox of claiming that there are *genuine factions* and tendencies in elections but that these differences (factions) are *narrowly confined* (if they are narrowly confined, they don't sound so different, after all). Since the Whig and Tory parties have different names, it is easy to see them as different in the sentence the way that Gagnon actually wrote it. Had he made the sentence about different factions, and written his paragraph as above, he would have invited, and would have had to answer, questions about what makes for real differences among people all of whom are in "the privileged classes."

Thus, in starting up a discourse analysis, one can ask questions like: What subjects (topics) and objects have been chosen for each clause? How does this choice shape our negotiations with the text? How does the finiteness marking of each clause shape the claims made for its validity and the ways we can interact over such validity? How could the clauses have been said or written differently and with what consequences in terms of negotiations over what claims are being made and how and why they are valid?

A.3 Ordering: the textual function

In any clause or in any sentence made up of several clauses, I have to choose what to put first. "First" here means anything that comes before the subject of clause or, if nothing comes before the subject, the subject itself. What goes first creates the perspective from which everything else in the clause or sentence is viewed. It is the launching off point for the rest of the information in the clause or sentence. It sets the context in which we view the information in the rest of the clause or sentence. Halliday (1994) calls what comes before the subject of a clause, or the subject itself if nothing comes before it, the "theme" of the clause or sentence. The remainder of the clause (everything after the theme), he calls the "rheme." The function served by picking a theme and rheme Halliday calls the *textual function*.

If I say, "Regrettably, the big girl crushed the small box," then I am viewing the claim that the big girl hit the small box through the lens of my regret about the matter. If I say, "The big girl, regrettably, crushed the small box," then I am viewing both the action of crushing and my feelings of regret about the matter through the lens of what I think or feel or have said or will say about the big girl.

We saw in section A.1 (p. 149) that there can be more than one clause in a sentence. This can happen in one of basically three ways: Two clauses can be conjoined, in which case they are both said to be "main clauses" (e.g. "Mary loves John and John loves Mary"); one clause can be embedded as a participant inside another clause, in which case the whole thing is said to be a "main clause" (e.g. "Mary thinks that the child loves her"); or one clause can be subordinated to another by use of grammatical words like "as," "while," "because," "so," and so forth, in which case the clause to which the subordinated clause is attached is said to be the "main clause" (e.g. "Mary loves John because he is nice," where "Mary loves John" is the main clause).

While each clause has its own theme, when one clause is subordinated to another, the clause that comes first can be said to be the theme of the whole sentence. To see something of how this works, consider Gagnon's sentence yet again:

11 As narrowly confined to the privileged classes as these were, the Whig and Tory parties none the less represented different factions and tendencies.

Gagnon places the subordinate clause "As narrowly confined to the privileged classes as these were" first in this sentence. Thus, we view his main claim ("the Whig and Tory parties none the less represented different factions and tendencies") from this perspective. It is (although background information) the information he and we "launch off" from in our consideration of his main foregrounded claim that the Whig and Tory parties none the less represented different factions and tendencies. If Gagnon had written his sentence as below, we would treat "The Whig and Tory parties represented different factions and tendencies" as the perspective from which we view or launch off to the rest of the information in the sentence:

12 The Whig and Tory parties represented different factions and tendencies, though they were narrowly confined to the privileged classes.

Given the way Gagnon actually wrote his sentence, the thematic clause about being narrowly confined to the privileged classes sounds like a *concession*. When it is not thematic, but placed at the end of the sentence, as it is in sentence 12, it sounds like an *after-thought*.

So, in starting a discourse analysis it is often helpful to ask questions like: How has the speaker or hearer chosen themes and rhemes for each of his or her clauses? How have whole-clause themes for sentences with more than one clause been chosen? How could these sentences have been said and written differently and with what communicative consequences?

A.4 Relating clauses: the logical function

If I have more than one clause in my sentence, I must choose how to relate them to each other. One way to relate clauses to each other is by subordinating one to another. In this case, the main clause is foregrounded "asserted" information and the subordinate clause is background "assumed" information. For example, if I say, "As nice as she was, the big girl none the less crushed the small box," I am asserting, as my main claim, the main clause "the big girl crushed the small box" and treating this as foregrounded. In turn, I am treating the subordinate clause "as nice as she was" as background information that I am assuming as taken-for-granted information that we can agree on. If I say "The big girl is nice, even though she crushed the small box," I am reversing matters. I am foregrounding the claim that the big girl is nice and treating the fact that she crushed the small box as taken-for-granted background information.

When I subordinate one clause to another, I can use small grammatical words to indicate the logical connection between the information in my two clauses. Thus, if I say "The big girl crushed the small box *because* it was ugly" I am using "because" to say that the girl's action of crushing the box was caused by its property of being ugly.

Rather than subordinating one clause to another, I can co-ordinate clauses, treating two clauses as equally foregrounded information. For example, if I say "The big girl is nasty and she crushes small objects," I am treating the two clauses as co-equal and both foregrounded pieces of information.

Finally, I can form two clauses that are independent of each other and placed in separate sentences. For example, if I say "The big girl crushed the small box. After that, it was quite ugly," I am using "after that" both to say that the box's being ugly temporally followed the act of the girl crushing it and to suggest that its being ugly was a result of her having crushed it.

The ways in which we relate clauses to each other constitute a part of what we might call the "logical function of language" (Thompson 1996). It is part of how we speakers and writers signal what we see as the logical connections between different pieces of information. To see how the logical function can work in communication, consider, once again, sentence 8 from Gagnon's text, reprinted below:

13 As narrowly confined to the privileged classes as these were, the Whig and Tory parties none the less represented different factions and tendencies.

Here Gagnon has made the clause "The Whig and Tory parties none the less represented different factions and tendencies" his main and foregrounded clause. He has subordinated the clause "As narrowly confined to the privileged classes as these were" to this main clause as backgrounded, assumed, taken-for-granted information. Of course, we could reverse matters if we wrote this sentence as below:

14 Although the Whig and Tory parties represented different factions and tendencies, none the less, they were narrowly confined to the privileged classes.

This version foregrounds or highlights (asserts) the social conflict between classes, while the version Gagnon actually wrote backgrounds such conflict.

Thus, a discourse analyst can always ask questions like: How has a speaker or writer connected his or her clauses so as to signal their logical relationships? What information is being foregrounded and asserted? What information is being backgrounded and assumed? How could things have been said or written differently and with what communicative consequences?

A.5 Cohesion

Speakers and writers have to do more than connect clauses within sentences. They must also connect sentences across whole texts. The grammatical devices we use to create such connections are called *cohesive devices*. They signal to the hearer the connections between the sentences of a text and are part of what makes a text sound like it "hangs together" (coheres).

There are six major types of cohesive devices (Halliday and Hasan 1976, 1989). Examples of each of them (numbered in reference to the following discussion) are seen in the little discourse below (note that the second sentence in 15 has been placed vertically):

15 The Federal Government expected Indian Nations to sign treaties.

However, though	=	6
most of	=	2
them	=	1
had *in fact*	=	6
done so,	=	3
the	=	2
Seminoles	=	5
would not ___.	=	4

Each of the numbered words or phrases is a cohesive device that signals to the hearer how the second sentence is linked (or how it coheres) with the preceding sentence. Below, I list the six major classes of cohesive devices and show how the member of that class represented in our example above functions. The numbers below correspond to those used in the example.

1 *Pronouns.* In the example, the pronoun "them" links back to the preceding sentence by picking up its reference from a phrase in that sentence ("Indian Nations").
2 *Determiners and Quantifiers.* The quantifier "most" links to the preceding sentence by indicating that we are now talking about a part ("most") of a whole that was talked about in the preceding sentence ("Indian Nations"). The determiner "the" in front of "Seminoles" links to the preceding sentence by indicating that the information it is attached to ("Seminoles") is information that is assumed to be predictable or known on the basis of the preceding sentence. In this case, it is predictable because the preceding sentence mentioned Indian Nations and Seminoles are an Indian Nation.
3 *Substitution.* The words "done so" are a dummy phrase that substitutes for (stands in for) "signed treaties" in the previous sentence. This

allows us both not to repeat this information and to signal that the second sentence is linked to the preceding one.

4 *Ellipsis*. The blank after "would not" indicates a place where information has been left out (elided) because it is totally predictable based on the preceding sentence (the information is "sign a treaty"). Since we reconstruct the left out information by considering the preceding sentence, this ellipsis is a linking device.

5 *Lexical cohesion*. The word "Seminoles" is lexically related to "Indian" since Seminoles are Indians. This links the two sentences together through the fact that they contain words that are semantically related.

6 *Conjunctions and other conjunction-like links*. The word "however" signals how the hearer is to relate the second sentence to the first. It signals that there is an adversative relation between the two sentences. "In fact" also links the second sentence to the first, though in a way that is subtle enough and hard enough to describe that it is possible that only native speakers would get its placement just right in a variety of cases. Related to this category are "discourse particles," words like "so" and "well" that also help tie sentences together into meaningfully related chains of sentences that "sound" like they go together.

Let's consider a moment how cohesion works in Gagnon's passage, reprinted below:

Also secure, by 1689, was the principle of representative government, as tested against the two criteria for valid constitutions proposed in the previous chapter. As to the first criterion, there was a genuine balance of power in English society, expressing itself in the Whig and Tory parties. As narrowly confined to the privileged classes as these were, they none the less represented different factions and tendencies. Elections meant real choice among separate, contending parties and personalities.

Gagnon devotes a great deal of the words and grammatical devices in this passage to cohesion. He uses the phrase "as to the first criterion" (in theme position) in his second sentence to tie back to the phrase "two criteria" in the first sentence. In the third sentence, he uses a pronoun inside a clause in theme position in its sentence ("as narrowly confined to the privileged classes as *these* were") and another pronoun in theme position in the main clause ("they") to tie back to "the Whig and Tory parties" in the preceding sentence. His final sentence about elections is not tied to the previous sentences in any explicit way (in fact, "elections" comes rather "out of the blue" here), for example, Gagnon does not use any logical connectors like "and therefore." Rather, his final sentence about elections is tied to the previous sentences by lexical (word-level) relations.

"Elections" is a word that is in the same semantic (meaning) family as the words in phrases like "different factions and tendencies," "the Whig and Tory parties," "balance of power," "valid constitutions," and "representative government" in the previous sentences (these are all words and phrases about governing and government). This connects "elections" back to these sentences. Gagnon seems to suggest, by this tactic, that his claim about elections – i.e. that they constituted a "real choice" – follows rather straightforwardly from the very meaning of what he has previously said. He treats his claim about meaningful elections as needing no more explicit logical connection to what has come before. He treats it almost as a mere restatement of what he has already said, despite the fact that a critical reader might worry about how meaningful (and for whom) these elections among the "privileged classes" were.

Thus, in starting a discourse analysis, the analyst can ask questions like: How does cohesion work in this text to connect pieces of information and in what ways? How does the text fail to connect other pieces of information? What sort of sense are these connections making or failing to make and to what communicative ends?

Speakers and writers use all of the above grammatical devices, and many others, to shape their texts "as if" they (the speakers and writers and the texts) had certain "goals" and "purposes." As listeners and receivers we "recover" these goals and purposes by paying attention to the uses to which these grammatical devices are put. Goals and purposes, in this sense, are not privately in people's heads, but publicly available in texts. Of course, they are always open to contestation and negotiation (as we have tried to do with Gagnon's text), but this negotiation is always shaped by the very grammatical devices that opened the negotiation in the first place.

References

Agar, M. (1994). *Language shock: Understanding the culture of conversation*. New York: William Marrow.

Anglin, J. M. (1977). *Word, object, and conceptual development*. New York: Norton.

Bakhtin, M. (1981). *The dialogic imagination*. Austin: University of Texas Press.

Bakhtin, M. M. (1986). *Speech genres and other late essays*. Austin: University of Texas Press.

Barsalou, L. W. (1987). "The instability of graded structure in concepts." In U. Neisser (ed.), *Concepts and conceptual development: Ecological and intellectual factors in categorization*. New York: Cambridge University Press, pp. 101–40.

Barsalou, L. W. (1991). "Deriving categories to achieve goals." In G. H. Bower (ed.), *The psychology of learning and motivation: Advances in research and theory, Vol. 27*. New York: Academic Press, pp. 1–64.

Barsalou, L. W. (1992). *Cognitive psychology: An overview for cognitive scientists*. Hillsdale, N.J.: Erlbaum.

Barton, D. and Hamilton. M. (1998). *Local literacies: Reading and writing in one community*. London: Routledge.

Bazerman, C. (1989). *Shaping written knowledge*. Madison: University of Wisconsin Press.

Bechtel, W. and Abrahamsen, A. (1990). *Connectionism and the mind: An introduction to parallel processing in networks*. Oxford: Basil Blackwell.

Bechtel, W. and Richardson, R. C. (1993). *Discovering complexity: Decomposition and localization in scientific research*. Princeton, N.J.: Princeton University Press.

Bellah, R. N., Madsen, R., Sullivan, W. M., Swindler, A. and Tipton, S. M. (1985). *Habits of the heart: Individualism and commitment in American life*. New York: Harper & Row.

Berkenkotter, C. and Huckin, T. N. (1995). *Genre knowledge in disciplinary communication: Cognition/culture/power*. Hillsdale, N.J.: Erlbaum.

Berman, R. and Slobin, D. I. (1994). *Relating events in narrative: A crosslinguistic development study*. Hillsdale, N.J.: Erlbaum.

Bernstein, B. (1974). *Classes, codes and control*. Vol. 1, 2nd edn, London: Routledge and Kegan Paul.

Bernstein, B. (1996). *Pedagogy, symbolic control, and identity: Theory, research, critique*. London: Taylor & Francis.

Billig, M. (1987). *Arguing and thinking: A rhetorical approach to social psychology*. Cambridge: Cambridge University Press.

Bloome, D. (ed.) (1987). *Literacy and schooling*. Norwood, N. J.: Ablex.

Bloome, D. and Egan-Robertson, A. (1993). "The social construction of intertextuality in classroom reading and writing lessons." *Reading Research Quarterly* 28(3): 304–33.

Bourdieu, P. (1977). *Outline of a theory of practice*. Cambridge: Cambridge University Press.

Bourdieu, P. (1985). *Distinction: A social critique of the judgement of taste*. Cambridge, Mass.: Harvard University Press.

Bourdieu, P. (1990a). *The logic of practice*. Stanford: Stanford University Press.

Bourdieu, P. (1990b). *In other words: Essays towards a reflexive sociology*. Stanford: Stanford University Press.

Bourdieu, P. (1991). *Language and symbolic power*. Cambridge, Mass.: Harvard University Press.

Bourdieu, P. (1998). *Practical reason*. Stanford: Stanford University Press.

Bowler, P. J. (1990). *Charles Darwin: The man and his influence*. Oxford: Basil Blackwell.

Brazil, D., Coulthard, M., and Johns, C. (1980). *Discourse intonation and language teaching*. London: Longman.

Bruer, J. T. (1993). *Schools for thought: A science for learning in the classroom*. Cambridge, Mass.: MIT Press.

Callon, M. and Latour, B. (1992). "Don't throw the baby out with the bath school! A reply to Collins and Yearly." In A. Pickering (ed.), *Science as practice and culture*. Chicago: University of Chicago Press, pp. 343–68.

Carbaugh, D. (1996). *Situating selves: The communication of social identities in American scenes*. Albany: State University of New York Press.

Carspecken, P. F. (1996). *Critical ethnography in educational research: A theoretical and practical guide*. New York: Routledge.

Chafe, W. L. (1979). "The flow of thought and the flow of language." In T. Givon (ed.), *Syntax and semantics 12: Discourse and syntax*. New York: Academic Press, pp. 159-81.

Chafe, W. L. (1980). "The deployment of consciousness in the production of a narrative." In W. L. Chafe (ed.), *The pear stories: Cognitive, cultural, and linguistic aspects of narrative production*. Norwood, N. J.: Ablex, pp. 9-50.

Chafe, W. L. (1994). *Discourse, consciousness, and time: The flow and displacement of conscious experience in speaking and writing*. Chicago: University of Chicago Press.

Churchland, P. M. (1995). *The engine of reason, the seat of the soul*. Cambridge, Mass.: MIT Press.

Churchland, P. S. and Sejnowski, T. J. (1992). *The computational brain*. Cambridge, Mass.: Bradford/MIT Press.

Clark, A. (1989). *Microcognition: Philosophy, cognitive science, and parallel distributed processing*. Cambridge, Mass.: MIT Press.

Clark, A. (1993). *Associative engines: Connectionism, concepts, and representational change*. Cambridge: Cambridge University Press.

Clark, A. (1997). *Being there: Putting brain, body, and world together again*. Cambridge, Mass.: MIT Press.

Clark, H. H. (1996). *Using language*. Cambridge: Cambridge University Press.

Collins, J. C. and Porras, J. I. (1994). *Built to last: Successful habits of visonary companies*. New York: Harper Business.

Crick, F. (1994). *The astonishing hypothesis: The scientific search for the soul*. New York: Scribners.

D'Andrade, R. (1984). "Cultural meaning systems." In R. A. Shweder and R. A. LeVine (eds), *Culture theory: Essays on mind, self, and emotion*. Cambridge: Cambridge University Press, pp. 88–119.

D'Andrade, R. (1995). *The development of cognitive anthropology*. Cambridge: Cambridge University Press.

D'Andrade, R. and Strauss, C. (eds) (1992). *Human motives and cultural models*. Cambridge: Cambridge University Press.

Darwin, C. (1859). *The origin of species*. New York: Modern Library.

Degler, C. N. (1991). *In search of human nature: The decline and revival of Darwinism in American social thought*. Stanford: Stanford University Press.

Douglas, M. (1986). *How institutions think*. Syracuse, New York: Syracuse University Press.

Duranti, A. (1997). *Linguistic anthropology*. Cambridge: Cambridge University Press.

Duranti, A. and Goodwin, C. (eds) (1992). *Rethinking context: Language as an interactive phenomenon*. Cambridge: Cambridge University Press.

Edwards, D. and Potter, J. (1992). *Discursive psychology*. London: Sage.

Edwards, J. A. and Lampert, M. D. (ed.) (1993). *Talking data: Transcription and coding in discourse research*. Hillsdale, N. J.: Erlbaum.

Elman, J. L., Bates, E., Johnson, M. H., Karmiloff-Smith, A., Parisi, D., and Plunkett, K. (1996). *Rethinking innateness: A connectionist perspective on development*. Cambridge, Mass.: Harvard University Press

Engestrom, Y. (1987). *Learning by expanding: An activity-theoretical approach to developmental research*. Helsinki: Orienta-Konsultit.

Engestrom, Y. (1990). *Learning, working and imagining: Twelve studies in activity theory*. Helsinki: Orienta-Konsultit.

Fairclough, N. (1989). *Language and power*. London: Longman.

Fairclough, N. (1992). *Discourse and social change*. Cambridge: Polity Press.

Fairclough, N. (1995). *Critical discourse analysis*. London: Longman.

Fausto-Sterling, A. (1985). *Myths of gender: Biological theories about women and men*. New York: Basic Books.

Fillmore, C. (1975). "An alternative to checklist theories of meaning." In C. Cogen, H. Thompson, G. Thurgood, K. Whistler, and J. Wright (eds), *Proceedings of the First Annual Meeting of the Berkeley Linguistics Society*. Berkeley, Calif.: University of California at Berkeley, pp. 123–31.

Fleck, L. (1979). *The genesis and development of a scientific fact*. Chicago: University of Chicago Press.

Foucault, M. (1966). *The order of things: An archaeology of human sciences*. New York: Random House.

Foucault, M. (1969). *The archeology of knowledge*. New York: Random House.

Foucault, M. (1973). *The birth of the clinic: An archaeology of medical perception*. New York: Vintage Books.

Foucault, M. (1977). *Discipline and punish: The birth of the prison*. New York: Pantheon.

Foucault, M. (1978). *The history of sexuality, Volume 1: An Introduction*. New York: Pantheon.

Foucault, M. (1980). *Power/knowledge: Selected interviews and other writings 1972–1977*. C. Gordon, L. Marshall, J. Meplam and K. Soper (eds). Brighton, Sussex: The Harvester Press.

Foucault, M. (1984). *The history of sexuality, Volume 2: The Use of Pleasure.* New York: Pantheon.

Foucault, M. (1985). *The Foucault reader.* Paul Rabinow (ed.). New York: Pantheon.

Freccero, J. (1986). "Autobiography and narrative." In T. C. Heller, M. Sosna, and D. E. Wellbery, with A. I. Davidson, A. Swidler, and I. Watt (eds) (1986). *Reconstructing individualism: Autonomy, individuality, and the self in Western thought.* Stanford: Stanford University Press, pp. 16–29.

Gagnon, P. (1987). *Democracy's untold story: What world history textbooks neglect.* Washington, D.C.: American Federation of Teachers, pp. 65–71.

Gardner, H. (1991). *The unschooled mind: How children think and how schools should teach.* New York: Basic Books.

Gee, J. P. (1985). "The narrativization of experience in the oral style." *Journal of Education,* 167(1): 9–35 [Reprinted in C. Mitchell and K. Weiler (eds), *Rewriting literacy: Culture and the discourse of the other,* New York: Bergin & Garvey, 1992, pp. 77–101].

Gee, J. P. (1986). "Units in the production of discourse," *Discourse Processes,* 9(4): 391–422.

Gee, J. P. (1990a). "Memory and myth: A perspective on narrative," introduction to A. McCabe and C. Peterson (eds), *Developing narrative structure.* Hillsdale, New Jersey: Lawrence Erlbaum, pp. 1–25.

Gee, J. P. (1990b). *Social linguistics and literacies: Ideology in Discourses.* London: Falmer.

Gee, J. P. (1991). "A linguistic approach to narrative." *Journal of Narrative and Life History* 1(1): 15–39.

Gee, J. P. (1992). *The social mind: Language, ideology, and social practice.* New York: Bergin & Garvey.

Gee, J. P. (1993). "Critical literacy/socially perceptive literacy: A study of language in action." *Australian Journal of Language and Literacy,* 16: 333–55.

Gee, J. P. (1996). *Social linguistics and literacies: Ideology in Discourses.* 2nd edn. London: Taylor & Francis.

Gee, J. P. and Crawford, V. (1998). "Two kinds of teenagers: Language, identity, and social class." In D. Alverman, K. Hinchman, D. Moore, S. Phelps, and D. Waff (eds), *Reconceptualizing the literacies in adolescents' lives.* Hillsdale, New Jersey: Erlbaum, pp. 225–45.

Gee, J. P. and Green, J. L. (1998). "Discourse analysis, learning, and social practice: A methodological study." *Review of Research in Education* 23: 119–69.

Gee, J. P., Hull, G., and Lankshear, C. (1996). *The new work order: Behind the language of the new capitalism.* Boulder, Co.: Westview.

Geertz, C. (1973). *The interpretations of cultures.* New York: Basic Books.

Geertz, C. (1983). *Local knowledge: Further essays in interpretive anthropology.* New York: Basic Books.

Goffman, I. (1981). *Forms of talk.* Philadelphia: University of Pennsylvania Press.

Goodwin, C. and Heritage, J. (1990). "Conversation analysis." *Annual Review of Anthropology* 19: 283–307.

Goodwin, M. H. (1990). *He-said-she-said: Talk as social organization among black children.* Bloomington: Indiana University Press.

Gould, S. J. (1993). *The mismeasure of man.* New York: Norton.

Green, J. and Bloome, D. (1997). "Ethnography and ethnographers of and in education: A situated perspective." In J. Flood, S. Brice Heath, and D. Lapp (eds),

Research on teaching literacy through the communicative and visual arts. New York: Macmillan, pp. 181–202.

Green, J. and Dixon, C. (1993). "Talking knowledge into being: Discursive practices in classrooms." *Linguistics and Education* 5: 231–9.

Green, J. and Harker, C. (eds) (1988). *Multiple perspective analyses of classroom discourse*. Norwood, N.J.: Ablex.

Griffiths, P. (1986). "Early vocabulary." In P. Fletcher and P. Garman (eds), *Language acquisition* (2nd edn). Cambridge: Cambridge University Press, pp. 279–306.

Gumperz, J. J. (1982). *Discourse strategies*. Cambridge: Cambridge University Press.

Gumperz, J. J. and Levinson, S. C. (eds) (1996). *Rethinking linguistic relativity*. Cambridge: Cambridge University Press.

Habermas, J. (1984). *Theory of communicative action*, vol. 1, trans. T. McCarthy. London: Heinemann.

Hacking, I. (1986). "Making up people." In T. C. Heller, M. Sosna, and D. E. Wellbery, with A. I. Davidson, A. Swidler, and I. Watt (eds) *Reconstructing individualism: Autonomy, individuality, and the self in Western thought*. Stanford, Calif.: Stanford University Press, pp. 222–36.

Halliday, M. A. K. (1989). *Spoken and written language*. Oxford: Oxford University Press.

Halliday, M. A. K. (1994). *An introduction to functional grammar*. 2nd edn. London: Edward Arnold.

Halliday, M. A. K. and Hasan, R. (1976). *Cohesion in English*. London: Longman.

Halliday, M. A. K. and Hasan, R. (1989). *Language, context, and text: Aspects of language as a social-semiotic perspective*. Oxford: Oxford University Press.

Halliday, M. A. K. and Martin, J. R. (1993). *Writing science: Literacy and discursive power*. Pittsburgh: University of Pittsburgh Press.

Hanks, W. F. (1996). *Language and communicative practices*. Boulder, Co.: Westview Press.

Harkness, S., Super, C., and Keefer, C. H. (1992). "Learning to be an American parent: how cultural models gain directive force." In R. D'Andrade and C. Strauss (eds), *Human motives and cultural models*. Cambridge: Cambridge University Press, pp. 163–78.

Havelock, E. A. (1986). *The muse learns to write: Reflections on orality and literacy from antiquity to the present*. New Haven: Yale University Press.

Heath, S.B. (1983). *Ways with words: Language, life, and work in communities and classrooms*. Cambridge: Cambridge University Press.

Heidegger, M. (1962). *Being and time*. New York: Harper & Row.

Heritage, J. (1984). *Garfinkel and ethnomethodology*. Oxford: Basil Blackwell.

Hicks, D. (1995). "Discourse, learning, and teaching." In M. W. Apple (ed.), *Review of Research in Education 21*. Washington, D.C.: AERA, pp. 49–95.

Hofstadter, D. and the Fluid Analogies Research Group (1995). *Fluid concepts and creative analogies: Computer models of the fundamental mechanisms of thought*. New York: Basic Books.

Hofstadter, D. R. (1997). *Le ton beau de Marot: In praise of the music of language*. New York: Basic Books.

Holland, D. and Quinn, N. (eds) (1987). *Cultural models in language and thought*. Cambridge: Cambridge University Press.

Hutchins, E. (1995). *Cognition in the wild*. Cambridge, Mass.: MIT Press.

Hymes, D. (1974). *Foundations of sociolingusitics*. Philadelphia: University of Pennsylvania Press.

Hymes, D. (1981). *In vain I tried to tell you: Essays in Native American ethnopoetics*. Philadelphia: University of Pennsylvania Press.

Hymes, D. (1996). *Ethnography, linguistics, narrative inequality: Toward an understanding of voice*. London: Taylor & Francis.

John-Steiner, V., Panofsky, C. P., and Smith, L. W. (eds) (1994). *Sociocultural approaches to language and literacy: An interactionist perspective*. Cambridge: Cambridge University Press.

Kanter, R. M. (1995). *World class: Thriving locally in the global economy*. New York: Simon and Schuster.

Kaplan, R. D. (1998). *An empire wilderness: Travels into America's future*. New York: Random House.

Keil, F. (1979). *Semantic and conceptual development*. Cambridge, Mass.: Harvard University Press.

Keil, F. (1989). *Concepts, kinds, and cognitive development*. Cambridge, Mass.: MIT Press.

Knorr Cetina, K. (1992). "The Couch, the cathedral, and the laboratory: On the relationship between experiment and laboratory, in science." In A. Pickering (ed.), *Science as practice and culture*, Chicago: University of Chicago Press, 1992, pp. 113–37.

Kochman, T. (1981). *Black and white styles in conflict*. Chicago: University of Chicago Press.

Kress, G. (1985). *Linguistic processes in sociocultural practice*. Oxford: Oxford University Press.

Kress, G. (1996). *Before writing: Rethinking paths into literacy*. London: Routledge.

Kress, G. and van Leeuwen, T. (1996). *Reading images: The grammar of visual design*. London: Routledge.

Labov, W. (1972a). "The logic of nonstandard English." In *Language in the inner city*. Philadelphia: University of Pennsylvannia Press, pp. 201–40.

Labov, W. (1972b). "The transformation of experience in narrative syntax." In *Language in the inner city*. Philadelphia: University of Pennsylvannia Press, pp. 354–96.

Labov, W. and Waletzky, J. (1967). "Narrative analysis: Oral versions of personal experiences." In J. Helm (ed.), *Essays on the verbal and visual arts: Proceedings of the 1966 Annual Spring Meeting of the American Ethnological Society*. Seattle: University of Washington Press, pp. 12–44.

Lakoff, G. (1987). *Women, fire, and dangerous things: What categories reveal about the mind*. Chicago: University of Chicago Press.

Lakoff, G. and Johnson, M. (1980). *Metaphors we live by*. Chicago: University of Chicago Press.

Laqueur, T. (1990). *Making sex: Body and gender from the Greeks to Freud*. Cambridge, Mass.: Harvard University Press.

Latour, B. (1987). *Science in action*. Cambridge, Mass.: Harvard University Press.

Latour, B. (1991). *We have never been modern*. Cambridge, Mass.: Harvard University Press.

Lave, J. (1988). *Cognition in practice*. Cambridge: Cambridge University Press.

Lave, J. and Wenger, E. (1991). *Situated learning: Legitimate peripheral participation*. Cambridge: Cambridge University Press.

Lemke, J. L. (1995). *Textual politics: Discourse and social dynamics*. London: Taylor & Francis.

Leont'ev, A. N. (1978). *Activity, consciousness, and personality*. Englewood Cliffs, New Jersey: Prentice-Hall.

Leont'ev, A. N. (1981). "The problem of activity in psychology." In J. V. Wertsh (ed.), *The concept of activity in Soviet psychology*. Armonk, N.Y.: M. E. Sharpe, pp. 37–71.

Levelt, W. J. M. (1989). *Speaking: From intention to articulation*. Cambridge, Mass.: MIT Press.

Levinson, S. C. (1983). *Pragmatics*. Cambridge: Cambridge University Press.

Levinson, S. C. (1996). "Relativity in spatial conception and description." In J. J. Gumperz and S. C. Levinson (eds), *Rethinking linguistic relativity*. Cambridge: Cambridge University Press, pp. 177–202.

Luke, A. (1995). "Text and discourse in education: An introduction to critical discourse analysis." In M. W. Apple (ed.), *Review of Research in Education 21*. Washington, D.C.: AERA, pp. 3–48.

Lynch, M. and Bogen, D. (1996). *The spectacle of history: Speech, text, and memory at the Iran–Contra hearings*. Durham: Duke University Press.

Macdonnell, D. (1986). *Theories of discourse*. Oxford: Blackwell.

Malone, M. J. (1997). *Worlds of talk: The presentation of self in everyday conversation*. Cambridge: Polity Press.

Margolis. H. (1987). *Patterns, thinking, and cognition: A theory of judgment*. Chicago: University of Chicago Press.

Margolis, H. (1993). *Paradigms and barriers: How habits of mind govern scientific beliefs*. Chicago: University of Chicago Press.

Michaels, S. (1981). "'Sharing time:' Children's narrative styles and differential access to literacy." *Language in Society*, 10(4): 423–42.

Michaels, S. and Collins, J. (1984). "Oral discourse styles: Classroom interaction and the acquisition of literacy." In D. Tannen (ed.), *Coherence in spoken and written discourse*. Norwood, N. J.: Ablex, pp. 219–44.

Middleton, D. (1997). "The social organization of conversational remembering: Experience as individual and collective concerns." *Mind, Culture, and Activity*, 4(2): 71–85.

Miller, C. R. (1984). "Genre as social action." *Quarterly Journal of Speech*, 70(2): 151–67.

Mills, S. (1997). *Discourse*. London: Routledge.

Minksy, M. (1985). *The society of mind*. New York: Simon & Schuster.

Mishler, E. G. (1986). *Research interviewing: Context and narrative*. Cambridge, Mass.: Harvard University Press.

Mishler, E. G. (1990). "Validation in inquiry-guided research: The role of exemplars in narrative studies." *Harvard Educational Review*. 60(4): 415–42.

Mishler, E. G. (1991). "Representing discourse: The rhetoric of transcription." *Journal of Narrative and Life History*. 1: 255–80.

Myers, G. (1990). *Writing biology: Texts in the social construction of scientific knowledge*. Madison: University of Wisconsin Press.

Nolan, R. (1994). *Cognitive practices: Human language and human knowledge*. Oxford: Blackwell.

Ochs, E. (1979). "Transcription as theory." In E. Ochs and B. Schieffelin (eds), *Developmental pragmatics*. New York: Academic Press.

Ochs, E. (1996). "Linguistic resources for socializing humanity." In J. J. Gumperz and S. C. Levinson (eds), *Rethinking linguistic relativity*. Cambridge: Cambridge University Press, pp. 407–37.

Ochs, E., Schegloff, E. A., and Thompson, S. A. (eds) (1996). *Interaction and grammar*. Cambridge: Cambridge University Press.

Ochs, E. and Schieffelin, B. (1983). "Foregrounding referents: a reconsideration of left dislocation." In *Conversational competence*, London: Routledge & Kegan Paul, pp. 158–74.

Ong, W., S.J. (1982). *Orality and literacy: The technologizing of the word*. London: Methuen.

Osborne, R. and Freyberg, P. (1985). *Learning in science: The implications of children's science*. Auckland: Heinemann.

Palmer, G. B. (1996). *Toward a theory of cultural linguistics*. Austin: University of Texas Press.

Philipsen, G. (1975). "Speaking 'like a man' in Teamsterville: Culture patterns of role enactment in an urban neighborhood." *Quarterly Journal of Speech*, 61(1): 26–39.

Propp, V. (1968). *Morphology of the Russian folktale*. Austin: University of Texas Press.

Psathas, G. (1995). *Conversation analysis*. Thousand Oaks, Calif.: Sage.

Quinn, N. (1987). "Convergent evidence for a cultural model of American marriage." In D. Holland and N. Quinn (eds) (1987). *Cultural models in language and thought*. Cambridge: Cambridge University Press, pp. 173–92.

Quirk, R., Greenbaum, S., Leech, G., and Svartvik, J. (1985). *A comprehesnive grammar of the English language*. London: Longman.

Reich, R. B. (1992). *The work of nations*. New York: Vintage Books.

Rumelhart, D. E., McClelland, J. L., and the PDP Research Group (1986). *Parallel distributed processing: Explorations in the microstructure of cognition: Vol. 1. Foundations*. Cambridge, Mass.: MIT Press.

Santa Barbara Discourse Group (1992). "Constructing literacy in classrooms: Literate action as social accomplishment." In H. Marshall (ed.), *Redefining student learning: Roots of educational change*. Norwood, N. J.: Ablex, pp. 119-50.

Schiffrin, D. (1994). *Approaches to discourse*. Chicago: University of Chicago Press.

Scollon, R. and Scollon, S. W. (1981). *Narrative, literacy, and face in interethnic communication*. Norwood, N.J.: Ablex.

Selzer, J. (ed.) (1993). *Understanding scientific prose*. Madison: University of Wisconsin Press.

Shapin, S. and Schaffer, S. (1985). *Leviathan and the air-pump*. Princeton: Princeton University Press.

Shore, B. (1996). *Culture in mind: Cognition, culture, and the problem of meaning*. New York: Oxford University Press.

Sinclair, J. M. and Coulthard, M. (1975). *Towards an analysis of discourse: The English used by teachers and pupils*. Oxford: Oxford University Press.

Sperber, D. and Wilson, D. (1986). *Relevance: Communication and cognition*. Cambridge: Cambridge University Press.

Star, S. L. (1989). *Regions of the mind: Brain research and the quest for scientific certainty*. Stanford, Calif.: Stanford University Press.

Strauss, C. (1992). "What makes Tony run? Schemas as motives reconsidered." In R. D'Andrade and C. Strauss (eds), *Human motives and cultural models*. Cambridge: Cambridge University Press, pp. 197–224.

Strauss, C. and Quinn, N. (1997). *A cognitive theory of cultural meaning.* Cambridge: Cambridge University Press.

Thompson, G. (1996). *Introducing functional grammar.* London: Arnold.

Toolan, M. (1996). *Total speech: An integrational linguistic approach to language.* Durham: Duke University Press.

Traweek, S. (1988). *Beamtimes and lifetimes.* Cambridge, Mass.: Harvard University Press.

van Dijk, T. A. (1985). *Handbook of discourse analysis: Vol. 1: Disciplines of discourse.* New York: Academic Press.

van Dijk, T. A. (ed.) (1997a). *Discourse as structure and process. Discourse studies 1: A multidisciplinary introduction.* London: Sage.

van Dijk, T. A. (ed.) (1997b). *Discourse as social interaction: Discourse studies: A multidisplinary introduction 2.* London: Sage.

van Dijk, T. A. and Kintsch, W. (1980). *Macrostructures: An interdisciplinary study of global structures in discourse, interaction, and cognition.* Hillsdale, N. J.: Erlbaum.

von Frank, A. J. (1998). *The trial of Anthony Burns: Freedom and slavery in Emerson's Boston.* Cambridge, Mass.: Harvard University Press.

Wertsch, J. V. (1998). *Mind as action.* Oxford: Oxford University Press.

Wieder, D. L. and Pratt, S. (1990a). "On being a recognizable Indian among Indians." In D. Carbaugh (ed.), *Cultural communication and intercultural contact.* Hillsdale, N. J.: Lawrence Erlbaum, pp. 45–64.

Wieder, D. L. and Pratt, S. (1990b). "On the occasioned and situated character of members' questions and answers: Reflections on the question, 'Is he or she a real Indian?'" In D. Carbaugh (ed.), *Cultural communication and intercultural contact.* Hillsdale, N. J.: Lawrence Erlbaum, pp. 65–75.

Wittgenstein, L. (1958). *Philosophical investigations.* Oxford: Basil Blackwell.

Index

Note: Page numbers in **bold** type refer to **figures**; page numbers in *italic* type refer to *tables*; page numbers followed by 'n' refer to notes